Ernest Marples

Ernest Marples

The Shadow Behind Beeching

David Brandon
and
Martin Upham

PEN & SWORD
TRANSPORT
AN IMPRINT OF PEN & SWORD BOOKS LTD.
YORKSHIRE - PHILADELPHIA

First published in Great Britain in 2022 by
Pen and Sword Transport
An imprint of
Pen & Sword Books Ltd.
Yorkshire - Philadelphia

ISBN 9781526760180

Typeset in INDIA By IMPEC eSolutions
Printed and bound in England by CPI Group (UK) Ltd, Croydon CR0 4YY.

Pen & Sword Books Ltd incorporates the imprints of Pen & Sword Books Archaeology, Atlas, Aviation, Battleground, Discovery, Family History, History, Maritime, Military, Naval, Politics, Railways, Select, Transport, True Crime, Fiction, Frontline Books, Leo Cooper, Praetorian Press, Seaforth Publishing, Wharncliffe and White Owl.

For a complete list of Pen & Sword titles please contact

PEN & SWORD BOOKS LIMITED
47 Church Street, Barnsley, South Yorkshire, S70 2AS, England
E-mail: enquiries@pen-and-sword.co.uk
Website: www.pen-and-sword.co.uk

or

PEN AND SWORD BOOKS
1950 Lawrence Rd, Havertown, PA 19083, USA
E-mail: Uspen-and-sword@casematepublishers.com
Website: www.penandswordbooks.com

Contents

Acknowledgements   6

Abbreviations   7

Introduction   9

Chapter 1   From Lancashire to the Army 1907–1945   13

Chapter 2   'I have done a certain amount of building myself …':
                Marples in Opposition, 1945–1950   20

Chapter 3   Power in Sight   28

Chapter 4   Into Government: Housing, 1951–1954   35

Chapter 5   Pensions and Pasture, 1954–1957   47

Chapter 6   Postcodes and Premium Bonds, 1957–1959   53

Chapter 7   Roads to 1939   64

Chapter 8   Roads in the 1950s   75

Chapter 9   Railways, 1918–1939   99

Chapter 10 Railways, 1945–1955   108

Chapter 11 BTC Modernisation Fails   135

Chapter 12 Superseding The British Transport Commission,
                1959–1961   149

Chapter 13 Beeching Goes Public   177

Chapter 14 The Beeching Report   197

Chapter 15 Private Life at the Ministry of Transport   226

Chapter 16 After Beeching: Barbara Castle and The Railways   236

Chapter 17 Seeking a Role, 1964–1978   246

Bibliography   268

Index   272

Acknowledgements

The authors would like to thank staff at the Postal Museum, the National Archive at Kew and the British Library for their professional support so readily given. After this book had been commissioned, the authors became aware of the recent deposit of Ernest Marples' personal papers with the Churchill Archives Centre at Churchill College, Cambridge. Especial thanks are due to Allen Packwood, director of the archives, who did everything he could to facilitate our work; to Tom Davies, who catalogued the papers so thoroughly and to the other staff for their generous support. Through their efforts we were able to have access to and make use of a mass of primary evidence much of which has not previously been available to researchers.

We would also like to thank John Scott Morgan for commissioning the current work and giving his enthusiastic support to the project.

Every reasonable effort has been made to trace copyright holders of material reproduced in this book but if any have inadvertently been overlooked the publishers would be glad to hear from them.

Abbreviations

AA	Automobile Association
ASLEF	Associated Society of Locomotive Engineers and Firemen
ATTC	American Telegraph & Telephone Company
AWS	Automatic Warning System
BR	British Railways/British Rail
BRB	British Railways Board
BRF	British Road Federation
BRS	British Road Services
BTC	British Transport Commission
CBI	Confederation of British Industry
CPRS	Central Policy Review Staff
DMU	diesel multiple unit
EEC	European Economic Community
ELSIE	Electronic Letter Sorting Indicating Equipment
ERNIE	Electronic Random Number Indicator Equipment
FTA	Freight Transport Association
GLC	Greater London Council
GWR	Great Western Railway
ITA	Independent Television Authority
LMS	London, Midland and Scottish Railway
LNER	London and North Eastern Railway
MG&N	Midland & Great Northern railway
NCB	National Coal Board

NUR	National Union of Railwaymen
NUT	National Union of Teachers
PTA	Passenger Transport Authority
POEU	Post Office Engineers' Union
PSRU	Public Sector Research Unit
RAC	Royal Automobile Club
RHA	Road Haulage Association
SMMT	Society of Motor Manufacturers and Traders
SR	Southern Railway
STD	Subscriber Trunk Dialling System
TUCC	Transport Users' Consultative Committee
TGWU	Transport & General Workers Union
UPW	Union of Postal Workers

Introduction

Ernest Marples (1907–1978) was one of the most significant and controversial British politicians of the mid-twentieth century. He initiated radical change in three government departments. In one of these, the Ministry of Transport, he controversially employed Dr Richard Beeching (1913–1985) to produce a detailed analysis of the state of the railway industry and to draw up a prescription for transforming it into a modern, efficient and profitable business. His findings were published on 27 March 1963. Officially titled *The Reshaping of British Railways* but usually known as 'The Beeching Report', it elicited an immediate and extraordinary furore and it has continued to be a source of often passionate argument down to the present time. In many quarters Beeching is regarded as the butcher of Britain's railways and his name lives on, continuing to attract opprobrium. However, the politician who actually gave him the job and set the parameters within which to work has been curiously neglected. This is his first biography.

Drawing on archive material, some of which has only recently become available for research purposes, the authors provide a biographical outline of the life of Ernest Marples. Underpinning this theme, the authors examine the development of railway and road transport from the early twentieth century to around 1968. They argue that the weakness of the transport policies initiated by successive governments throughout this period contributed to the creation of a serious crisis for the country's road and railway system by the late 1950s. By this time the nationalised railways were making unacceptable financial losses while the road system was woefully overstretched and incapable of coping with a seemingly exponential increase in demand and usage. This crisis required radical action.

The measures brought about by Marples must be seen in the context of the wider economic, social and political changes shaping the United Kingdom after the Second World War. By that time there had been major growth in the influence and power of the pro-road lobby. Road haulage had clearly shown its superiority over rail for certain logistical tasks. Equally, growing numbers of people felt that it was their right, not simply a privilege, to enjoy the personal freedom and flexibility which they saw as being offered by private motoring. While large numbers of people had a sentimental attachment to the railways, this did not necessarily extend to using them. Their old-fashioned image compared unfavourably with the modishness increasingly associated with the private car.

The railways had been nationalised after the Second World War along with a number of other industries, often ones that were run-down but necessary for the effective functioning of what remained a predominantly free enterprise economy. The concept of state ownership was always somewhat anomalous in such an economy and, perhaps with the railways in particular, there were always powerful enemies who viewed nationalised industries with hostility and wished to see them fail. Marples was a businessman with financial interests in building roads. Was he being an honest broker as Minister of Transport when he employed Beeching, who has been seen as the destroyer of much of Britain's railway system?

The relative lack of attention accorded to Ernest Marples is surprising given his prominent political role in the 1950s and 1960s. He significantly shaped the post-war history of the Conservative Party. Despite a fairly humble background, Marples had, by 1939, amassed considerable wealth from property, before enlisting in the army and serving until 1944. First elected to Parliament in 1945, he became the key figure influencing Opposition housing policy. At the same time he was co-founder of Marples-Ridgway, which became a thriving civil engineering contractor. As junior Housing Minister to Harold Macmillan from 1951 to 1954 he ensured delivery of the incoming Conservative government's manifesto pledge, then thought rash, to build 300,000 houses a year. After an unhappy spell at the Ministry of National Insurance, he was forced out of the Anthony Eden government, only returning to office as Postmaster General once Macmillan had succeeded Eden: he revolutionised Post Office accounts, launched postcodes and the Subscriber Trunk Dialling system usually known as 'STD'.

After his triumph in the 1959 general election, Macmillan as incoming Prime Minister brought Marples into the Cabinet as Minister of Transport. His brief was urgently to tackle the serious problems that were being brought about by changing transport use, and he quickly made his mark. The British Transport Commission was dismantled and the loss-making railway system was identified as requiring early remedial action. It was clear that this would involve a controversial increase in the closure of unprofitable services. Marples inaugurated the country's motorway system and introduced a tranche of new, and again often controversial, regulations applying to motorists. He masterminded Beeching's appointment as first chairman of a new British Railways Board, defending his plans against a restive Conservative Party. In 1963, the publication of the Beeching Report proved unexpectedly turbulent for the Macmillan government: if the Report itself did not arouse enough acrimony, the Profumo scandal forced the establishment of Lord Denning's famous inquiry into a murky pool of scandalous and profligate behaviour among elements of Britain's social and political elite. Marples, although an outsider, was fortunate not to be implicated when his relationship with a former prostitute became known to Denning. In the autumn of 1963 Macmillan was forced by ill-health to give up the premiership and a vulgar Conservative leadership contest ensued. While Marples continued as Minister of Transport under Macmillan's successor, Sir Alec Douglas-Home, the Conservatives were clearly losing momentum and credibility with the electorate.

The October 1964 general election swept the Conservatives away and Marples never held office again. He had made many enemies and few new friends. Dr Beeching was increasingly uncomfortable under Harold Wilson's Labour government and left before his term of office was completed. While Labour was not noticeably friendlier to the railways than the Conservatives, despite various election pledges about ending the closure programme, Wilson eventually appointed Barbara Castle as Minister of Transport. She introduced the concept of the 'Social Railway', whereby identified lines would be kept open with public subsidy if it was evident that their withdrawal would cause severe hardship. This approach was a marked contrast to the Conservatives' narrower accountancy-based focus on railway finances. Some would see Castle's years at the Ministry of Transport as those when perceptions of Britain's railways started at last to become more positive.

Marples meanwhile was estranged from (and eventually dismissed by) Edward Heath, Home's successor as Conservative leader, and he left politics after receiving a peerage in 1974. His business affairs were growing increasingly tangled. When he fled to Monaco in 1975, the Inland Revenue was in close pursuit. This was an anticlimax for a man of undoubted drive and energy who once had seemed destined for very high, possibly even the highest, political office. He never managed, however, totally to divest himself of the reputation of being a maverick. There were senior figures in his party who never fully trusted him and despite enjoying years of patronage from the wily Harold Macmillan, he remained what he had always been, something of an outsider. His descent into relative obscurity with a somewhat besmirched reputation was more rapid than his rise to fame. Dr Beeching, on the other hand, glad to be away from the spotlight of what was, for much of the time, very hostile publicity, went back to private industry. He held senior management posts at ICI and was also involved with Redland and AEI. His effective chairing skills were recognised when he was appointed to head a Royal Commission on the Judiciary. In 1965 he was made a life peer as Baron Beeching of East Grinstead. Many may not have liked him but, unlike Marples, there were few who questioned his probity.

Chapter 1

From Lancashire to the Army 1907–1945

E rnest Marples was born at 45 Dorset Road, Levenshulme (now Greater Manchester) on 9 December 1907, to Alfred ('Alf') Ernest Marples, an engine fitter and later foreman engineer at Metro-Vickers, Trafford Park, and Mary ('Pol') Hammond. Alf was a socialist, shop steward and crown green bowling enthusiast while Pol made bowler hats and hatbands at Christie's of Stockport before her marriage and after giving birth to Ernest. Alf, a close friend of Ellis Smith (later MP for Stoke-on-Trent), was loath to leave his bowling club but in 1923 the family found a new home in Henshaw Street, Stretford. The young Ernest's upbringing, like all domestic arrangements in this traditional home, was in the hands of Pol, who tirelessly worked for Ernest to 'make something' of himself. The house, he later recalled, smelled permanently of boiled cabbage, emblematic of the English cooking of that period. Young Ernest's entrepreneurial skills were early in evidence when he sold 'Batty's Famous Football Tablets' outside Saturday matches at Maine Road or Old Trafford. His lifelong adherence to the fluctuating fortunes of Manchester City date from this time.

His grandfather Theo, at one time Chatsworth head gardener and seemingly one of a long line of Marples there, also took a lively interest in pets, founding one journal, *The Pigeon Fancier*, and later re-launching it as *Our Dogs*, which he ran from an office in Oxford Road. He was chief judge and referee at Crufts for many years. Ernest often stayed at his grandparents' old beamed cottage in Hazel Grove and seems to have adored his grandfather.

His schoolfellows, perhaps with the benefit of hindsight, later recalled a small boy with fair hair, self-assured to the point of overconfidence, irrepressible, interested in making money and capable of doing anything well. By the time he was sent to Victoria Park elementary school, he must already have acquired his lifelong habit of early rising. There he was taught by Dr John Corlett, a former National Union of Teachers (NUT) organiser. Corlett was to enter Parliament at the same time as the younger man, though his tenure as Labour MP for York was brief.

Walking and rock-climbing seem to have been a passion from early on. By the time he was at secondary school the young Ernest (never Ernie) was part of a group of boys from the Manchester suburbs, 'the Bogtrotters', who were committed to major walking and climbing expeditions in the nearby Peaks, the Lake District or North Wales, which places they reached by train or bus. They were not above straying into the Chatsworth estate, though being young and fit were never caught by Theo's successors. As a young man he also excelled at ballroom dancing, later claiming to have won several prizes. Contemporaries recalled him as a fitness fanatic, forever climbing, cycling or skiing when not fishing in nearby canals. These pursuits would be added to, once his income was secure. Pol, who tended to be over-protective, worried about his climbing. In the end he had to steel himself against the maternal embrace. When he finally left for London she was in floods of tears.

A scholarship to Stretford Grammar followed but the school could not hold him. He later recalled running away to find work with a steamship company, thus (in his words) 'sacrificing a good, free education on a scholarship for quick cash gains'. The folly of this bargain was pointed out to him by one of the clerks and he returned to school. Another example of his early entrepreneurship was a holiday job as gatekeeper at the local football ground. The fruits of his experience were, he claimed, recorded in a notebook entitled 'Mistakes I have made'. When he did leave school he was articled to an incorporated accountant in Manchester, passing his final examination as a chartered accountant in 1928 at the age of twenty-one. Some of his work was in Liverpool; while doing that he lived at 16 Church Street, Wallasey (a local connection he would be careful to point out to voters in 1945). Auditing the books of bankrupt firms gave him (he later drily claimed) important insights into the behaviour of nationalised industries.

He then decided to seek his fortune in London, departing with only £20 in his pocket, borrowed from his mother. There he stayed at the Tottenham Court Road YMCA while he found work as a trainee accountant. Possibly at this time he also took a part-time job as a bookie's clerk, an occupation that eventually led to him learning tic-tac. Indeed he briefly became a bookie himself, offering odds on horses and dogs at White City. The year 1930 may have been a turning point. Ernest obtained a mortgage for a small house in Notting Hill and then let it as a bed and breakfast location to cover his outgoings. He lived in the damp basement and cooked the breakfast himself, carrying it upstairs on trays. But, as he later recalled, 'I lived free and my time was my own to tackle a deal.' Other Victorian house acquisitions followed in better areas such as Bramham Gardens, with the young landlord converting them into flats. By 1934 he had moved to 18 Courtfield Gardens, SW5, which became home for two years. His observation of construction gave him a useful practical knowledge of the building trade. He still found time to turn out for Dulwich Hamlet, a noted local amateur football team.

Fate now intervened. While climbing rocks near Tunbridge Wells he met Jack Huntington, a civil servant, the two forming what Ernest himself dubbed 'a close and intimate friendship' that lasted over thirty years. Huntington was fourteen years Ernest's senior yet seems almost to have adopted the younger man. It appears to have been a genuinely Socratic relationship. They shared a flat before the war; after the war Huntington lived in a house owned by Marples. As Marples tells the story Huntington treated him to his first dinner at the Café Royal in gratitude for making him train and improve his fitness as a climber. Huntington extended the younger man a substantial loan to facilitate the establishment of Kirk & Kirk, a contracting business. 'Hunti's' bounty was greater still, for he expanded the cultural and intellectual horizons of the young Ernest, introducing him to Marcus Aurelius, Aristotle and Thomas Aquinas.

On the eve of the Second World War Ernest's most major project to date, the erection of a modern block of 130 flats with bathrooms, was completed. The new acquisition, Harwood Court, was in the Upper Richmond Road, London SW15, a Putney property he would retain until the 1970s. Ernest lived at No. 3, his last London address before joining up.

By the standards of the time, the young Ernest Marples was an experienced traveller. There is photographic evidence of him climbing mountains in Austria in 1936, 1937 and 1938; in the Bavarian Alps in 1936; and, shortly before the war, observing German house prefabrication methods at close hand. He first reached his beloved Davos, Switzerland, in March 1939 and as early as 1934 he may be seen sailing to the Canaries on a trip that also took in Madeira. He later claimed 'a first-hand knowledge of Germany and Germans' due to his enthusiasm for and experience of mountaineering there.

An agile, active and increasingly prosperous young man was not likely to lack female companions. He may have known several young women during the 1930s, including one in Switzerland. While little is known of his first marriage to Edna Florence Harwood on 6 July 1937, he had known her for at least three years: she had joined him in Austria in 1934, on a 1935 climbing holiday in the Lakes and another such in Austria and Switzerland the following year; the well-travelled pair visited Paris in 1937 and even reached Dakar before war ended such trips for the duration. At the time of their marriage Edna may only have been sixteen, though photographic evidence suggests her physical maturity. If this is so, her parents' consent would have been required. The couple set up house in Pembridge Gardens, Notting Hill.

By 1938, Ernest had become (in the words of his *Oxford Dictionary of National Biography* obituary) 'a man of some substance'. With Huntington's financial assistance he now diversified from landlordism into building contracting. His new firm, Kirk & Kirk, had taken on the erection of the Poplar power station, a project doomed to be delayed by the outbreak of war. More significant yet, Kirks employed a young consultant, Reginald Ridgway. Their meeting would prove to be the foundation of Ernest's post-war financial independence and wealth.

In July 1939, still only thirty-one, he volunteered for the London Scottish Territorials, and was posted the next month to the 3rd battalion 97th AA regiment. He was a gunner, later appointed to 368 heavy anti-aircraft battery. He rose to be battery quartermaster sergeant and (eight months after joining up) regimental sergeant major, later claiming this was a regimental record. Late in January 1941 he was discharged as a warrant officer on appointment to a commission, transferring to the Royal Artillery as second lieutenant (becoming substantive lieutenant in November). The Marples thoroughness was soon on display. Francis Boyd (later of the *Manchester Guardian*), who served under him, thought him the only efficient officer in the battery and observed his resentment at his lower status among fellow officers. He still had a Manchester accent and the coming years were to replicate this pattern of disparagement within the Conservative parliamentary ranks. By June he had been promoted to acting captain but rose no higher. He never saw combat. On 17 November 1944 he was invalided out of the army after sustaining a bad cut to his knee which had become infected with tetanus. He left with the honorary rank of captain after war service lasting five years and four months, all of it in Britain. He was awarded both the Defence Medal and the standard War Medal 1939/45.

For many, wartime service with its experience of collective action shifted their thinking to the political Left. Ernest of course had a solid Labour background so might have been expected to reproduce this political trajectory. However, he did not serve overseas and while he certainly saw action as an AA battery commander, he did not face the enemy on the battlefield. Moreover, his pre-war experience was quite distinct from that of his parents and not just spatially. When in later years he spoke of his father he presented the older man as resistant to change whereas his own adult work experience had been of self-help. All this may have contributed to Captain Marples' inclination not to shift Left. Once recovered from the tetanus, still only thirty-seven and 'full of vigour', he knew there would be a general election before long, though he could not have foreseen that Labour would precipitate it by withdrawing from the coalition while hostilities still raged in the Far East. The UK, especially its major cities, was substantially bombed-out. A gifted entrepreneur with a track record in building would surely find ample opportunities in poorly-housed Britain.

We may speculate that Ernest's marriage to Edna had not been a happy one. He had of course volunteered just two years afterwards; many husbands waited to be called up. There followed six years of postings around the UK. While the couple certainly holidayed in Scotland in 1942, Ernest, for whom leave would have been restricted, was clearly seeing other women and going on Scottish holidays with them. The marriage was dissolved in 1945.

Yet Captain Marples opted for a political career. His ability to combine it with continued entrepreneurial activity would be demonstrated only later. But where? Though it was seventeen years since he had left Manchester his roots remained there and many friendships from his earlier life persisted. Moreover, the north-west was broader than the two great metropolitan cities which dominated, and contained many constituencies that had retained their Conservative allegiance through the inter-war years; there had been no general election since 1935. Suburban Manchester certainly offered possibilities to a young man with a good war record. Then there was Liverpool, a largely Conservative city that still reflected its former aristocratic patronage. Beyond Liverpool lay the spacious suburbs of the Wirral, with their apparently impregnable Conservative constituencies. If he was going to play to the regional strengths that marginalised him in the army, Captain Marples was spoiled for choice.

The path which took Ernest to the Wallasey nomination is obscure. The constituency was a county borough (then located in Cheshire) comprising small towns snaking along the top of the Wirral and linked by the railway tunnel under the Mersey to Liverpool; it excluded Birkenhead. The seat had been safely Conservative between the wars, lately represented by Lieutenant Colonel Moore-Brabazon. But Brabazon had succeeded to the peerage, precipitating an April 1942 by-election. This contest had been triumphantly taken by former Wallasey mayor and local councillor George Reakes, standing on the Independent ticket. In this Wallasey adhered to a pattern of revolt in English towns, some of them later emblematic of Conservatism.

Though it had been ruptured by 1939, Reakes' background was vintage Labour. His early patron had been Walter Citrine, one-time Wallasey parliamentary candidate and general secretary of the TUC during the 1926 General Strike. Reakes secured election in 1942 as an outspoken backer of Churchill, advocating a vigorous prosecution of the war, though – in a pattern that would continue – Churchill necessarily endorsed the unsuccessful Conservative candidate. There had certainly been discontent among the local Conservatives at having a carpetbagger thrust upon them. By 1945, with the national party truce abruptly ruptured, Reakes might have survived by reverting to his Labour allegiance, but he was estranged from local party leaders whom he had tactlessly described as 'a collection of potted Hitlers'. In Wallasey as elsewhere Labour was determined to put up a candidate, thereby severing him from a potential area of support. While continuing as a National Independent candidate, Reakes declared in his election address that 'on all major issues I supported Mr Churchill and the National Government'. 'A vote for me,' he added, 'is a vote for Mr Churchill and Mr Eden.' His actual programme, reflecting the national mood, resembled Labour's, for he advocated common ownership of land and mines while opposing the 'nationalisation of our daily life'.

Wallasey Conservatives were determined to recover a seat they had lost in 1942. In this era before the Maxwell-Fyfe reforms it did an aspiring Conservative no harm to be a man of means. We know Ernest visited Conservative Central Office in February 1945 and he must have been adopted in Wallasey soon after, because by March he was putting himself about in the constituency. From April until polling day (5 July 1945) he spent whole weeks there. The first task he faced was to demarcate himself from Reakes. It was therefore something of a triumph to elicit a telegram from Churchill himself which was then reproduced as an election leaflet. 'In reply to your enquiry,' the war leader wrote, 'I do not look upon your oponent (*sic*) Mr Reakes as in any sense a supporter of mine.' Down in London, Huntington had unearthed an interesting political fact – that Churchill, in seeking to reverse a defeat on education policy had sought and obtained a March 1944 vote of confidence in the House: Reakes had on that occasion opposed him. Here was the Achilles heel of a candidate who vaunted his support for the Prime Minister. As Marples tells the story, he kept pressing this inconsistency until 'Reakes's confidence oozed away'. To Marples there were only three issues at stake: support for Churchill, the establishment of a permanent headquarters in Wallasey, and his own relative youth and service (at thirty-seven he was far younger than the fifty-six-year-old Reakes, while the Labour candidate was past sixty). His campaign was not without personal mishap, including a climbing misadventure in Snowdonia from which he did not extricate himself until 3 a.m. When Wallasey declared on 5 July 1945, Marples had won comfortably with 18,448, nearly 43 per cent of all votes cast. But the incumbent Reakes still took 14,638 and the Labour-Co-op candidate almost 10,000. Ernest's own recollection of the election focused on the 1944 no-confidence vote, but arithmetically the truth lay rather with Reakes who, when seconding the vote of thanks to the returning officer, remarked, 'Mr Churchill has won Wallasey with the aid of the Co-op and Mr Marples gets the divi.' For Ernest Marples, no subsequent Wallasey election would be closer.

The wartime government had faced a major challenge to ensure that some 3 million men under arms were not, as in 1918, often unable to cast their ballots. As a result, voting was staggered through July and the national picture emerged only on the 26th of that month. It revealed, startlingly, a huge surge to Labour. Attlee's party had won the popular vote for the first time and, more important, gained a crushing predominance in the House of Commons. Captain Marples' initial experience of full-time politics would be in Opposition to an unprecedentedly powerful Labour government.

Chapter 2

'I have done a certain amount of building myself ...': Marples in Opposition, 1945–1950

E ven on the Left it is now accepted that the astute Attlee erred by partnering housing with health in his government. Labour's determination to build a national health system required great energy, leaving little time for housing. Creating the National Health Service was a full-time political job, given to Attlee's most energetic and charismatic minister, Aneurin Bevan. Bevan himself saw the two policy areas as inextricably combined. This giant department was only broken up in January 1951, by which time Bevan had been replaced by Hugh Dalton. He had clashed with Bevan over whether a council house should have one or two WCs. Bevan's insistence on two led Dalton to deem him 'a tremendous Tory' (see Thomas-Symonds, *Nye: Political Life of Aneurin Bevan*, 2015). Ultimately, this failure to focus on housing performance would prove electorally fatal, giving Marples, and the Conservatives, their opportunity. For now, their parliamentary attention was fixed on the scale and dominance of the new administration.

From the time of his election, Marples worked assiduously to make his mark. This was not easy in Opposition. His party was bruised by unexpected defeat with a large margin. What was an ambitious thirty-seven-year-old to do? His approach reflected his pre-war experience and wartime experience: the need to get organised. First he needed a London base. In this era, in-house working accommodation for MPs was scarce and beyond the expectation of newcomers. To build a reputation for the assiduous constituency work promised to his Wallasey voters he needed a London office. With his significant personal resources he would not need to skimp. He required easy access to the House of Commons and accommodation large enough to function both as home and constituency office. Identification of the ideal spot seems to have taken some time, but by 1947 he was installed in 33 Eccleston Street, London SW1, a short bike ride from Parliament for a fit and energetic man. This distinguished house, part of an early nineteenth-century stuccoed terrace, was three bays wide and included an attic and a basement. Decorating the first floor of the whole terrace was a beautiful continuous cast iron lotus pattern balcony. Marples filled the interior appropriately, acquiring Regency furniture, including a bed reputed once to have belonged to Queen Caroline, sister to Napoleon Bonaparte. Some of its furniture appeared in the 1948 British film *The First Gentleman*, starring Cecil Parker. In time Eccleston Street would become more than his office. It would provide a married home for him and his second wife Ruth, as well as an admirable space where the Conservative Great and Good might sample Fleurie wines and fine dining while mingling with celebrities. Eventually it became an important dining venue for political guests starting, in July 1948, with Anthony Eden. At one point in the mid-1950s the couple even had a beehive on the balcony (Marples' ebullient claim the bees gathered nectar from Buckingham Palace gardens remains unproven). By the 1960s they were a celebrity couple. He had become a good cook, but Ruth was even better. Great care was taken over the menus. Efficient record-keeping ensured that guests were not served the same menu twice. Nor was their home open only to Conservatives. Labour figures like Charles Pannell crop up, plus industrialists and academics, like Beeching and Crowther. The Eccleston Street visitor book falters only in May 1975, by which time the couple were in France.

The place needed considerable work to make it fit for purpose, but this was underway in the second half of 1946. Marples approached refurbishment in his usual constructive spirit, seeking out expertise: when his first choice as interior designer disappointed, a Professor Richardson was brought in to finish the job. And now, uniquely among the 1945 intake, he brought in time and motion experts Urwick, Orr & Partners to plan his time. They allocated the job to a Mr A. Stephenson whom Marples directed to consult Rose Rosenberg, erstwhile secretary to Ramsay MacDonald and an early example of his ability to find personal friends across the political divide. Stephenson began to log how the new MP spent his days. His observations disclosed a threefold division of politics, business and 'health & culture'. Politics split neatly into parliamentary duties and constituency work. For the former there was 'Miss Campbell' to whom the new MP hoped to delegate a considerable amount and anticipated providing her with staff. For Wallasey there was 'Miss Cox' operating from the promised new local HQ.

Business, in 1946, meant three things to Marples: Kirk & Kirk, the Status Leisure Corporation and his landlord role at Harwood Court and the Wetherby Trust. 'Mr Encke' was deemed to represent him 'to the fullest extent' at Kirk & Kirk; he was given the additional duty of liaising with 'Mr Grundy' at Status Leisure; management of Harwood Court and the Wetherby Trust had rested with 'Miss Baron' for some years. It was anticipated that all the property records would be consolidated at Eccleston Street once its refurbishment was complete.

That left health and culture. Stephenson saw that Marples had to read *Hansard*, *The Times*, *The Economist* and the *Sunday Times* as well as books. He programmed recreation from noon until 1.00 on Mondays and Wednesdays plus half an hour of squash on Tuesdays, Thursdays and Fridays. Engagement of a chauffeur was anticipated 'if Mr Marples can accustom himself to travelling as a passenger in his car'. The ambitious Marples stipulated his own availability for parliamentary conversations and interviews that would promote him nationally: in November 1946 Stephenson watched him spending no fewer than sixty-two hours this way. He concluded that meeting his own high standards of efficiency would leave the Honourable Member for Wallasey working as much as 100 hours a week. This, he drily observed, would require ample opportunity for recuperation. His remarkable document – surely a unique insight into the life of a new MP – was submitted to Marples on 11 November 1946 (MPLS 1/1). The young, comfortably off bachelor, not yet forty, had insufficient hours in his week.

'Captain Marples' took his oath on 2 August 1945, first addressing the House on the 22nd, his debut a question to the new Prime Minister being on Palestine. On 17 October 1945 came his sixteen-minute maiden speech, characteristically devoted to a call for the rationalisation of controls. He advocated that one department should be responsible for issuing builders' licences, collecting and collating all the information required by government. His target was the redoubtable Bevan and the exchange opened a decade of jousting between the two. 'Like a previous speaker,' Marples began, 'I have done a certain amount of building myself' before revealing he lived in just such a block. 'I am still the landlord.' He challenged Bevan on the upper ceiling for building prices (£1,300 in London, £1,200 outside) and accused him of waging class war over housing policy. The post-war transition provided ample convenient political targets: difficulties in getting building licences; lenience governing quantity specification; blurred lines of responsibility for raw material supply; the need for a single authority governing building permission. 'The Government have the control, and they should take the responsibility,' he concluded. He had identified homes as his policy priority.

In the next housing debate he targeted high building costs. These he scorned on rational grounds (high costs meant fewer houses built) and on traditional Conservative grounds – high costs meant high subsidy. Pursuing the rational argument, he advocated removing allocation powers from local authorities and inviting a financial contribution from those who became more prosperous while in subsidised housing. He recalled that pre-war costs had been split equally between materials and labour but alleged labour's share to be now far higher. Since the extra had not gone to profit and building output had fallen, the culprit must be the Ministry of Works, which produced and distributed building materials. Left to themselves, builders' merchants would surpass its performance. This was rhetorically powerful, delivered with authority by one steeped in the building trade: Attlee's structural error in combining housing with health left exposed a vulnerable flank. No other Conservative was interested in housing before the 1950 annual conference. The Conservative ranks were dominated by public school and Oxbridge boys, many of independent means and none versed in the building trade. Had the Hon. Member for Wallasey heard (or heard of) the famously phlegmatic Attlee's advice to a new member to 'specialise and keep out of the bars'? By making this his specialism, he need not fear rivals.

While Churchill's government certainly prioritised housing after 1951 it would not have created the NHS. But Labour had problems of its own. Bevan, as we have seen, wanted to build to the highest standards, irritating his Cabinet colleagues by refusing to compromise; there were crippling shortages of raw materials that pitched house-building against manufactures for export; ahead of them lay the horror year of 1947 spanning a severe winter and a massive sterling crisis. War and Truman's abrupt termination of the American loan would leave Labour in a cleft stick: exports were vital to earn foreign currency, but materials were urgently needed at home. On 13 November 1945 Marples intervened on the Furnished Houses (Rent Control) Bill, carefully acknowledging his interest as 'a landlord of furnished rooms'. He was letting many flats to other members, and (he revealed), on both sides of the House. He was drawing up a template for the long years of Conservative opposition. This pattern was sustained during 1946 as he elicited written replies on sundry aspects of the building trade. The early spring brought a break from politics when he became the first Englishman to climb the Matterhorn since war ended, an impressive feat at any time, but doubly so since undertaken in a snowstorm. Back in London, the autumn brought speeches on timber for scaffolding, the mobile repairs labour force, the Building Industry

Production Council and the municipal housing allocation. He pursued his incentives theme during detailed arguments over the productivity of labour, advocating the return of piece rates to replace time rates. Of Bevan he remarked, 'Unless he brings about payment by results for the building trade, he will never succeed in building houses for our people' (House of Commons papers, 21 November 1946). That winter he intervened in a debate on the government's Cotton Bill, spoiling it with a personal attack on Sir Stafford Cripps he came to regret: '… the speech was my worst … they expected thoughtful constructive criticism from me'.

Although Marples was building a reputation in the House, his business affairs were not going well. He had gradually become disillusioned with the poor performance and excessive caution of Kirk & Kirk (builders of Harwood Court). His suggestion to appoint Urwick Orr to review its operations was spurned. But there was hope. Kirks had, in 1938, appointed as its new general manager R.J. ('Reg') Ridgway, a man with quite different ideas. The company had a chance to bid for a new power station at Brunswick Wharf (Poplar) even though it lacked relevant experience. Ridgway stepped into the breach, personally preparing all the designs, drawings, calculations and programmes. He seems to have been key to Kirk & Kirk landing the contract. Marples noticed and soon he and Ridgway resolved to form a new company free of the timidity (as they saw it) of Kirk & Kirk. This took time, but by the end of 1948 they had formed the private limited company Marples, Ridgway and Partners Ltd to carry on business as civil engineering contractors. Marples took 80 per cent of the equity of the new venture and became its chairman, Ridgway took 20 per cent and was appointed general manager. It was incorporated on 21 December 1948 and proved long lived, being dissolved only on 4 November 2013 following the death of Lady Marples, though it had long ceased trading. The new company even took over the Brunswick power station contract from the unadventurous Kirk & Kirk. This step rationalised Marples' business interests, marking an organic shift from the residential to the broader construction market. In time it would bring schemes such as the superstructure and river works of the Skelton Grange Power Station in Leeds: during the next two to three years the two men fashioned a major construction company that would eventually blossom into a major exporter of British design expertise. Of course, building opportunities were plentiful in war-damaged Britain. Birkenhead had been savagely bombed on the night of 15 March 1941. Travelling from Woodside Station to London on parliamentary duty, the young MP would have been familiar with the derelict sites and gutted buildings of 1940s Britain. Blitzkrieg had destroyed 225,000 houses, severely damaging 550,000 more.

Marples' Commons interventions and questions display two principal interests: the building industry, its raw materials and labour force and the provision of housing; and the preoccupations and concerns of the broader Merseyside area – not just the Wirral. He learned to sharpen his argument and imbue it with broader Conservative values, identifying inefficiency with a bloated state. Bevan, he believed, thought it his own responsibility to build the houses whereas it was the building industry that had to deliver. He would illustrate his theme with examples from his own firm's practice: materials shortages caused layoffs if bureaucratic procedures led to delays. 'What is wanted on a site is not necessarily a 100 per cent correct decision but a speedy decision.' This focus on speed allowed him to juxtapose, perhaps inaccurately, the natural dynamics of the industry he knew best against a lumbering state bureaucracy. He would excoriate Labour ministers but always treat Labour MPs courteously, especially those from the building trade. Though a convinced Conservative he was more socially akin to the other side of the House.

'Perhaps I may declare my own interest in this matter. My interest is to build houses under contract for the local authorities, and I say here and now, that I, as a contractor, working for a local authority, cannot build them as quickly, or as cheaply as private enterprise building for speculation, which is something I do not and cannot do. As far as I am concerned, the point of view which I am now putting forward is really against my private interests.' He contrasted the performance of councils which took a year to complete a dwelling with private builders who took eight months: '… private enterprise is cheaper, quicker and better than local authority building under contract'. This was disingenuous for the Conservatives' later building success would not have come without a decisive council contribution. For now, his solution was subsidy to private enterprises so that they would build, while leaving the allocation (based on physical need) to councils. Marples became secretary of the Conservative Party's Housing Committee but may have had few rivals. In 1947, he published his only book, an extended essay advocating co-partnership. It is as near as we can get to a statement of philosophy from this most pragmatic of politicians. *The Road to Prosperity: An Industrial Policy* draws freely on his business experience and seems to be occasioned by anxiety that the defeated Conservative Party would drift into an accommodation with the new status quo, exactly what did happen, with a few exceptions, after 1951.

Like many Conservatives of the 1945 intake, Marples sought inspiration in Party Chairman Fred (Lord) Woolton. Woolton liked to minimise global differences on the Left, the better to lump together opponents from Attlee to Stalin. Marples followed, dubbing Labour 'the Socialist Party', spicing his text with plentiful quotations from Lenin. Perhaps conscious of missing a university education – and knowing from Jack Huntington what he had missed – Marples dropped intellectual names with undiscriminating enthusiasm. That said, the case for co-partnership – essentially schemes to broaden share capital ownership – is laced with plentiful examples from British practice. We may speculate that apart from the sheer pleasure of appearing in print for the first time, Marples must have derived the greatest satisfaction from Woolton's willingness to pen an introduction. 'He is the son of a working man: he was nurtured in a Socialist home and became a Conservative by conviction and an employer of labour through his own courageous adventuring in life'. To Woolton, Marples embodied the spirit of free enterprise. Marples would eventually repay him after 1951 by turning his housebuilding rhetoric into reality. If *The Road to Prosperity* was a product of the Cold War era, the bastion of free enterprise was the United States. Between January and March of 1949, Marples made his first visit, courtesy of the Anglo-American Parliamentary Group, a selection suggesting he was regarded as a coming man of British politics, someone influential Americans might wish to know. This first trip marked the start of a strong relationship between Marples and the USA, enriched over time with personal links and eventually also with strong company ties.

Back in London, Marples, who seldom lacked female company, would start seeing Anne Bailey, a young woman of thirty. Meanwhile in Wallasey, the February 1950 general election presented a more orthodox political challenge than 1945. He faced only Labour and Liberal opponents and, while Labour now had a younger candidate, the incumbent's advantage had shifted to him. His 1945 victory had been on a minority vote predicated on Labour's perverse decision to oppose Reakes. This new contest would be fought on Labour's record. Marples seems to have enjoyed his campaign, drawing large audiences to meetings, relishing his depiction by opponents as 'a bigger and better villain than in 1945', dismissing as 'wild' the charge that he had voted against the health service. His eye for a good photo opportunity was often on display: he hired a nineteenth-century horse-drawn coach and donned a

Regency coachman's coat to drive it round Wallasey; he campaigned against Labour's sugar packaging, inaccurately labelled with its gross, not its net weight. He boasted of having conducted nearly 5,000 personal interviews locally and promised to extend his constituency service with a new branch in Moreton, reflecting boundary changes which brought that town, as well as Saughall Massie and Leasowe into the constituency for the first time. Not only the *Liverpool Daily Post* but even the *Sunday Express* carried pictures of him on the summit of Snowdon. That same day he was the 'victim' (in reality the beneficiary) of a mock 'kidnapping' by Liverpool University students on their panto day. The *Daily Express* covered an attack on him by Labour's Bessie Braddock, choosing to illustrate it with a picture of the large lady herself; Marples too was photographed, but by contrast training with the Chelsea football team. Surprisingly, neither the Conservatives nationally nor Marples locally made much of housing, which suggests the issue lacked salience for all the local bomb damage on Merseyside. The *Wallasey News* for 25 February hailed his 'decisive victory' with a doubled Conservative vote. It was impressive – his 33,904 represented over 57 per cent of votes cast, leaving Labour's John Hindle far behind at 18,989 (below 32 per cent) and the Liberals on less than 11 per cent.

Chapter 3

Power in Sight

In retrospect the period between the two general elections of February 1950 and November 1951 may seem a mere prelude to the long period of Conservative dominance of government which was about to begin. In practice Labour had built a substantial following and was not easily dislodged. True, its majority had fallen from 146 to 5, but it was still a majority and only the second the party had ever enjoyed. For all Marples' Wallasey landslide, the national Labour vote was huge. It exceeded 13.25 million, suggesting the people were still generally sympathetic to its reform programme, despite austerity. The Conservatives still had a battle on their hands to win the electorate's hearts and minds and this was a scenario in which the newly returned Wallasey member would have to play his part. For all their party's enduring popularity, the Labour leadership, by 1951, was visibly exhausted, worn out by eleven years of continuous involvement in government. Bevin was dead, replaced, inadequately, by Morrison. Cripps was dying. The energy of the administration emanated from its younger figures, Bevan above all. Attlee might have made him Foreign Secretary in Bevin's place: instead, in January 1951, he made him Minister of Labour. Bevan also faced an emerging rival in Hugh Gaitskell, who became Chancellor when ill-health finally forced Cripps out. When Gaitskell sought economies in the NHS budget to fund rearmament for the Korean War he precipitated the resignation of Bevan and the young President of the Board of Trade, Harold Wilson.

Labour was still in government and so it was a Labour King's Speech on which Ernest Marples intervened on 13 March 1950, prefacing his remarks by admitting 'I am never quite sure what are the rules of this House as to how often a person should declare his interest in a particular industry, but as this is a new House I should like to declare my interest by saying that I am a building contractor, mostly in the heavy civil engineering line now and erecting fairly large buildings, but in the past erecting a great number of buildings for local authorities.' Any politician needs luck, and luck now attended the Member for Wallasey, moving his central area of expertise to the centre of politics. He was secretary of the Conservative Parliamentary Housing Committee which put him at the heart of policymaking. October 1950 brought the annual Conservative Conference, an event that Harold Macmillan, hoping for a defence appointment, did not even attend. The Conference for once gave expression to a widespread and controversial issue. A motion attacking Labour's housing record was debated. It made repeated calls, evoking cheers, for a commitment to build 300,000 dwellings a year. This would surpass Labour's record by 50 per cent. Woolton, in the chair, could not avoid an amendment specifically committing the party to achieving this figure as a minimum. It was carried unanimously. Wise heads were shaken; Churchill himself defined it only 'as a target ... in time of peace' – the Korean War having broken out that summer. Even cautious Conservative historians such as Blake in *The Conservative Party from Peel to Churchill* believe the stance on housing to have been an asset when Britain returned to the polls the following year (1970: 268). On 6 November 1950 Marples rose in the House to make an hour-long speech. It consolidated his reputation as a housing expert and exhibited his growing confidence. Marples later claimed that an informal backbench meeting of Conservatives had pressed his case for moving the amendment on Churchill as the only MP who could stand up to Bevan. The amendment regretted that 'the Gracious Speech shows no resolve to ensure a steady increase in the rate of house building up to at least 300,000 houses a year'. His job was to make the case for Woolton's great promise, asking if it were physically possible to build 300,000 houses a year and, if so, how? He began with the main Labour defence: that present resources were being driven as hard as they could, illustrating his point with reference to school-building where the number of places were up 50 per cent at roughly equal outlay.

On-site building materials were, he insisted, the biggest single factor in falling productivity. For timber, where he disputed that there was a world shortage, he proposed spending the dollars necessary to accumulate a stockpile sufficient for a further 100,000 dwellings. For cement he proposed a reduction in the amount required per house and scorned the continued use of 1890 standards, offering practical suggestions such as the part use of timber to support a floor. When Bevan, opposite, silently assented, Marples turned on him. 'Why have they not carried out these economy measures?' Next came bricks, where industrial output was below pre-war levels: internal partition walls could be built with breeze blocks instead of leaving them for the exterior; 5,000 extra workers should be recruited to raise industry output; local authorities with brickyards should be prioritised in central allocation of resources. If those measures were not enough, labour should be imported. More houses could be had either by increasing output or by taking on more workers. Payment by results, universally applied, was the answer, plus shorter apprenticeships and higher pay. These practices, he pointed out, had been deployed by Morrison when building the Festival of Britain site on the South Bank. This had lured away men from a power station Marples Ridgway was building on the other side of the Thames! Workers 'ought to go back to building new houses', quite achievable even with present controls. As a first step, private enterprise should be allowed to build more houses, and not only under direction by local authorities. This was precisely the step Labour feared would compromise resources.

Labour had dabbled in prefabricated houses under a short-term 1947 programme. Marples now called for it to be long-term. He proposed reducing the share of three-bedroom houses (then still above 50 per cent) to devote more homes to the needs of the old. If there were more but smaller units, those in large houses would trade down, releasing new letting stock. The government should set councils free to pursue perceived local needs, whether for a large number of smaller houses or a smaller number of larger ones. Earlier completions might be achieved without checking every gadget: a second WC and an outside tool shed were examples he gave of what might be added later. Heckled by Labour members, he replied 'If Hon. Gentlemen opposite object to that, they have to ask themselves whether they want to house 13 families with one lavatory each, or 12 families with two lavatories, leaving one family homeless. It is a choice of evils, and we must decide where the balance of advantage lies.' He asserted, without authority, 'we believe that housing is the first social priority, subject only to the overriding needs of defence'. The government's capital investment programme entailed too much unnecessary industrial building while new houses were not replacing those destroyed in the Blitz quickly enough. The government was complacent and lacked 'drive and energy'; a bold claim to make of the volcanic Bevan, but he went further. Recalling the minister's 1945 aim of cutting building costs he quoted Girdwood Committee figures showing that these rose by 12.5 per cent in just two years. 'Our censure on the Right Hon. Gentleman is for building far too few houses, building too expensively, and building too late.'

Bevan's reply suggests he knew that something significant had occurred. No one on the Opposition front bench could have opened the debate, he jeered, leaving it to the one man with the terminology. 'Therefore, the Hon.

Member is repeating this afternoon, with an air almost of discovery, merely what we have been doing for five years.' In parliamentary terms, Bevan was a street-fighter; personal attacks were in his repertoire. Kirk & Kirk, charged the minister, had failed to build houses and then walked away to build power stations instead. The government was already doing most of what Marples was asking for; only determined government mobilisation of resources had allowed even present performance; US softwood stockpiling (which Marples had proposed to emulate) had caused global shortages; ending timber licensing would bring waste; the housing programme was sustained in 1945–1947 only by substituting cement for scarce softwood. While the government had already allowed the private sector to build, results had been patchy. 'We on this side have not said we are going to build an additional 100,000 houses … because we are putting up real houses. We are building houses, not votes.' After this telling concession, there was more: 'anyone … can build a house today which will be a slum tomorrow, but we insist upon building houses for people which they will want to live in today and which they will want to go on living in 10 years' hence, as otherwise we should have these houses on our hands. Therefore, I will not reduce building standards'. Churchill, replying for the Opposition, deemed Marples' speech 'admirable'. So too did Churchill's successor but one. 'One of the best speeches heard from a backbencher in a long time' observed Harold Macmillan (noted in *The Macmillan Diaries 1950–1957* – Catterall 2011: 26). Sadly, Marples' own diary, which might have recorded his feelings, is lost. The Conservative amendment fell by 288 votes to 300.

Churchill was older than most key Labour figures but he was surrounded by men in their fifties such as Macmillan, Butler and Eden. Among ambitious Conservative MPs there were numerous younger men still. Marples, now forty-three, had applied himself in the House since 1945 and would reap his reward in the new decade. He began consciously preparing for future parliamentary debates. Adjectival phrases start to appear in the appointment diary – 'corrosive bitterness', 'gritty cantankerousness', 'mental nakedness' (MPLS 42). Was he searching for *bon mots*? He was a man with a plan and in March 1951 the Conservative political centre turned his speech into a powerful polemic which cemented his growing reputation ('Housing', Ernest Marples MP, March 1951).

This was a masterly amalgam of Conservative prejudice (distaste for 'red tape' and promotion of private enterprise) and practical knowledge. It scorned Bevan's claim that 200,000 was the highest housing output figure the economy could bear and put flesh on Woolton's conference pledge. Practical examples from Marples' amendment speech were included to give an air of solidity to the argument that the country could now build the houses required. Essentially the argument was for increasing output from the present workforce, raising the numbers employed on housing and increasing the 'usefulness' (i.e. efficiency) of unskilled labour with new methods and materials. The key tactical shift the Conservatives would make in housing policy on resuming office was clearly signalled; they would abandon Labour's commitment to three-bedroom houses for all new stock.

The energetic Marples was starting to attract attention. In April he met Geoffrey Crowther, seemingly for the first time. That May he made his first appearance on the Home Service's *Any Questions*. In July he was for the first time pictured with Ruth ('Miss R.') Dobson, his future wife, at a company function. That same month, Young Conservatives rallied at the summit of Snowdon where they were greeted by 'Mr Ernest Marples MP, Mountaineer and Authority on Housing'. Yet some feared he would overplay his hand. In the papers of the Central Office chairmen may be found a curious unsigned letter. Its author complains that Ernest Marples is 'somewhat importantly letting it be known that he is writing the Conservative Policy approach to housing and leasehold reform', grumbling that in the process he planned to ignore the views of a great many established interests. 'I should be sorry,' laments the author, 'if the Conservative Party were to be committed by a not very experienced Member of Parliament', especially since 'he is one of our bright young men: he is very good on platforms; he has boundless energy, and a considerable sense of publicity'. These qualities, the author continues, are dangers as well as assets, though he concludes, 'I don't want you to do anything with him'. The recipient is R.A. Butler, then chairman of the Conservative Research Department. Who, writing to Butler, would have been able to affect such an authoritative tone? Contextually the author can only have been Woolton or the party leader. Since Woolton was on friendly terms with Marples and had recently contributed a foreword to his book, the likely author must have been Sir Winston Churchill ('Strictly Private' to R.A. Butler, 21 September 1950, Conservative political archive, 20/1/1).

On the government side, Attlee's dilemma was acute. He had a majority, albeit small, and there was little evidence of popular discontent with Labour rule. But maintaining government with a majority of five was onerous. Attlee felt the loss of Bevin deeply and the recent resignations reflected a deep split over Labour's future direction. He and his surviving principal colleagues had been running the country for eleven exhausting years and these had taken their toll. On top of everything else, and just six years after 1945, the country was again at war. Gambling that a new election might enhance his greatly diminished majority, Attlee fatefully called another for 25 October 1951. British general elections consist of hundreds of simultaneous contests. In Wallasey, Marples faced a new Labour candidate in the twenty-seven-year-old Fred Jarvis, his Labour rival Hindle having 'defected' (in Marples' words) to nearby Runcorn. Jarvis was in the Wallasey Youth Parliament and a Liverpool graduate – an indisputably local candidate. He was quick off the mark, attracting 800 to his first rally at the Grosvenor Ballroom. There he defended nationalisation, accusing Marples of warmongering and plotting to cut welfare. But he was orthodox in his defence of the government's rearmament programme. On 19 October at Gorsedale School, Jarvis hosted the redoubtable Bessie Braddock who charged that Marples had moved out of house building and into power stations because he could make more profit that way. The Liberals, crushed in February 1950, were in no position to run a candidate, settling instead for inviting the main party champions to debate. This invitation Marples declined, preferring to set out his own stall. When he joined neighbouring Tories in a rally at Birkenhead Town Hall, he concentrated on housing ('How to build our houses', *Liverpool Evening Express*, 13 October 1951; *Daily Mail* interview 18 October). In the *People* (21 October) he expounded Churchill's housing plan. His election address stepped away from the issue, declaring the election was about a rise in the cost of living and the 'administrative failures' of the socialists.

In the end Marples took 37,423 votes against 21,718 for Jarvis (who later rose to be general secretary of the NUT). He had defied Jarvis' local roots and marginally strengthened his majority. Overall, the poll was lower, though Jarvis achieved a record Labour vote. A gleeful Marples toured the constituency the next day with a loudspeaker. With the Conservatives set for government, the local press speculated that he might be appointed Housing Minister. Whatever were his own personal prospects, the long years of the Conservatives in Opposition were over. The national result was freakish, for Labour once again outpolled the Conservatives, taking its popular vote almost to 13.5 million. However, in the House of Commons the Conservatives edged ahead with 321 seats to Labour's 295. This, in the context of Liberal collapse, meant an overall Conservative majority of just 17. Despite this, exultant Tories behaved as if they had won a landslide. With the Speaker due to retire, Marples was prominent among those wanting another Conservative in his place. The Leeds MP James Milner, chairman of Ways and Means, had reasonable expectations of becoming the first Labour Speaker but talks between the 'usual channels' broke down and he was thwarted. The vote – the first ever contested vote for a Speaker – followed party lines and elected W.S. Morrison. Marples' partisanship, uncharacteristic though it was, would return to haunt him.

Chapter 4

Into Government: Housing, 1951–1954

After the turbulent 1940s, the 1950s could be said to have lacked drama. While globally this was the decade of the Mau-Mau emergency, the Suez fiasco and the space race, British domestic politics and economics exuded a powerful sense of continuity. The principal public figures had come to the fore in the 1940s and politicians, most of them male and middle-aged, shared a background in the forces or the war effort. Dominant figures such as Churchill himself, Eden, Macmillan and Attlee, had all served in the First World War. Perhaps as a result, this was a decade of growing corporatism, with potentially antagonistic forces yoked in tripartite institutions for the common good. Post-war exhaustion and the austerity that followed seemed of themselves to require an era of social peace. Starting in October 1951, this was a prolonged period of Conservative rule as Prime Ministers – Churchill, Eden, Macmillan, Home – succeeded each other like the heirs of Banquo; if doom cracked it was only at the very end. In the early years after 1951, the very restraint of the new Conservative administration towards Labour's transformative legacy underpinned this apparent continuity. Political conflicts (four general elections, Suez) might occur but the impression abides, in England at least, of a country slipping back into something like the 1930s, albeit with a sense of gathering prosperity that Macmillan would later memorably articulate.

And yet it was not the 1930s. Important demographic shifts were underway. A post-war baby boom had important implications, first for school-building, then (by the 1960s) for the expansion of university provision. House building increased steadily through a combination of municipal provision (for rent) and liberal (and taxpayer-subsidised) access to mortgages. Conscription lasted until 1960, providing a further common experience for the adult male population. The new National Health Service (whose burgeoning costs had worried even Bevan) faced increasing user demand from a population whose expectations were rising. Women, displaced at first from paid work by servicemen returning from the war and required to bear the babies and raise children, began to drift back into jobs, albeit often part-time ones. Unemployment was not eradicated but overall economic growth was steady and sufficed to occupy a growing workforce. As a result, living standards rose steadily. Three factors above all illustrate this odd conflation of continuity and change. Each would play a part in the increasingly flourishing career of Ernest Marples: the provision of housing; the expansion of private transport at the expense of public transport, this becoming his responsibility in the 1960s; and the arrival of commercial television, which would preoccupy him during his second spell as a government minister.

Following the narrow Conservative victory of October 1951, Churchill summoned Harold Macmillan to Chartwell, inviting him to be the minister who would 'build houses for the people'. Macmillan, who specialised in global affairs, had little interest in housing and was disappointed; he had harboured hopes of one of the greater offices of state. As we have seen, Labour had bundled housing with health, necessarily the second priority of Bevan who was determined to establish what became the NHS. Churchill adopted Attlee's structural adjustment of 1951: Macmillan would be head of the Ministry of Housing *and* Local Government. Knowing he needed help with his new portfolio, Macmillan's mind turned to the able backbencher who had moved the Opposition amendment to the 1950 King's Speech. G.W. Moseley, Macmillan's assistant private secretary who later took on the same role for Marples, in 1982 recalled that Churchill himself 'regarded Marples as the obvious man for the job', a view passed on by phone. Marples wanted to be the minister himself, an ambition he discussed with Colin Coote, *Daily Telegraph* editor. Whether on Coote's advice or not, he acquiesced. Another illustration of Macmillan's eye for talent was the appointment of Reginald Bevins as his parliamentary private secretary. Bevins, the same age as Marples, had a parallel career: both were pre-war socialists; both served in the Royal Artillery; both became Merseyside MPs. In 1959 Bevins would succeed Marples as Postmaster General, and this time the job came with a seat in Cabinet (see D. Campbell-Smith, *Masters of the Post*, 2011: 418–419). Churchill consented to Marples serving him as parliamentary secretary at the newly fashioned ministry. Macmillan later told his biographer that Marples had no vision but was a 'doer', a remark freighted with the *hauteur* that had already coloured the younger man's parliamentary experiences. Indeed, given Marples' prominence in the national housing debate it seems legitimate to speculate why he did not receive the housing job himself as some on the Labour side had expected. Perhaps the Prime Minister retained his earlier misgivings? At all events, between them the two men would exert considerable influence on post-war Britain.

A third figure now came into play in the shape of Sir Percy Mills, a Birmingham industrialist and an old ally of Macmillan. He was brought in as advisor and wasted little time in establishing ten regional housing production boards. Thus the triumvirate of men who in the 1960s would accomplish a transport revolution was formed a decade earlier. At the heart of it was Macmillan's nexus with Marples: 'in fact he made me PM', he later told Anthony Sampson. A working partnership grew between the two, developing into friendship in Macmillan's old age and cemented on Marples' side with (in Macmillan's words) 'complete loyalty … ingenuity and untiring energy', a view confirmed posthumously by Nigel Fisher (MPLS 8/2).

Marples saw the older man as 'more patient', tactful and understanding; for his part Macmillan thought Marples 'one of the cleverest men I have ever met in a limited, practical field'. Mills would also figure in Marples' political life for over a decade, entering the Cabinet nearly three years before him, providing a valuable sounding board on Post Office matters before Marples succeeded him as Postmaster General in January 1957, continuing as Minister without Portfolio (1961–1962) before falling (unlike the younger man) in Macmillan's celebrated 'Night of the Long Knives'. He was already a frequent Eccleston Street lunch guest.

By 22 November 1951 Macmillan was ready to lay proposals for 'smaller and simpler houses' before Cabinet; Churchill encouraged him *not* to avoid a row with Labour over this aim, perhaps believing that the public would reward a government that prioritised output. After this it is striking how little attention the Cabinet paid to housing before the Coronation in June 1953, beyond acquiescing reluctantly in the distasteful but necessary business of providing subsidies to local authorities. Pragmatism, not ideology, was to rule the day. Labour had tried to meet the housing shortage through the construction of prefabs and repairs to existing structures. Its housing policy rested on two Acts of Parliament. The 1946 Act made large subsidies available to councils to build council housing, allowing them to borrow from the Public Works Loan Board. The 1949 Act shifted councils into a central position in the burgeoning welfare state by offering the possibility of public subsidy to owner-occupiers and landlords seeking to improve their properties. Councils might now build for the whole population, not just the needy. Alongside these two principal statutes, the 1946 New Towns Act set up development corporations to establish new towns, ten in all, before the programme began to suffer cuts the following year. Meanwhile, the Town and Country Planning Act 1947 took powers to plan the use and development of land and levied a development charge on builders. This charge irked Conservatives, but for all their complaints, Labour had built 1.5 million public homes by 1951. This Conservative government aimed to replace the state with the market as the determinant of land use. In 1952, the Cabinet set up a committee to reform the 1946 Act; it favoured local authority planning but was critical of the Central Land Board and the development charge. Macmillan urged reduction if not abolition of the development charge but had to settle for compensation being paid only when planning permission was refused or land compulsorily purchased. It is important not to overstate the shift in housing policy from Labour to Conservative: even the reduction in standards was prefigured in a Labour housing circular of April 1951.

As we have seen, Macmillan had been loath to take on the housing job, reluctant even to chair the party's Housing Committee. The new administration carried round its neck an apparent albatross: Macmillan grumbled that he had no idea how to fulfil the apparently infeasible pledge to build 300,000 homes a year. Matters were further complicated because the Chancellor of the Exchequer, R.A. Butler (RAB), like his Labour predecessor, was determined to ease balance of payments pressure. Imports of raw materials, domestically in short supply, were frowned upon. This problem was eased with the appointment of the affable Viscount Swinton as Minister of Supply, and further lightened when Churchill tended to back Macmillan against the Treasury. But unlike his boss, Marples was not new to the issue. He had specialised in it in Opposition; he knew it as landlord and partner in a thriving construction company; he had penned the 1951 pamphlet that fleshed out the Woolton commitment. Sensing an opportunity, he energetically set to work. Of course, the pamphlet had explicitly favoured private enterprise output over contracting-out from local councils. Now, faced with the political imperative of fulfilling Woolton's pledge, the two men abandoned ideology, unsentimentally agreeing that subsidising councils to build for rent was the only possible route to success. Pragmatism triumphed. They also discovered they shared a negative view of the new permanent secretary, Sir Thomas Sheepshanks, who was quickly circumvented by Mills' new regional boards. The new parliamentary secretary would later claim credit for resolving the matter recalling that he directly broached with Sheepshanks a minister's powers to force civil service resignations!

Marples chaired gatherings of civil servants and builders in a ministry room furnished with cupboards. Some contained scale models of system-building while others held the wine for which he was starting to acquire a connoisseur's reputation. (In those days he stored large quantities at the Army & Navy wine cellars in Victoria Street.) In Marples' own recollection, Macmillan had appeared 'within five minutes' of his arrival at his new office, exclaiming, 'How are we going to build these houses?' To this Marples claimed to have replied that it could be done only his way and not by Civil Service methods, meaning the otiose Sheepshanks. Macmillan was willing to give him control and it was organised ingeniously: departmental meetings (to be chaired by Marples) were set for Tuesdays and Thursdays when Macmillan was in Cabinet. They were subsequently rubber-stamped by a general council with the minister himself presiding. Late in 1951 the Cabinet set Macmillan a series of annual new build targets: 230,000 houses in 1952, 260,000 in 1953 and 300,000 in 1954 (Great Britain figures).

At the Ministry, Marples' personal secretary was Barbara John. His days soon developed a rhythm: most evenings, if in London, he made time for squash; lunchtimes saw him on the tennis court; Saturdays would find him watching Manchester City, and in November the following year he witnessed England's famous 6–3 drubbing by Hungary, deriving afterwards some inspiration from a conversation with the chastened full-back Alf Ramsay. He kept a high profile in Wallasey, with eight recorded visits in 1952 including the opening of the New Brighton cricket pavilion; in the evenings there were visits to Covent Garden, the Old Vic and (the hit of the season) *South Pacific*; the following year he saw *Aida* at Covent Garden, spoke at a summer Conservative rally and attended the party's Annual Conference.

On 7 November 1951 Marples rose to address the House for the first time as parliamentary secretary to the Ministry of Housing and Local Government, generously welcomed to his new appointment by his Labour predecessor Arthur Blenkinsop: '… the only Member from his benches who has had the courage to put forward practical proposals with regard to the housing problem. We are therefore, if anything, rather sorry to find that he has not been appointed to the higher office'. Shortly afterwards, Marples resigned as Managing Director of Marples Ridgway, though Ridgway, like Mills, frequently lunched at Eccleston Street and the two must have discussed company affairs; he still attended the company AGM. While he retained 80 per cent of company shares, the key political question would be his income – from this date for as long as he was a minister, he received no dividends, director's fees, salary or other sums apart from expenses incurred on the company's behalf. His appointment diary makes it clear he kept in close touch with Ridgway, lunching with him most weeks in 1954 for example and frequently in the previous two years. He would be haunted by his business interests, especially after he became Transport Minister.

On 4 May 1952 the *News of the World* ran a simple Q&A with Marples (billed as 'No. 2 to Mr Harold Macmillan') on how the government could build the promised houses. Marples was keen to insist that the government was building 'the people's houses'; photographs abound of him shovelling concrete, up ladders and appearing to help out with brick production. Under the 1952 Housing Act, local authorities were allowed to sell council houses, and the value of buildings without a licence increased. By 1953, however, only 20 per cent of contributions of total homes were from the private sector. That year's Housing Act raised council subsidy, thus encouraging publicly funded building. On 19 June, Cabinet authorised David Eccles, Minister of Works, to raise the ceiling for unlicensed house building. Eccles had wanted £500, as for industrial and agricultural buildings, but had to settle for doubling to £200. Macmillan backed him. This was a significant step away from state control. Eccles (not in the Cabinet) was only one of those pressing for acceleration in private activity. A more formidable proponent was Fred Woolton, who weighed in with a June 1952 memorandum advocating a property-owning democracy built on a greater element of owner-occupation. Macmillan pleaded for time to learn whether window fittings (of timber or steel) could be had in sufficient number. It was the old problem of resources but he was careful to bring forward other suggestions such as borrowing for housing at lower rates, or over a longer period; a special saving system, directed towards house building to stimulate the sector and save at the same time. On 9 July 1952 Macmillan praised Marples' 'excellent paper' on the Rent Restriction Acts.

By September, Macmillan was being forced to guard his other flank. He had already clashed with Butler over his wish for complete removal of the development charge for private house building levied under the Town and Country Planning Act. Butler thought this likely to promote inequality and was unimpressed by Macmillan's claim that any exploitation might be dealt with by compulsory purchase orders. Once again, the Cabinet faced a contradiction between its desire to build without subsidy and the very real constraints Labour had confronted. The Rent Restriction Acts, chafed at by landlords seeking to recover their outlay on improvements, illustrated this further. Only in October did Macmillan achieve Cabinet backing for easing them to free cash resources for repair work.

In autumn 1952 Marples, who favoured flats and hoped that people would learn to love them more, attempted to build 'High Paddington'. This was a proposal from the future architect of the Barbican estate Sergei Kadleigh for an 8,000-resident estate above Paddington Goods Depot. It was publicly opposed by John Betjeman, a firm believer in low-rise housing with gardens. This was a battle postponed because the real drive for high-rise building occurred later after Macmillan had been succeeded by Duncan Sandys. Nevertheless, they did build 252,000 homes in 1952 and that autumn Macmillan received a standing ovation at the Conservative Party Conference. Marples himself opened the first tenant-owned house in Wallasey in November.

On 14 October 1952 Cabinet had approved a 'rent and repair' Bill to plug the gap before major legislation (based on valuation) was possible. Landlords could raise rents under certain conditions, such increases to be based on the repair element (8 per cent) of the gross rateable value. Macmillan's approach was to blame deficiencies in Labour's 1948 Act for making it impossible to have a revaluation before 1955 or 1956, presenting his policy as a stopgap. Rents must rise to improve the housing stock in its millions; where else was the revenue for improvements to come from?

On 13 November 1952 Macmillan got his Housing White Paper through Cabinet but had to leave Marples holding the fort in the House. While there Marples said, 'The party opposite never built 200,000 houses in any year except one, and they only did so then by their "finish the houses" campaign, whereby they dropped everything in order to put a roof on houses which were standing without roofs … only in one year were more than 200,000 houses built, and that was the year when the building programme was almost wrecked.' Macmillan was pleased with Marples' performance, observing that he closed the debate on a White Paper to reform the Town and Country Planning Act 'very well indeed' (*Diaries*, 1966). Marples himself was more self-critical. Stokes for the Opposition had sat down unexpectedly early, leaving the minister floundering and unready. Marples' own notes, intended, as ever, to promote self-improvement, emphasised the need to relax before speeches.

The sector saw increased focus on conditions in the 1950s. The White Paper, *Housing – The Next Steps*, published on 3 November, surveyed the housing scene and attempted in visionary terms to scope out plans for when the target had been hit. It damned rent structures as 'hopelessly illogical', arguing that inadequate rent levels made it impossible for landlords to maintain their properties. However, the housing shortage meant rents could not be totally decontrolled.

The House Repairs and Rents Act 1954 permitted limited increases in rents on properties which had been let before September 1939 and which had been maintained in a good state of repair. Rent control *was* lifted from newly built and converted dwellings, but without the results for which Macmillan had hoped.

Macmillan then, and subsequently, had talked in Cabinet of 'The Grand Design', a futuristic vision of housing policy. In the White Paper three months later, Macmillan cheered Cabinet with news of 318,750 housing completions during the year. Faced with this success, no one quibbled that they had needed the municipalities to deliver. Hennessy's brutal comment in *Having It So Good: Britain in the Fifties* (2007: 21) that 'Macmillan's push for the magical 300,000 new homes a year was overwhelmingly a state enterprise' was the simple truth.

Macmillan now proposed increasing owner-occupancy by reducing the subsidy for local authority housing and cancelling rent controls in the private sector. He argued that private rents should increase to encourage landlords to make improvements. Rent increases would be linked to the revaluation of property to decide a so-called 'fair' rent. The government subsidised the temporary repair of dilapidated or condemned buildings in the private sector under 'Operation Rescue'. The proposals were incorporated into the 1953 White Paper and then, later, into the 1954 Housing Rent and Repair Act.

Macmillan should have been in a confident mood in 1953, but he chose to disguise it: '… after wandering for fourteen months among these wretched trees, I can scarcely see the wood at all', he grumbled on 22 January. In fact, the completions target was almost certain to be met – the development charge was gone, he had Cabinet backing for other ways of encouraging private building and looked forward to extending the free licence to all new houses over a certain size. However it was the old housing stock that presented the chief problem. Councils were raising rents and private landlords wanted to do the same. The revenue (meaning landlord income) was needed to refurbish the stock. He now urged a revaluation of rates and proposed, once this had happened, to attach to the new rateable value a maximum rent for the property concerned. Landlords would also have to maintain properties in a state of 'good tenantable repair'. He identified two problematic categories of house: the dilapidated and the condemned. The former might be made habitable while the latter – slums – would have been cleared by now had it not been for the war. He proposed that local authorities acquire them without compensation and in time they might use the sites for development. And, crucially, he had secured Butler's agreement to a rates revaluation. By Cabinet on 16 April, Macmillan felt confident enough to declare his intention to switch to refurbishing old stock once the 300,000 target had been reached.

Mother Nature intervened on the night of 31 January 1953, assailing the English east coast with disastrous floods. A combination of intense low pressure heading down the North Sea, hurricane-force winds and a high tide produced a huge mound of water that pushed south down the North Sea, raising sea levels 8 feet above normal. Communities from the Tees to the Thames were affected, 307 people being killed and some 40,000 rendered homeless. As parliamentary secretary it fell to Marples to visit Canvey Island, one of the worst-hit spots, where 13,000 needed evacuation and fifty-nine people had died. Canvey Island had faced its purgatory in the small hours of 1 February. On arrival he faced rough handling by aggrieved (and now homeless) residents. Since the country had no flood warning system this disaster can have been no surprise. Back in the Commons, much of the government defence fell to the Home Secretary David Maxwell-Fyfe. But when it came to housing matters Marples had to front for the department while Macmillan was touring his share of the flood-hit areas. He stumbled over the department's failure to requisition property to rehouse the homeless and had to be rescued by the Speaker, but otherwise seems to have handled some lively questioning with his usual aplomb.

It is fascinating to watch Macmillan, the future Prime Minister, at this early date sketching out the policies with which he later became identified. He was determined to promote owner-occupation, urging the sale of council properties on often-reluctant councils, encouraging New Town corporations to sell freehold sites and slashing the ratio of new private building to council building from 1:5 to 1:2. Britain's 3.75 million owner-occupied properties he deemed occupied by those with a stake in the country, contrasting them unfavourably with council tenants who were subsidised to the tune of £770 a year. He recognised however that renting would be the principal form of tenure for the majority. On private building for rent he was pessimistic: eyebrows might have been raised in the building trade had it been known that Her Majesty's Minister for Housing and Local Government, and a leading

Conservative, had told his Cabinet colleagues, 'the days of the great landlords are finished'. By 28 April Marples was warning the House 'my Right Hon. Friend has told local authorities that they ought now to be turning their attention to slum clearance. It is primarily for each authority to decide the pace of its own operations according to the needs of its area, but he is studying the whole question of unfitness and disrepair with a view to a comprehensive plan in which a renewed slum clearance drive would have a prominent place'.

However, Macmillan got his way. Butler, reluctantly, acquiesced in deferral of a rents Bill though Macmillan's blandishments had convinced few that Tory canvassers would be able to overcome 'wicked Tories to raise rents' headlines. Harry Crookshank, Lord Privy Seal, produced a timetable whereby a Rating Revaluation White Paper would be discussed in early summer at which time Macmillan would warn councils of the contents; by then local elections would be over, avoiding any electoral risk. With luck legislation would be completed then or in the autumn. The 'Grand Design' would thus be the central platform during the next session of Parliament, preceded by its own White Paper. In fact, events moved faster and by 21 May Marples was on his feet in the Commons introducing the Second Reading of the Rating and Revaluation Bill. On 30 June it was the Second Reading of the New Towns Bill.

Speaking to the Housing Repairs and Rent Bill in November 1953, Bevan's response had encapsulated the Labour attack: 'he [Marples] did exactly what he said he was going to do. He "clawed back" workers from housing repairs to new building. Does he deny it? Does he deny that it was his intention to use repair workers on new house building? We should like to know, because the accusation made against us is that we neglected this problem, and the reason why we were attacked for neglecting it was because we did not bring in legislation to deal with the Rent Restriction Acts. But we were doing something far more important than that – we were repairing the houses'. Nevertheless, with Marples doing the heavy lifting, the Conservatives would deliver Woolton's pledge. It just took nifty ministerial footwork and a cheerful willingness to ignore the instincts of a party warming to the notion of a property-owning democracy. Of course housing was not the only government department fighting for scarce resources against a Chancellor prioritising restriction of supply to protect the balance of payments. In this ministerial infighting Marples excelled, though his very success marred the performance of others.

Cabinet met on 18 January 1954. That year's Housing Repairs and Rents Bill proclaimed an intention to provide for the clearance and redevelopment of areas of unfit housing accommodation; to secure or promote the reconditioning and maintenance of houses; and to amend Labour's housing legislation and relax rent control. On 13 April 1954 Marples moved its Third Reading, with Macmillan winding up: by now his combative exchanges with Bevan were conducted on equal terms. The resulting Act attracted ire from Labour who saw it as impoverishing people with higher rents. At its Second Reading (some months earlier), Marples was gratified to be congratulated on his performance by Henry Brooke, successor to Macmillan as chairman of the party's housing committee. Though a graceful performer in the House, he remained self-critical, believing he needed to improve, even contemplating a five-year plan to raise his game.

During the calendar year 1954 the once despaired-of house building target was again met, a perfect backdrop to the general election everyone expected the following year. This was the kind of success the public could understand. Standards had been compromised, for example by building two- rather than three-bedroom houses, but even so it burnished the reputation of the government as an administration that got things done. That year the Ideal Home Exhibition (sponsored by the *Daily Mail*) celebrated government success and the parliamentary secretary made sure he was on hand to be photographed welcoming the Queen to a three-bedroom 'people's house'.

On 18 October that year Marples left Housing and Local Government. As the dynamo of the ministry he might legitimately have expected promotion. Instead he would enter the doldrums. Historians of the 1950s vary in their assessment of Marples. To David Kynaston in *Family Britain* (2010: 281) he was 'super-energetic'; Richard Lamb, in *The Macmillan Years: The Emerging Truth* (1995: 14) dismisses him as 'pedestrian': to Charles Williams, reflecting contemporary Conservative snobberies, he was 'bumptious and talkative' (*Harold Macmillan*, 2009); Peter Hennessy manages 768 pages of *Having it So Good* (2007) without mentioning him. Without doubt he deserves greater credit than Macmillan for the achievements of the Ministry after 1951; he, unlike his chief, had a plan to hit an output target no one believed in. Curiously he came in his old age to believe his greatest achievement at housing was to push for the first Clean Air Act.

The Conservative achievement in meeting the Woolton pledge cannot be gainsaid. But there was a price. The completions figures related to dwellings, not houses, and some were decidedly modest in scale, contrasting with Bevan's aspirational approach. The Marples/Macmillan target was hit early. However, as Horne observes, their performance in slum clearance and dwellings renewal was less impressive. Moreover, performance in sectors with less clear-cut goals, such as school building and road construction, had been poor, reflecting the two men's success in corralling scarce resources. Macmillan and Marples may have delivered the numbers, but the real shift in type of housing provision came in Eden's time with the appointment of Duncan Sandys to the housing portfolio. It was Sandys who put through a November 1955 measure biasing development in favour of tall construction. Hennessy points out that 'over the four years 1956–60, high rise blocks increased from three per cent of new public housing provision to fifteen per cent' (Hennessy 2007: 493).

Chapter 5

Pensions and Pasture, 1954–1957

On 18 October 1954 Churchill moved Macmillan away from housing to his long-coveted position of Minister of Defence. Marples moved too, but only sideways, replacing Robin Burton as parliamentary secretary to the Minister of Pensions, Osbert Peake. While Peake's office was elevated to Cabinet rank, Marples became merely one of two parliamentary secretaries, co-equal with John Smyth. He must have resented this reduction in status after being Macmillan's effective deputy for so long but he dutifully followed the advice of the Whips' Office and knuckled down. It was poor reward for one of Churchill's most successful junior ministers, the man whose legwork had allowed the Conservatives to deliver their eye-catching 1951 manifesto pledge. It also suggests Macmillan had little clout in the administration – if indeed he had tried to help Marples up the ladder at all. Six months later, Macmillan would reach the Foreign Office and eight months after that the Chancellorship. These rapid promotions for his old chief, bringing him into contention for the top job, were dog years for Marples.

On 7 April 1955, the long-awaited transition from Churchill to Anthony Eden took place. Eden wasted no time, calling a general election for 26 May. While few seats changed hands in this contest, the position of the Conservative government was greatly strengthened, leaving them a majority of sixty seats over all other parties. Marples' result in the Wirral confirmed that it was now very much a safe seat. When Macmillan moved from defence to become Eden's Foreign Secretary, Marples must have had some expectation of personal advancement. If so, he was disappointed. Macmillan then continued his dizzying rise, replacing Butler at the Exchequer in December. He was in no doubt about Marples' abilities, deeming him 'a very capable man' and lamenting that he was being left to languish as Under-secretary for Pensions. The next month he advocated his cause (and that of Julian Amery) in a private meeting with Butler and Eden, discovering that the Chief Whip (Buchan-Hepburn) was 'very prejudiced' against both. Worse (for Marples) was to come.

He remained joint parliamentary secretary to the Ministry of Pensions and National Insurance until 20 December 1955 when Peake was replaced as minister by John Boyd-Carpenter in what turned out to be a general reshuffle. Two new parliamentary secretaries (Edith Pitt and Richard Wood) arrived to replace Marples and Smyth. Were there doubts in Conservative circles about his business interests? Perhaps worried about this, he had written to the Attorney General on 3 August 1955 asking if he had to get rid of his shares. The Attorney had replied that in the case of a controlling interest divestment should occur 'if there is any danger that a conflict may arise or appear to arise between his public interest and his public duties'. The Attorney objected to the proposed shares disposal because Ridgway might be inferred to be acting as 'cover' for Marples in the event that he re-acquired his former holding.

Just before Christmas 1955 Marples was summoned to 12 Downing Street, official home of the Chief Whip. Sherry was offered but the mood was far from festive. Buchan-Hepburn opened by remarking 'this is going to be rough on you'. Marples could not expect promotion. If he moved at all the best he would get would be a sideways move and that to a 'worse' ministry. Eden, the Chief Whip reported, thought he might prefer to return to business. In that event a baronetcy would be offered. Buchan-Hepburn then ventured an extraordinary statement: 'everyone knows you have done well. It isn't as if you were a dud. You have done awfully well and Harold speaks highly of you'. Talent, it seemed, was not valued in the new administration. Marples' own notes portray an embarrassed Buchan-Hepburn 'ill at ease', speaking in muddled sentences. He summarised the situation in his own words to the Chief Whip: he faced a forced resignation disguised with an honour. 'I am not personally acceptable to the Prime Minister although I am efficient.' The deflated Chief Whip replied, 'it's just that Anthony wants to put his chaps in and there isn't room for you'.

Marples now wisely played for time, consulting Hugh Massingham (opposed), lunching with Ridgway (in favour). Massingham additionally stressed the need to keep in with Macmillan. This was critical advice for he also briefed him on the best way to approach the now Chancellor. By 4 p.m. Marples was seated in Macmillan's room in the House, briefing him about Buchan-Hepburn's performance on which, Marples records, he 'concentrated fiercely'. Macmillan regretted his own failure to get Marples a job. 'I tried all I could', he reported regretfully, perhaps recalling his September conversation with the Chief Whip and Butler, though it is hard to credit the impotence of this consummate player of the political game.

Then, extraordinarily, this newly appointed Chancellor of the Exchequer exclaimed, 'it is a rotten government and probably will break up.' Eden was bringing in all the 'party boys'; at the Exchequer, he himself had fought to bring onto his staff people like Percy Mills. Then, decisively, Macmillan added, 'don't accept a bloody thing from them. Go on the back benches ... when you see the Chief Whip show him you mean business. Threaten him you mean to work hard at politics'. Over time, he himself would get more power and indeed 'do something' for him. A grateful Marples came away thinking Macmillan 'genuinely angry'.

At 5 p.m. he returned to 12 Downing Street and, largely, followed Macmillan's advice. 'Firmly and happily' he reminded the Chief Whip of his earlier 'bad advice' to go to Pensions where he had passed fifteen unhappy months. He was prepared to resign but he refused to camouflage the resignation as a business move ('I have all the money I want') and declined the honour. To his astonishment Buchan-Hepburn immediately accepted this and even attempted to withdraw his earlier remarks. Marples found this sincere if baffling. One hour later they had a third meeting at which he was offered parliamentary secretary at the Ministry of Fuel and Power under Aubrey Jones whom he considered a close friend. After further consultations with Massingham and his fiancée Ruth, he phoned the Chief Whip refusing the job and the honour and promising to tell the truth about his resignation. He went home to down a bottle of wine with Ruth. For the first time in four years he was out of government. The couple departed the next day for an extended Christmas holiday in Davos.

Whether by accident or design Marples did not entirely follow Macmillan's advice. He might have cultivated expertise and burnished his reputation on the back benches. Instead, and remarkably after an active decade in the House, *Hansard* records not a single contribution to the House of Commons during the whole of 1956. But 1956 was no run-of-the-mill year and offered much for an ambitious MP to comment on. The country had a relatively new Prime Minister whose Chancellor Harold Macmillan introduced premium bonds in his April budget. That July the Clean Air Act, a belated response to London's smogs, received Royal Assent while October saw the Queen open Calder Hall, Britain's first nuclear power station, presaging a secular shift in energy sources. In foreign affairs, February brought the celebrated Twentieth Congress of the Communist Party and its assault on the policies and methods of Stalin by Khrushchev. That same month, Guy Burgess and Donald Maclean, the celebrated 'Cambridge spies' who had disappeared in 1951, resurfaced in Moscow. However, it was the Suez Crisis and its impact on British politics that would rescue Marples' government career. On 5 November Britain and France invaded Egypt in response to the nationalisation of the Suez Canal by President Nasser. Israel joined the action. Eden sought to avoid giving a clear denial of collusion with the Israeli government even though its participation in the conflict was plain to see. On 20 December, just a year after instructing his Chief Whip to sack Marples, Eden fatefully told the Commons 'there was not foreknowledge that Israel would attack Egypt. There was not.'

While Marples had not troubled the clerks of the House of Commons, he had not been idle. His appointments diary for 1956 records plenty of political activity: a February lunch with Percy Mills (similarly out of favour), meetings with Macmillan and Mills in March, appearances on *Any Questions* in April and November and a meeting with the Wine Trades Association. His social life was also full: two weeks skiing in Davos at the end of March; visits to Glyndebourne as well as Wimbledon and Queen's. There was Ascot and of course a regular fixture list of First Division matches. Were these the actions of a man conscious of his own abilities and anxious to keep in the public eye yet with a rich hinterland and private business interests to pursue? He may even have lunched with Macmillan on 21 December. If so, it may be highly significant, with the older man fewer than three weeks away from No. 10. His business was going well. Marples Ridgway grew from strength to strength in the expansionary 1950s. Among its greatest achievements (as main contractor) was the Allt-na-Lairige Dam near Loch Lomond for which the company obtained the services of noted engineer Eric Geddes. Its reservoir serves the Glen Shira hydroelectric scheme – the power station is two miles downstream, on the River Fyne's east bank. It is still the only large pre-stressed concrete dam in Britain, though completed in 1957.

The year 1956 was also memorable in Marples's private life. In 1951 he had met Ruth Alianore Bradfield (née Dobson) and the two had become close. She was the daughter of a master lace dresser prominent in Nottingham business circles. 'Ri' (as she was known to her family) had been an actress and a model. The two shared a passion for tennis and were both enthusiastically sociable. They were married in Westminster on 7 July with Reg Ridgway and Jack Huntington serving as witnesses. He was forty-eight and she was thirty-seven. Ernest's marriage to Edna Harwood had of course been dissolved the year of his election to Parliament. Ruth too had been married, aged only twenty and on the eve of war, to John Butlin Bradfield, a Nottingham auctioneer; this too had been dissolved. Unusually, her marriage to Marples had a settlement attached (witnessed by Huntington and Harry Waugh). Since the couple did not have children it is worth noting that the settlement anticipates this possibility, suggesting they may have hoped for offspring. The settlement dissolved the Wetherby Trust shares into the Harwood Trust, giving Ruth an income. She moved from her home in Chapel Street, Westminster, into Eccleston Street, and from this time on became a full and equal participant in Marples' affairs, political and social. Until Ernest's rapid decline into Alzheimer's, their marriage was overwhelmingly happy, though Ruth later confided to friends that he had 'never been easy to live with'. After his death she emerged as a formidable defender of his posthumous reputation.

On their wedding night the couple departed for an extended honeymoon, returning only on 2 September. While they were away Anne Bailey, late in July, had given birth to a son, Ellis Lincoln Bailey. Bailey herself would later allege that Marples had continued to see her although she had, by this time, both married and served a jail sentence, possibly for prostitution. Her account of continued dalliance during the Marples' engagement singularly failed to convince Lord Denning when he investigated her story during the backwash of the Profumo affair seven years later. The date of the birth matters because Bailey would allege that Marples had been 'good to her' afterwards, implausibly because the newly-weds were honeymooning out of the country. There was never any suggestion, even at the height of the post-Profumo scandal, that Marples was the father.

For Britain, Suez was a national calamity, but it broke the clouds over Marples' career. The ill-timed Egyptian invasion had coincided with American presidential elections in which Eisenhower, the Republican candidate, could not be seen to acquiesce in neo-imperialist ventures. His administration aggressively sold sterling and the franc, precipitating a run on both, and it refused to sell Britain oil. This was a major crisis in what the post-Churchill Conservatives liked to consider Britain's 'Special Relationship' with the United States. On 24 November the UN General Assembly censured Britain and France. Behind all lurked doubts about Israeli collusion and the veracity of Eden's statements to the House of Commons. Macmillan, as Chancellor, had warned of the gathering crisis afflicting sterling and late in November shared with a nervous Cabinet his fear of devaluation. Eden, convalescing in Jamaica after a nervous disorder and recurrent fevers, had left Butler and Macmillan managing the government. The initial public reaction to Suez had been euphoric but by mid-December Conservative popularity was at rock-bottom. Knowing the game was up, but fearing Eden would oppose withdrawal, Butler and Macmillan encouraged him not to come home while they organised an effective surrender; once he reappeared in London it was too late, and on 9 January 1957 he resigned to depart for a long Jamaican convalescence. Harold Macmillan replaced him the following day.

Chapter 6

Postcodes and Premium Bonds, 1957–1959

MMacmillan succeeded Eden as Prime Minister on 10 January with low political expectations, even warning the Queen that his government might not last. While he still had control of patronage he was determined to use it. He seems first to have considered Marples as replacement for Aubrey Jones at the Ministry of Fuel and Power, an appointment that might have gratified Marples after his experiences only a year before (see the hint in 'E.M.A.' 'Note for the Record', 29 October 1959, PREM 11/4943). In the end Jones moved from Fuel and Power to Minister of Supply, procuring defence equipment. Macmillan had found a better role for Marples, making him Postmaster General, but he took care first to obtain assurances of a clear demarcation of interests between him and Marples Ridgway (Marples to the Prime Minister 15 January 1957, Prime Minister to Marples, 16 January 1957, PREM 11/4943). Marples later drily attributed his Post Office appointment as being to the only government department Marples Ridgway was not supplying (*The Times*, 21 July 1976).

The office of Postmaster General was one in which a showman might excel – his immediate predecessor had been the avuncular, if partisan, wartime 'radio doctor' Charles Hill, now Chancellor of the Duchy of Lancaster. Though not a Cabinet position, at least not in Macmillan's first administration, the Postmaster General headed a large nationalised industry and effectively ran his own department. When the call came on 12 January 1957, Marples was in Davos, rounding off his backbench year with an extended bout of skiing and Christmas socialising. He was abruptly summoned and offered the job. If he could not be in the Cabinet (and Macmillan may not then have felt secure enough to go that far), becoming Postmaster General was the next best thing, especially since it also conferred membership of the Privy Council. In time Marples would discover ample scope for his accountancy skills and unveil several long-simmering Post Office projects that he might implement. STD, mechanical sorting, the electronic phone exchange and new uniforms for postmen could all be introduced by an energetic minister seeking to be noticed. By 28 January he was comfortably in post, pondering how to handle party political broadcasts. This year brought several one-on-one meetings with the Prime Minister (as well as formal dinners) at 10 Downing Street. Being Postmaster General was his rehabilitation after the humiliations of 1954. His Labour 1960s successor, Tony Benn, told an *Any Questions* audience that Marples was the best Postmaster General the country had ever had.

The Post Office

The 1950s Post Office was an institution central to the nation's life and a substantial contributor to the Exchequer. It was a quasi-public corporation which held a monopoly of phone services and supply. Phone users were reminded of their subscriber status by fixed connection of the handset to the wall: these sets were manufactured exclusively by the Post Office and rented to subscribers. General post offices, the only permitted location for stamp purchase, were then as familiar on British high streets as W.H. Smith and Boots the Chemist. They also occupied first place for savings in a country where the majority lacked bank accounts. Transactions handled on the public's behalf exceeded £5 billion, an immense sum by 1957 standards. Marples understood this centrality in the life of the nation and wanted to capitalise on it, urging his staff to focus on counter services where the aim should be 'to please as well as to serve the customer'. The Royal Mail also enjoyed a monopoly of letter and parcel carriage. This immense trading organisation received over £400 million annually from the public in exchange for its services and now it was answering for the first time to an entrepreneur. Though effectively a nationalised industry, its Crown Agency status meant it was not liable for taxation. Its workforce, then exceeding 350,000, enjoyed Civil Service status. Over time this strange phenomenon came to puzzle and frustrate a minister with an accounting background. It certainly stimulated his thinking about the role of public industries in that pre-privatisation era. Marples eventually concluded that the post and phones should be discrete businesses but for now there was little government appetite for separating them.

In 1955 the Churchill government had granted the Post Office a measure of self-contained finance. Commercial accounts governed policy and limited the Exchequer's annual claims on it to £5 million. Bizarrely, its ancient monopoly required that all revenue had to be paid to the Treasury while parliamentary authority must still be sought for expenditure. To accommodate this anomaly a dual accounting system was run, with the Post Office's own accounts reflecting the accurate trading picture. This absurdity affronted Marples. His first thought was that a better way of reporting the required two sets of accounts (cash and commercial) was to plough depreciation charges back in and put borrowing arrangements on a more realistic basis. He spent considerable time fighting even this issue through government against heavy Treasury resistance. This involved political infighting but Marples knew he had the backing of a Prime Minister who watched his activities 'with admiration' (Prime Minister's Personal Minute to Postmaster General, 17 March 1959, POST 122/169).

It took Marples three years as Postmaster General to turn the Post Office into a trading organisation. By Christmas 1958, Macmillan had forced his plan onto the Chancellor (Derek Heathcoat-Amory) though it still took months to agree a solution. Marples wanted regularisation of Post Office/ Treasury relations: the separation of their accounts; the replacement of the estimates procedure with other forms of parliamentary control; the retention nonetheless of Civil Service status by Post Office staff. Only in April 1959 did the two jointly propose a trading fund that would hold income and investment with the year's financial record stated in commercial accounts accompanied by a report to Parliament from the Postmaster General (*Future Status of the Post Office*, Memorandum by the Chancellor of the Exchequer and the Postmaster General, 11 April 1959). Their continued differences over details required reference to Cabinet. For all his energy Marples can have derived only deferred gratification from seeing the 1961 Post Office Act come in under his successor Reginald Bevins. It created a Post Office fund under the management of the Postmaster General: all income was paid into the fund and all expenditure met out of it. This enabled the Post Office to operate as a business with the financial status of a public authority. Even this the Treasury ponderously viewed as 'a major constitutional innovation'. Marples joyously flagged up his triumph in a Wirral speech, rallying most of the press, including *The Times*, the *Daily Telegraph*, the *Daily Mail*, the *Scotsman* and the *Glasgow Herald*. The announcement of a trading fund, delivered in Wallasey on 18 September 1959, with an election approaching, attracted plenty of press coverage in what had become the Marples style.

That said, the real radical surgery – most obviously the separation of post and telecommunications, had to await his Labour successor Tony Benn, an occasion on which he was invited to comment in the house magazine (*Masters of the Post*, 458). The Cabinet discussed the Post Office in July 1959 but a White Paper embodying change was delayed by the general election. When it finally appeared (as *The Status of the Post Office*, Cmnd. 989, March 1960), Marples had moved on. The first Post Office commercial accounts were presented by Bevins. Marples still contrived to leave his fingerprints on the news.

One pet project the Prime Minister could count on his loyal lieutenant to develop was Premium Bonds. Macmillan's only (1956) budget had disclosed a penchant for popular capitalism: he himself had handpicked the first-ever winning bond at a Trafalgar Square ceremony which we would now call a 'media event'. This cunning inducement to save caught the public imagination and was an instant success with bonds worth £5 million sold on the first day. The Opposition was critical: Shadow Chancellor Harold Wilson dubbed the Bonds 'a squalid raffle' and lamented a 'national demoralisation' but Macmillan's Treasury tenure had merely been a prelude to a premiership allowing him to restore to office the lieutenant with whom he shared a popular touch. Marples moved early to automate prize-winner selection helped by the team behind the Second World War code breaker, Colossus. They had already created ERNIE (Electronic Random Number Indicator Equipment) to pick bond numbers. Marples was not blind to the publicity-gathering implications of the sobriquet. At ERNIE's Lytham St Anne's home at 9.15 a.m. on 1 June 1957 he flicked a switch and sixteen minutes later the first randomly selected winning Premium Bond number was produced. Generations of ERNIEs followed, and National Savings were still using the acronym in 1999.

As Postmaster General his responsibilities included: broadcasting matters (licensing, allocation of frequencies, matters concerning radio interference) as well as the government's relations with the Independent Television Authority (ITA) and the BBC; the core postal, telecommunications and other activities that comprised Post Office services; and attending the Post Office board. His time as Postmaster General was not marked by innovation in broadcasting, perhaps because the easy wins lay elsewhere, and so what follows focuses principally on post and telephone services. July 1958 brought a government decision to defer the establishment of an independent committee to review the operations of the BBC and the recently established ITA but by February Marples had ascertained that both wanted to go ahead in view of the lengthy list of matters requiring review ('Broadcasting Developments', 17 February 1959, CAB 129/96/34). These included longer broadcasting hours; pressure from film companies for subscription services; controversies over advertising in ITA channels; and that old chestnut, the issue of BBC funding.

He was given the Merseyside entrepreneur Kenneth Thompson (MP for Liverpool Walton and some two years younger), as Assistant Postmaster General and took Commons questions for the first time in the new post on 30 January 1957. By then he was in the thick of it. Marples ran the Post Office through a 'Postmaster General's Policy Discussion' meeting once or twice a month. Attendees included Thompson and the Post Office Director General. At such meetings he pressed for a more commercial approach, qualified by putting the customer first – two objectives that might seem incompatible. It was certainly productive: in less than three years this team pushed through three White Papers, the last firmly establishing the Post Office as a trading department.

Even his very first day hinted at an exciting three years to come. After a press call, he visited Shell-Mex House to inaugurate the country's first private teleprinter automatic switching system installed by the Post Office for Shell and BP. He used a press conference to make known his curiosity about the public's opinion of Post Office services, conveyed his excitement at the prospect of deepening its use of electronics and declared his view that the growing use of the telephone needed to be accommodated within building design (*Post Office Magazine*, March 1957). Shell-Mex House was a corporate event, but contemporaries J.R. Baxter, his assistant private secretary and later private secretary to Thompson, recalled his easy conversations with staff at all levels. Nor was this feigned. He quickly set a schedule of sub-post office visits, delighting in turning up unexpectedly at even the most remote location.

It remains an impressive schedule: Edinburgh, Glasgow and the Outer Hebrides (February 1957), and six visits in South Wales the same month. March 1957 brought his overnight trip on the 'Down Special', the travelling post office or 'Night Mail'; in January he found time to help out at the Liverpool switchboard and accompany Postman Walter Perry on his Liverpool morning round, observing Perry's difficulties with letter boxes too low, too small or too high. (He subsequently directed the Post Office to work with the British Standards Institution and the Design Council to produce twelve prototype standard letter boxes later to be displayed at the Building Exhibition at Olympia). In January 1958, he and Ruth picked one for their Eccleston Street home (*Marples Papers 8/2*). Over time personnel relations became formalised. The new Postmaster General approved existing union agreements and kept them on schedule. Ron Smith became general secretary of the Union of Postal Workers (UPW) around this time. Marples found him comfortable with change: STD, ERNIE and mechanical sorting. Later, Charles Smith became general secretary of the Post Office Engineers' Union (POEU). Handing over to Reginald Bevins in November 1959, Marples counselled that he should 'keep sweet the two Smiths', advice Bevins was careful not to follow (D. Campbell-Smith, *Masters of the Post: The Authorized History of the Royal Mail*, 419).

Though back in harness, Marples was determined to maintain his regular pre-appointment regime: each day began with a game of tennis and there was time for business interests, regular meetings with Ridgway and attendance at the company's December AGM; visits to the Beaujolais vineyards and tasting of the 1955 vintage; Christmas departure for a skiing holiday in Davos or Zermatt (for a full month in 1957–1958); the uninhibited couple returned the following April. He made the most of his time, using the rail sleeper service to reach his constituency in the summer months. The much-travelled pair spent all August 1958 in Venice, by way of Ostend. That year was an important one in another way: after many years as an amateur fancier of Beaujolais wines, Ernest finally achieved his ambition of buying a chateau and vineyard. The location was Fleurie, an estate of 45 acres on the right bank of the Rhône, north of Lyons. On their many visits the couple would live in a nearby cottage 'Les Laverts', 'an absolute gem'. When in residence the couple flew the Union flag. A stay in the cottage also became a coveted reward for later acolytes like Mark Schreiber, social friends and the couple's extended family. The vineyard itself thrived and by 1964, the year Marples finally left office, his *cru* was awarded a gold medal at Paris's Exposition Agricole.

Marples' last Commons appearance as Postmaster General was on 20 July 1959, rather prosaically to announce proposals to improve the signal in the Highlands and Islands. His plans on leaving the Post Office included the extension of STD to 60 per cent of all calls, maintaining the UK's global lead in mechanisation, joining a Commonwealth global cable venture, cutting waiting times for new phones to a few weeks, redesigning post offices and exchanges and expanding the telex service. But by 5 November he had been succeeded by Bevins. His farewell message to the staff contained a fair amount of boasting but his thirty-three months had been a time of real achievement (*Post Office Magazine*, No.10, October 1959).

Macmillan's aim, at least until the 1959 election, was to demonstrate that nationalised industries could be run efficiently (Letter to the Chancellor of the Exchequer, 16 December 1958, POST 122/169). Marples reminded government colleagues that the Post Office had to balance its budget after making allowance for depreciation (on a replacement basis), pension liability and an Exchequer payment in lieu of tax. In return he wanted the necessary investment to meet burgeoning demand for a phone service. During his first fifteen months the Post Office had raised £50 million of extra revenue: it was funding half its investment programme from its own income. Still, he worried that looming pay awards would upset the balance, and by July 1957 was sounding the alarm, warning Cabinet of severe increases in charges ('Post Office Finance', memorandum by the Postmaster-General, 12 July 1957, CAB 129/88/8). The only way to avoid 'chronic deficit' was to raise an extra £63 million in the eighteen months to the end of March 1959. He had concluded there must be higher postal charges, even if opposition to them was led by the Prime Minister himself. He proposed raising the cost of an inland letter from two pence halfpenny to three pence and imposing the full cost of a telephone on residential subscribers. By these means, he would transform a current year deficit of well over £6 million into a £5 million surplus. Investment in the phone service was about to pay off, but this was an uncomfortable reminder that in the staff-intensive letter business revenue would be hard to come by.

In December 1957 Marples moved the Second Reading of the Post Office and Telegraph (Money Bill) in a lengthy, characteristically expansive speech. Its object was to meet the cost of Post Office capital expenditure for two years, authorising the Treasury to issue up to £75 million and defining ways it might be borrowed. Provision was made for repaying the Exchequer. Actual capital expenditure would be £180 million, with £105 million found from internal sources. The speech was notable for anticipating a revolution in the sorting process, spearheaded by the introduction of postal codes; for heralding STD; and for its interest in a standardisation of design of post offices and telephone kiosks ('branding', as we would call it today). The situation was akin to his honeymoon days with Macmillan at Housing. The Bill completed its Third Reading in January 1958 and became law that April. He had appointed Esso chairman Sir Leonard Sinclair to lead a committee to look at 'one of the major headaches of the Post Office, the telegraph system' but Sinclair's June 1958 report was a damp squib, doing little but recommending a price hike.

In May 1958 he offered the House his view that government should distinguish between capital investment allocations in a revenue-producing industry that traded and straight expenditure from taxation. He thought it obvious: 'there is a difference between a revenue-producing concern and one which takes its money purely from taxation'. Post Office capital investment was scheduled to fall by £10 million pounds in the four years from 1956–1957 (though he had obtained extra cash for the last two years in the cycle). 'I wish I had the same freedom in the Post Office as I have in my own business,' he lamented, insisting 'there must be a steady programme, and one cannot turn that programme on and off as though it were a tap. The business will not be efficient if one does'. He selected the example of roads: 'the telephone cables which should be laid when the roads are being made must be thought of at the same time. Automatically, investment on [*sic*] the telephones service should be increased if investment on roads is increased.'

Telephones

The Post Office was no slumbering behemoth. Its phone engineers were experimenting dynamically. Phones might take the lion's share (about 80 per cent) of all Post Office capital investment but that would soon pay off. The Postmaster General faced an important tactical decision on whether to introduce STD universally or go ahead with it as soon as areas were ready. He opted for the latter. His White Paper, *Full Automation of the Telephone System* (Cmnd. 303, November 1957) heralded slashed call charges once STD arrived in the New Year. That day he wrote to phone managers warning them of the changes under way and urging them to sell the good news of an increased range for the hated minimum three penny call. The trick was to cut the number of charging units by 90 per cent, substituting direct dialling for operator-handling in trunk calls. He partnered it with standard charges and establishing 'local call areas' which would steadily extend. Hitherto manual operators alone had been able to measure the charge for a distance call: this could now be done via automation. The White Paper promised full automation: eventually all calls would be dialled and phone numbers of three and four digits would grow to as many as ten. He hoped for savings as high as £15 million a year. Five months later Marples took the transition to cheap, quick and easy calls further. Some trunk charges were cut and he extended the cheap rate period to cover the entire night, while stretching the trunk dialling facility beyond its initial Bristol pilot area (it took time to reach the whole country). There was to be two-penny a minute trunk dialling for all. On 5 December 1958 STD was formally inaugurated for all subscribers in

Bristol and this time (after several disappointments trying to launch his eye-catching schemes) Marples persuaded the Queen to inaugurate it.

He had a good record in securing investment. While the longed-for Post Office Tower would not be built on his watch, he was on hand to witness the Lord Mayor of London in July 1958 lay the foundation stone of the city's new telecoms centre in Farringdon Street. It would be the Post Office's largest commercial building since the war. Characteristically he worried that automation would remove the human element from the phone service. Operators would, after all, continue to have a role when problems arose. An illustrated employee information booklet of March 1959 informed staff of the need for 'new language': 'It is as a customer that we will now think of each telephone subscriber'. Phone operators were enjoined to be themselves and sound like human beings. On the inside cover was a handwritten note from the Postmaster General: 'This tells you about our plans for the telephone service and the part you can play in it. Our aim is not only to serve but to please the customer. We can do it. And we can have fun doing it.' A week before Christmas 1958 Marples had been pictured trying out the new trunk dialling call box. One civil servant, Toby O'Brien, remembered him as 'always extremely good with the press' (Letter to Lady Marples, 24 June 1982, Marples Papers 8/2). Nor did he forget Parliament. When universal STD arrived, he wrote to all MPs showing in detail how their constituencies were affected. He would be less successful at this kind of management in his transport years.

In 1959, seeking to erect the 450-foot-high Post Office Tower, Marples once again encountered a formidable foe. The Tower was needed to sustain radio waves in an increasingly high-rise city. Marples had prepared the planning ground with prior approval from the London County Council planning committee and the Fine Arts Commission. But Evelyn Sharp, formerly deputy secretary at the Ministry of Housing and Local Government was now permanent secretary. Even her reputation as a promoter of modernist high-rise blocks did not dispose her to favour this techno-marvel, as she deplored its design. Once she got wind of his intentions she buttonholed him, followed up with a letter recording her 'horror' at his plan and threatened to bring it before the Housing Advisory Committee. As it happened, the Post Office had over several years eliminated every other way of dealing with the problem. The Tower would be built but by Ernest's Labour successor Anthony Wedgwood Benn. For now, erection was significantly delayed and it was only opened in 1965 (POST 122/1172). Marples was not the last minister to receive rough treatment at Dame Evelyn's hands, as readers of Richard Crossman's *Diaries of a Cabinet Minister* will know.

Life was easier abroad, where Marples liked showing off the Post Office and basking in its reflected glory. He showcased it in Nigeria and Libya in September 1957, then in Nassau (Bermuda) and New York for ten days in early summer 1958; that October saw him boosting exports at the Brussels World Fair. Come January 1959 and the US Postmaster General was in London while later that month Marples flew to New York to visit the American Telegraph & Telephone Company (ATTC). His industry was already nationalised, a prospect ATTC feared and combated by cultivating US public esteem.

Royal Mail

One Post Office division was devoted to telegrams. The publicity-conscious (and newly-married) Marples was delighted to announce the wedding greetings telegram ('well in time for Easter weddings') on 1 March 1957. The Christmas post – then a major annual event – provided another opportunity to address the public: that December, television audiences saw him appeal to them to 'post early', 'write clearly', 'pack safely'. Marples constantly sought efficiency gains in the labour-intensive delivery business and tried to quantify them but was frustrated in those places where staff had to traipse up long paths or drives to the door. He worried about static or declining Post Office revenue at a time when the number of addresses requiring deliveries was rising and fretted about long queues at Crown post offices. He pulled in Lewis Casson and others to smarten the buildings up.

Nor was technological excitement lacking on the postal side where more profound change was underway. Since the early 1950s a new automatic sorting machine had been developed by the Post Office's Dollis Hill engineers. The happily-dubbed Electronic Letter Sorting Indicating Equipment (ELSIE) was triggered by introduction of a postcode which it translated into binary form using dots printed through phosphor tape on to the envelope. The dots could then be read by a sorting machine. The format of the postcode was a six-character alphanumeric: three letters designated the geographical area while two numbers and a letter identified the individual address. Norwich, the site of the launch, was 'NOR' followed by a space, then a two-digit number (which, unlike the current format, could include a leading zero) and a single final letter (instead of the two final letters in the current format), for example, 'NOR 09N'. Luckily, Norwich had eight ELSIES, making it an obvious choice to launch what Marples knew would be a world first. Sensing the publicity opportunities, he had tried, but this time failed, to get the Queen to inaugurate the new system. He made up for her absence by inviting a posse of international reporters to hail this British 'first'. It was a world-beating innovation from the country that had launched the Penny Black. He came to Norwich in July 1959 for the official launch of the experiment in front of the national media. In fact ELSIE failed to work on this occasion and the whole thing was an elaborate deception. Whether Marples knew of the subterfuge is unknown, but the whole amusing tale is told by Campbell-Smith in *Masters of the Post: The Authorised History of the Royal Mail*, (2011: 405–406). In less than three months, each of the city's 150,000 private and business addresses would receive a code. It was, in Campbell-Smith's words, 'an experiment in automation which would be in advance of anything else in the world'.

Chapter 7

Roads to 1939

Early days on the roads

The 'Railway Age' may be said to have started in 1830 with the opening of the Liverpool and Manchester Railway, the progenitor of the long-distance inter-city main line. Stagecoach operators could not compete in terms of price and speed and most of them quickly went out of business as the new-fangled railways spread across the land in the following years. Britain's roads remained busy through the rest of the nineteenth century, much of the traffic feeding into or being distributed from the growing railway system. These roads were largely designed for horse-drawn traffic which moved slowly by later standards. Even late in the nineteenth century the roads were administered by nearly 2,000 local bodies many of which were very reluctant to spend money on systematic maintenance or improvement work. When there had been heavy rainfall, the roads turned into quagmires. In dry periods they became dustbowls. There were incessant complaints when motor vehicles began to appear. Their greater speed caused them to throw up dense clouds of dust to the great annoyance not only of the motorists themselves but other road users and passers-by. The area around the roads became covered with a patina of dust and dirt. Many early cars were driven recklessly and with braking systems yet to be perfected accidents were frequent. These early vehicles were mechanically unreliable and sometimes suffered the ignominy of being rescued and towed away by horses.

Before 1914 demand grew among the motoring public who, at that time, were almost exclusively well-to-do and frequently highly influential, for the development of the administrative systems, money and other resources needed for a greatly improved national road system. From earliest times it was a source of annoyance to motorists that governments siphoned off much of the revenue extracted from them for purposes other than improving or maintaining the roads. On this issue, if not necessarily on any other, the various road users' organisations were in concert.

The 'Age of the Road' might be said to date from the time in December 1894 when a Mr Henry Hewetson imported the first motor car into England. He drove it from the docks and across London, his progress watched by gaping crowds when, to their great amusement, he was stopped by the police for not being preceded by a man on foot with a flag to give warning of the vehicle's approach. The car was a Benz manufactured in Germany. This was evidence that countries industrialising later than Britain could leapfrog the painful processes associated with playing a pioneering role and set themselves up competitively in new industries in which Britain had no initial advantage.

The beginning of a road users' lobby can be traced back to 1886 when a conference was convened in Gloucester by the two main bodies representing cyclists: the Cyclists' Touring Club and the National Cyclists' Union. Their concern was the clouds of dust that were produced by the motorised users of the unmetalled roads of the day. This dust got into all those places, both mechanical and personal, where it was most unwelcome. As a result of this meeting, the Roads Improvement Association was set up in 1886 to persuade politicians to use public funding to improve road surfaces. A problem for road users was the enormous differences between the standards of road building and maintenance pursued by different local authorities. The Local Government Act of 1888 gave county councils the responsibility for maintaining major roads and improvements and greater uniformity followed.

Motor cars began to come into their own after the 'Red Flag Act' was repealed in 1896. This had been passed in 1865 and decreed that any mechanical vehicle using the public roads should be preceded by a man on foot and should not go faster than 4mph in the country and 2mph in the town. 'Mechanical' at this time largely meant steam-powered vehicles. By the 1890s this Act, although widely ignored, was holding back the use of the new internal combustion horseless carriages, much to the chagrin of their users. As their numbers spread, at this time only among the better-off, so bodies emerged to represent their collective interests as road users. In 1897 the rather aristocratic Royal Automobile Club (RAC) was formed. Its members were convinced that cars were desirable, had come to stay and their aim was to exert pressure on public bodies to make the changes necessary to ensure that roads were made safer for motorists. The close links the RAC had with the cyclists' organisations faded with the realisation that their respective interests were antagonistic, not mutual. More impatient to achieve changes favourable to motorists was an offshoot of the RAC, the Motor Union. This left the RAC in 1907 and in 1910 it merged with the equally militant

Automobile Association (AA). Both organisations fought against what they saw as unfair legal restrictions on motoring and unnecessary persecution and prosecution of motorists by the police. They particularly objected to the use of speed traps and the AA became involved in the strictly illegal practice of employing scouts at the roadside to give motorists advanced warning that there were speed traps in the neighbourhood. The motorists' organisations were also opposed to any idea that there should be tests and a system of licensing for those using cars and other self-propelled vehicles. They objected to registration plates as these allowed vehicles and their owners to be identified.

Motorists may have felt that they were singled out for unfair treatment but others who used the roads felt that they were being disadvantaged by the increasing numbers of self-propelled vehicles. Vast numbers of horse-drawn conveyances used the roads as did cyclists and pedestrians. Also using the roads were animals, often being driven to market. Complaints were mostly about the dangerous and inconsiderate manner in which motorists drove their vehicles and also, of course, the all-pervasive dust that their machines threw up on dry, unmetalled surfaces. The arrogance of the rich motorists who considered themselves above the law created an anti-motoring lobby in Parliament. *The Economist* commented drily in 1913: 'The vehicles of the rich kill and maim far more people than the vehicles of the poor ... But then nearly all politicians and officials constantly drive at an excessive speed themselves.' The Chancellor of the Exchequer, Herbert Asquith, in 1907 suggested that a motor car would be 'almost an ideal tax, because it is a tax on a luxury which is apt to degenerate into a nuisance'. Despite the unpopularity of motorists with the bulk of the population, the motoring clubs were beginning to accrue some negotiating strength because in 1903 they managed to have the speed limit raised to 20mph.

Into the 1920s

After the First World War the motoring organisations vociferously opposed almost every attempt to improve road safety. Both the AA and the RAC condemned all speed limits, driving tests, compulsory insurance, pedestrian crossings, speed traps and motorised police patrols and punishments handed out for motoring offences. These organisations put accidents largely down to 'human error' on the part of road users other than motorists and they used the occurrence of such accidents as propaganda in their campaigns for improved roads and new roads. The Pedestrians' Association, strident in its opposition to motor vehicles, in 1938 pointed to '100,000 killed and three million injured on the roads of Great Britain since the Great War'. The Society of Motor Manufacturers and Traders described this as 'hysterical'. Although the pro-road lobby was growing, its campaigns could not prevent a surge of road safety legislation in the 1930s including compulsory third-party insurance, mandatory driving tests and penalties for careless and dangerous driving.

When the Great War ended there was much talk about nationalising the railways and introducing a ministry to control both the railways and the roads. This created great concern in the pro-road camp which feared that railway matters would dominate the activities of this ministry to the detriment of the road interest. A pro-road group of MPs emerged, around 280 in number at the time, who campaigned vigorously against both the nationalisation proposal and the likelihood of the ministry being in thrall to the railway lobby. In the event, the railways were not nationalised and the Ministry of Transport, when created in 1919, proved to have many officials who were firmly in favour of road transport. It has continued, in its various guises, to be contentious ever since – by generally showing preference to bodies lobbying on behalf of road haulage and private motorists over public transport operators and non-car users.

The railways were quick to exploit the potential of motor vehicles as feeders to and from their trains. As early as 1903, for example, the Great Western Railway (GWR) operated two primitive motor buses from Helston Station to the Lizard. The use of buses enabled them to tap into sources of traffic which were useful but which were unlikely to warrant the investment needed to build and operate a railway line. The use of such vehicles was early acknowledgement of the flexibility and potential of road transport.

By the turn of the twentieth century the railways in many urban areas found themselves starting to experience keen competition from electric tramcars which could pick up and set down their passengers far more conveniently than trains. Although a few stations, usually located in inner-city areas, had closed by 1918 as a result of competition from trams, it was not until the years immediately after the end of the Great War that the growth of road transport began to pose a serious threat to the railways. Large numbers of cheap and relatively efficient army surplus trucks and buses became available for the first time. Many demobbed men had, in their war service, become skilled in motor maintenance. Many operators started with just one vehicle adapted to carry goods on weekdays while being convertible to use as a charabanc for weekends. In 1921 there were 128,000 goods vehicles, nearly 350,000 by 1930 and over half a million in 1938. The Railways Act 1921 was intended to create a coordinated transport system based on the supposedly complementary nature of road and rail. However, between 1924 and 1934 the railways lost about a quarter of their goods traffic to road transport. In no year between 1918 and 1939 did the volume of the freight carried by the railways reach the pre-1914 level. As early as 1919 when there was a national railway strike from 22 September to 5 October, the pattern of the future was clear, as *The Times* indicated: 'The triumph of the motor lorry, demonstrated so plainly in the prompt collection and distribution of milk and food during the strike, has done more to advertise the possibilities of motor transport to the people of this country than even the much greater success achieved by the motor lorry during the war'. The ability of road haulage vehicles to keep many essential services going was also confirmed graphically in the General Strike of 1926.

Hauliers quickly realised that they enjoyed far more flexibility in their operations than did the railway companies. They could appear overnight and tout for whatever business seemed to offer the quickest and best returns, their low overheads meaning that, in the absence of government regulation, they could undercut railway fares and rates. Lorry operators benefited from the convenience that came with being able to offer a door-to-door service without the necessity for transhipment. Railway freight operations, however, usually involved the transhipment from goods depot to local delivery vehicles of consignments which might then be damaged in the process. Journey times of goods conveyed by rail might be extremely slow where wagons found themselves shunted, sorted and then re-sorted several times on journeys of any length. It was not unknown for highly perishable soft fruit, for example, to take so long to get to market by rail that it was ruined by the time it got there. Dr Beeching stated in his report of 1963 that even then 'nearly all freight [traffic] moved by the staging of wagons from marshalling yard to marshalling yard, with variable and accumulated delays within them, so that the overall journey was bound to be slow and unpredictable'. Where short and medium distances were involved, road haulage often had the advantage in speed, even before Britain had motorways. Eliminating the need for transhipment reduced the hauliers' insurance costs. The haulage industry came to be dominated by small independent businesses with only a handful of vehicles, although there were some much larger companies. All were capable of taking traffic away from the railways.

Many railway stations were inconveniently located for the places they purported to serve and particularly for local, short journeys they began to lose business to bus operators. Rural branch lines were often hard hit because bus operators could handle the limited passenger traffic on offer much more cheaply and usually more conveniently for the passengers.

Over the course of the next decades the railways either found themselves conveying the various traffics for which they were better suited than road vehicles or carrying the sort of consignments that simply did not interest road hauliers. Railway charges tended to be based on the value of the goods conveyed rather than the cost of conveying them. Road haulage rates, on the other hand, were lower for valuable merchandise and relatively higher for less valuable commodities. Hauliers therefore tended to concentrate their activities where there was a lucrative heavy and regular demand for loads of fairly valuable merchandise. This left the railways to handle traffic that the road operators did not want but which the railways, under their 'common carrier' regulations dating back to the nineteenth century, were legally required not to turn away. Much of it was loss-making.

Regulation in road transport

From 1929 railway companies obtained legal powers to operate buses although, as has been pointed out, some companies had begun this activity back in the 1900s. The 'Big Four' bought some bus companies outright and obtained large shareholdings in others. The Road Traffic Act of 1930 established a system of regulating and licensing bus services. Proposals for new bus routes had to be presented to traffic commissioners, a system which allowed the railways to object to the granting of a road service licence. Public service vehicles had to possess up-to-date certificates of fitness and the timetables agreed with the traffic commissioners and advertised publicly had to be observed. Fare changes could only be made with the agreement of the commissioners. Infringements of the rules could lead to an operator losing its licence.

In 1933 road haulage came under new regulations. These provided licences to haulage companies who were now restricted to operating only within the terms of the licence with which they had been issued. Railway companies also bought into the road haulage industry. They took over Carter Patterson, the parcels carriers, and the removals company Pickfords, allowing some degree of coordination in appropriate road and railway activities. The idea of regulation of road haulage and the bus industry undoubtedly owed much to Herbert Morrison, a leading figure in the Labour Party. It was hoped that it might go some way towards stemming the flow of traffic away from the railways. Also in the 1930s, Neville Chamberlain, when Chancellor of the Exchequer, increased vehicle excise duty which placed an added financial burden on the road haulage industry. The impact of this was soon lessened by the outbreak of the Second World War.

The road haulage industry quickly gained a reputation for rogue or 'cowboy' operators, especially among many of the smaller companies who were prepared to run vehicles that were not roadworthy, were actually dangerous or carried loads that were unsafe because they were poorly secured. When official measures were taken to control some aspects of hauliers' operations, the *Commercial Motor* of 29 March 1932 complained bitterly: '… long distance haulage is in the position of a criminal in the dock'. Compared with the number of infringements of the law perpetrated by companies in the industry, very few road hauliers actually appeared in court. This did not prevent the formation of the Road Haulage Association in 1932, backed by various pro-road organisations, to counter what was seen as the undue preference of governments towards the railways.

Motor coaches posed a significant challenge to the railways from the 1920s. They proved ideal as a cheap and largely working-class means of transport for such events as day trips, works outings and visits to sporting occasions. Many of the vehicles were luxurious and had the advantage of being able to pick up and drop their passengers more conveniently than the railways. They were also able to take their passengers to places inaccessible by the railways. Most manual workers had a week's unpaid holiday before the First World War and some white-collar workers had two. A slowly increasing number of blue-collar workers were allowed two weeks holiday but the Holidays with Pay Act of 1938 increased the number of workers receiving holidays with pay from about 4 million in 1937 to over 11 million in 1939. Wages did not always allow workers and their families to travel and pay for accommodation and in 1937 it was estimated that less than one in three of the population actually went away for a holiday. Coach proprietors cashed in, their cheap prices attracting large numbers of money-conscious families to use the coach to travel to their holiday destinations or, for those with limited means, to partake of the day tours and excursions that were becoming widely available. Before the Second World War, most people travelling for recreational purposes still used trains, but by 1951 the proportion of holidaymakers using them had fallen to 47 per cent.

In Britain before the First World War, motor cars were expensive luxuries largely available only to the rich and it was to this market that the nascent car industry largely directed its efforts. The first major attempt to produce a cheap, basic but mechanically reliable car aimed at a mass market was the Model 'T' Ford introduced in 1912 and selling in the UK for £135. It was capable of a maximum speed of 40mph but in 1914 motorised road transport was still in its infancy. After the war ended, however, some British companies began to investigate ways to increase output levels including the production of cheaper models. A pioneer of small, standardised family cars was the Austin Seven which first appeared in 1921. Models of this sort boosted the automotive industry by increasing its potential market. With growing sales, unit costs and prices could come down. A marked fall in prices and significant improvements in the technical performance of motor vehicles combined with a rise in real incomes greatly to assist the growth of motor transport in the inter-war years. Hire-purchase arrangements became widely available. By 1938 the motor car was no longer a luxury available only to the well off. In that year there were 3 million motor vehicles on the road compared with 230,000 at the end of the Great War. Car ownership, however, was still very much in the minority. Cars were for the middle class and, at the upper end of specifications, for the seriously wealthy. Buses, motorcycles, motorcycle combinations and push-bikes were the working-class means of transport. It was significant that when Wythenshawe was planned as a very large overspill township for Manchester's slum clearance programme, it was entirely dependent on road transport with a comprehensive system of bus routes. An east to west railway passed along the northern periphery of Wythenshawe but despite the township being a planned development on a 'greenfield' site, no attempt was made at that time to involve railways in its transport infrastructure.

Ongoing technical improvements led to motor vehicles becoming more powerful, reliable and cheaper to run. The introduction of pneumatic tyres, for example, allowed higher speeds, lower fuel consumption and a more comfortable ride. The technology of road vehicles grew far more rapidly than that of the railways. Petrol was cheap until the railway companies persuaded the Exchequer to tax it in 1928. In 1939 more of Blackpool's visitors arrived by railway but cars, motorcycles and coaches, the latter getting faster, larger and more luxurious, were gaining ground. The tonnage of traffic passing over the Preston to Blackpool road, which was the busiest holiday road in Britain, doubled between 1922 and 1925 and had more than doubled again by 1935.

A revolution was taking place. As H.V. Morton in his *In Search of England*, published in 1926, wrote: '… never before have so many people been searching for England … The popularity of the cheap motor car is also greatly responsible for this long overdue interest in English history, antiquities and topography. More people than in any previous generation are seeing the real country for the first time'. The irony was of course that ever-increasing influxes of motorised vehicles began to change the nature and appearance of rural Britain. The 'real country' was changing.

As Dyos and Aldcroft argue in *British Transport* (1971), referring to the inter-war years: 'Never before had any one industry produced such profound change in such a short time as that around motor transport. It greatly facilitated the movement of goods and people and created new employment and investment opportunities which did much to relieve the gloom of those years.' In the late 1930s between 1.3 and 1.5 million people derived their livelihoods from the manufacture, operation and servicing of motor vehicles. The manufacture of motor vehicles and cycles employed nearly 400,000 people by 1939, making it the fourth largest industry in Britain. For the carriage of perishable commodities such as milk, fruit, vegetables and flowers, the motor vehicle was a godsend, particularly over short distances. The location of factories was no longer largely tied to areas where railway facilities were available. The new light industries such as electrical, chemicals and motor vehicles grew up largely around the west and south Midlands and the periphery of London, and road haulage was ideally suited to their needs. Road transport had far greater flexibility than the railways to deal with changing market demands. Dyos and Aldcroft again: 'The social habits of the people, the pattern of trade, the location of industry, sport and entertainment were all affected by this new medium of transport'. As Thorold, in *The Motoring Age* (2003) said, 'The private motorist revelled in his or her deliverance from the mass travel of the railways. It meant that you could drive alone or with spouse or lover or friends; the choice was yours'. He added, '… your individuality and your social status were made manifest in your car. Car advertising was full of glamour, snob appeal and suggestive erotic imagery'.

This may have been so but, above all, people enjoyed the unprecedented mobility that came with the private car. Despite the impression we have of dismal economic conditions in the inter-war decades, the low prices and increased real wages for many of those in work meant improved living standards and prospects for large numbers of the occupied population and their families.

The behaviour of many road users was basically 'every man for himself'. Parking was becoming a serious issue as the number of vehicles increased and drivers parked almost wherever they wanted, showing supreme contempt for the safety or convenience of others. Interestingly, cars were playing a growing role in certain types of crime, proving usefully quick means of escape from the scene of misdemeanours. Car usage brought selfish and anti-social behaviour to the fore. Motorists objected to being required to have licences conditional on their fitness and the passing of a test. Why should they be able to demonstrate knowledge of the rules of the road? After all, driving was supposed to be about individual freedom. Many did not see why they needed to have third-party insurance. They were incensed by the imposition of the 30mph speed limit in 1935 and the requirement from June 1935 that driving tests were compulsory for anyone who had not held a licence before April 1934.

From the earliest days of private motoring, car owners felt that the various taxes and dues they paid as motorists were not reciprocated by national or local government in terms of improvements to the road system. In 1920 government funding became available to assist local authorities towards the cost of maintaining roads but they still had to find the bulk of the cost themselves. A number of ring roads and bypasses such as that avoiding Kingston upon Thames were built in the inter-war years as were a handful of more ambitious schemes like the East Lancashire Road. In 1929 the Local Government Act made county councils responsible for all roads outside the major urban areas. In the late 1930s the ministry produced a more ambitious programme, little of which took place because of the onset of the Second World War. In 1937, *The Economist* had observed that while Britain had the densest traffic of any country, very little was being done to accommodate it. No proper national road policy existed and huge numbers of deaths and injuries were being incurred annually on the roads. In fact, only 4 per cent was added to Britain's total road mileage between 1899 and 1936. In November 1938, the *Manchester Guardian* revealed that road users were producing not far short of £100 million annually for the Treasury, only about a quarter of which was actually being spent on roads.

The Cyclists' Touring Club became increasingly disillusioned with most of the other participants in the road lobby for their stance totally in favour of motorised transport and its users, seemingly at whatever cost. They eventually went off on their own but not before one of their members wrote in the *CTC Gazette* in June 1933: '… with every road widened and cemented, wire fencing in place of hedges, and everything done to move a maximum mileage in a minimum time at minimum cost the whole policy is anathema for scenery, quietude and rural simplicity. The commercial transport interest will never rest content until the countryside is scarred with cement tracks, and every secondary road is turned into a trunk road!'

It became clear from events in this period that Transport was not a particularly fashionable or desirable ministerial portfolio. Most ministers were not of particularly high calibre and were not always effective in fighting the corner for their departments against other departments competing with them for resources. Few remained in the post long enough to make a serious impression.

Sir Eric Geddes was the first Minister of Transport and had wanted a ministry with comprehensive powers over all forms of transport with the intention of producing the best balance between all modes of land, sea and air transport. Such an aim was never achieved. In 1941 the Ministry became the Ministry of War Transport, having absorbed the Ministry of Shipping. From 1946 to 1970 it returned to its title of Ministry of Transport except for the years 1953 to 1959 when it when it was known as the Ministry of Transport & Civil Aviation.

The motor lobby, which had made its appearance with the forerunner of the RAC in 1897, was deeply concerned because Geddes was an ex-railwayman and they felt that he would be in thrall to the still very influential railway lobby in Parliament. Pro-road interests clearly had influence even at this early date and what emerged was a separate department particularly concerned with road construction, improvement and development. This marked the start of a process whereby the number of civil servants involved primarily with road matters grew, later on massively exceeding those concerned with the railways. The road lobby enjoyed a useful coup in 1930 when it managed to get the 20mph speed limit abolished. A surge of road casualties led to a 30mph limit in built-up areas being introduced in 1935. However, despite constant pressure from road interests, Tory and the Tory-dominated national governments were not prepared to fund the resources to make a major impact on road building, maintenance and improvement in the economically troubled inter-war years. Issues around road transport were to become of major concern and urgency after the end of the Second World War.

Chapter 8

Roads in the 1950s

The Transport Act of 1947

The Bill which became the Transport Act of 1947 came under sustained attack both within and outside Parliament. Over 800 amendments were moved in the Commons and more than 200 in the Lords. The Road Haulage Association (RHA), avid to emasculate or, ideally, totally destroy the Bill, lobbied tirelessly among its many sympathisers in both Houses. With large-scale funds at its disposal, the RHA also sent many thousands of letters to affiliated bodies and those considered to be sympathetic, urging them to contact their MPs, of whichever party, condemning the Bill in the most forthright terms and demanding that they vote it down. The extreme *bête noire* for the RHA was the proposal in the Bill to limit to forty miles the range of operation of 'C' licence commercial vehicles. These were the vehicles used for carrying their owners' goods, as distinct from those operated by hauliers plying for hire. The idea was that this restriction on the 'C' licence holders would encourage businesses to use the comprehensive network of longer-distance facilities which it was intended to create under the Road Haulage Executive of the British Transport Commission (BTC). The RHA and its allies lobbied hard and successfully and the issue of 'C' licences went unrestricted. This was a significant victory for the road lobby because even before the Act the number of 'C' licence vehicles was more than double that of all the other commercial vehicles and their numbers were expanding rapidly. The decision not to exercise any control of the movements of these vehicles meant a lost opportunity to develop an effective coordinated inland transport system. It was highly ironic that a vehement opponent of proposed curbs on the 'C' licence holders was the Cooperative Movement. This was closely allied to the Labour Party and the trade unions but found itself at odds with the Labour government because it operated large number of 'C' licence vehicles.

The Transport Act of 1947 set up a Road Transport Executive which was split into separate Road Haulage and Road Passenger Executives in 1949.

The Act attempted to bring the long-distance 'A' licence road hauliers under public ownership. Some operators sold out voluntarily and others were compulsorily purchased. This was a formidable operation which brought over 40,000 vehicles into the orbit of British Road Services (BRS) by the early 1950s. Unfortunately, the integration of road and rail haulage was effectively stymied by the failure to bring the 'C' licence holders into the state sector. The Road Passenger Executive brought the provincial bus operators in the Tilling and Scottish Motor Traction groups under the BTC wing but not the many companies in the British Electric Traction group. They and a number of usually small so-called 'independent' operators fought hard against the threat of nationalisation. Birch Bros, for example, a well-known private operator who ran an express service from Rushden in Northamptonshire to London, placed slogans on the exterior of its vehicles such as 'Don't let nationalisation take you for a ride!' and 'If this bus were nationalised to subsidise British Railways, fares would rocket!' The pre-nationalisation railway companies had stakes in most of these bus companies but that did not prevent railways and buses continuing to operate in competition on many routes.

A major intention of the Act was the creation of 'Area Schemes' for the bus industry. These would have led to the greater coordination and integration of bus services in the designated metropolitan areas but nothing came of this part of the Act. These Schemes, had they been implemented, might have produced better coordinated public transport able to compete more effectively with the rise of private motoring.

The impact of the car

Around the start of the twentieth century, the car had been seen as a rich man's toy and symbol of conspicuous consumption, hated by ordinary people because it covered them with dust and endangered their lives. In the 1950s it was to become the private transport of choice for large swathes of the population and was increasingly cheap enough to be available to all but the poorest. With the decline of public transport particularly from the 1950s, the car became virtually a necessity for increasing numbers of people, especially in rural areas.

In 1976, Perkin, in *The Age of the Automobile* described the private car as: 'the most universally desired of all the desirable consumer goods of twentieth-century society'. He continued: 'The motor vehicle, public and private, has come to dominate our lives, to determine where we live, where we work, where we spend our leisure time and take our holidays, the shape and size of our cities and towns, indeed, a large part of our whole physical environment.'

The benefits and the negatives that road vehicles produce are inextricable from each other. By the 1950s the descendent of the horseless carriage was killing and maiming huge numbers annually; creating noise, vibrations and toxic fumes; disturbing the ecology of the countryside; dividing residential, shopping and other areas into almost inaccessible segments because of the speed and density of traffic on the roads that cut a swathe through them; and bringing towns and cities and many beauty spots and tourist destinations into gridlocked suffocation and requiring ever more land in an already crowded island for roads, parking and other activities ancillary to motor vehicle use. Non-renewable resources were squandered with cavalier abandon and massive global oil and automotive businesses strutted around with the power to tell elected governments what to do, rather than the other way round. Wars were fought to gain access to or maintain supplies of oil. This was the age of the road but the demands of road vehicles and road users were increasingly spiralling out of control. Something had to be done. But just what could be done when no government seemed prepared to recognise and face up to the issue?

Britain's infrastructure was desperately run down when the Second World War ended. Overseas investments which had helped to cushion the economy during the pre-war depression had largely been sold off to pay for war supplies. Enormous debts and interest obligations had to be repaid, not least to the USA. When Lease-Lend finished suddenly in August 1945, Britain was hard pushed to pay for vital imports of food and raw materials. More loans from the US and Canada bridged the gap until Marshall Aid came to the rescue in 1948. Balance of payments crises followed every second year into the 1950s and were tackled through drastic measures such as the devaluation of the pound in 1949 and by austerity measures including petrol rationing until 1950, food rationing until 1954, import quotas and the direction of scarce supplies such as steel to the export industries.

The paradox was that despite these factors Britain was soon achieving a higher rate of economic growth than at any time since the middle of the nineteenth century although that growth was well below the average of the other advanced western countries. Increasing generalised affluence was a major factor in the headlong rise in the number of private cars and other motor vehicles. Goods vehicles constituted a small minority of this increase but they carried an increasing proportion of the consumer goods of the rising affluent society. Their numbers increased from 560,000 in 1946 to 1,173,100 in 1956. Lorries helped to account for the railways' share of freight traffic declining from 54 per cent in 1952 to 32 per cent in 1972.

Undoing the Transport Act of 1947

The BTC was established with the intention of planning and creating an integrated national transport system to replace the somewhat chaotic and wasteful structure evident in the inter-war years. The Labour government of 1945 was committed to the principle of integrated public transport but what resources were available had to be prioritised and most went to the repair and maintenance of the railway infrastructure. This was still the situation when the Conservatives were returned to office in 1951. The 1953 Transport Act favoured cars and road haulage over the railways and in the post-war boom the Conservatives encouraged increased car ownership. Road haulage was now viewed as the major overland freight mover and it formally achieved this position in 1955. The road haulage industry was denationalised in 1953 and a much slimmer BRS was left to compete with the private sector. During the years of Conservative government, concepts of public transport coordination and integration simply evaporated. Gone was the notion of creating a transport system in which each form of transport concentrated on the role for which it was best suited and was planned to complement the other transport modes.

The favourable financial position enjoyed by the BTC until 1953 owed much to the increasing profitability of BRS. From 1948 to 1953 it earned surpluses of over £15 million. This income was crucial for the BTC but a mouth-watering temptation to the Conservatives avid to bring the bulk of BRS back into the private sector. Huge numbers of vehicles belonging to BRS were sold back to the private operators at knock-down prices. Virtually all the restrictions involving road haulage were removed, constituting a body blow for the railways. It was payback time for what was seen as the socialist dogma of the Labour government which had won such a decisive victory in 1945.

Pressure from the road lobby

There was widespread agreement that a greatly improved road system was essential for the reconstruction of the British economy after the Second World War. This was an acknowledgement of the crucial role played by

Britain's roads in the life of the nation, not least during the war. There was great admiration for the German autobahn network and after the war the British road lobby tried to persuade the Labour government that the country, as part of its reconstruction, needed a network of new, fast roads. In 1945 a delegation from the British Road Federation (BRF) and the Society of Motor Manufacturers & Traders visited Germany to inspect the autobahn system. The Labour Party supported this view when Alfred Barnes, Minister of Transport, told the House of Commons on 6 May 1946 that: '... a road plan would form the framework upon which the planning of town and country would be based'. A motorway system was to be created within ten years, amounting to about 800 miles. Motorways would link the West Midlands with Hull, South Lancashire, Bristol, the Scottish border and London. Connected with this would be greatly improved road links between Manchester, the Wirral and North Wales. It was an ambitious plan but it was not to be. When Marshall Aid ceased there was a desperate need for a big increase in exports, a shortage of essential materials and a lack of capital for investment. The projected motorways and road improvements were victims of the time of austerity. Soon, investment in roads fell below pre-1939 levels.

During the Second World War Britain's automotive industry was given over to assisting the war effort and found itself after the war unable to respond effectively to a world crying out desperately for more motor vehicles, especially cars. The continental manufacturers had largely been destroyed and the Americans were preoccupied with trying to meet the insatiable demands of their own market for automobiles. British manufacturers were unable to step into the void because much of their plant was worn out and unsuitable for peacetime forms of production and because of the chronic shortage of steel and other essential raw materials. Government policy was one of 'Export or Die', directing the industry to export much of its output. Domestic demand was dampened down by means of quotas and purchase tax. Things did not improve in the 1950s as 'stop-go' economic policies forced the government to squeeze the home market and restrict the growth of car sales. Petrol tax and car licence duty were repeatedly raised and for a time and petrol rationing, which had been abolished in 1950, was reintroduced temporarily in 1956 as a result of the Suez crisis.

The disgruntlement felt in some quarters was voiced by *The Economist* of 25 October 1952: 'For fifty years, motoring has been overtaxed. Motor cars have been treated as if they were visible symbols of the selfishness of arrogant wealth. That attitude largely explains the wasted years between the wars, when the development of the motor industry and of roads was strangled by taxation. If, instead, automobile development had been encouraged, some millions of man-years wasted in unemployment might have been used to good account, and by 1939 this country would have been equipped with a greater engineering industry, a fine road system, a stronger balance of payments, and a significantly higher standard of living.'

After the Second World War, the big players in the increasingly influential road lobby were the major oil and rubber companies, the big automotive manufacturers, road construction and maintenance companies, road haulage concerns, the leading motoring associations and the trade unions representing workers in the automotive and road transport industries. These were all capable of lobbying individually but there were also organisations of a more collective nature. The BRF had been formed in 1932 with the purpose of counteracting what it claimed was the 'sinister and distorted' propaganda of the railways who, it asserted with considerable hyperbole, were seeking to 'enslave' British industry. The BRF had been a major opponent of Labour's intention to nationalise much of the road haulage industry. It later campaigned energetically and successfully for the denationalisation of the bulk of BRS. The BRF was described in the House of Commons in 1960 as 'the strongest lobby'. Other organisations included the Society of Motor Manufacturers and Traders (SMMT), the RHA and the Freight Transport Association (FTA). The RHA made absolutely clear what it stood for: '… the complete freedom of choice in transport services by trade and industry and for full and natural development of each form of transport … without fixed and political distortion'.

In 1955 the Roads Campaign Council was created largely on the initiative of the SMMT and with the support of the RHA, the AA and the RAC. It hired a right-wing pressure group then called 'Aims of Industry' to publicise the case for a large motorway building programme. The Confederation of British Industry (CBI) often worked closely with the road lobby. Those organisations that belonged to the catchall road lobby tended to believe that their interests would be best served by Conservative governments and they made many contributions to Conservative Party funds. In the run-up to the 1959 general election, the RHA described the Conservative Party as 'the answer to the hauliers' prayers'.

It is perhaps not surprising that the various bodies that constituted the road lobby did not always enjoy harmonious relationships. The Transport

& General Workers Union (TGWU) was wracked by tensions between the interests of those members who worked in vehicle manufacturing and others employed in the bus industry. There may have been this schism among its members but the union was a major player in shaping the Labour Party's policies as well as being a consistent contributor to the party's funds. The various elements that constituted the TGWU did not expect to gain a sympathetic hearing from the Conservatives.

There was a supporting cast of professionals such as surveyors, town planners and others employed by local authorities whose interests were closely linked to road and motorway building. The County Surveyors' Society for example, although it only had a small membership, provided regular advice to the Association of County Councils. One of the most prominent advocates of motorways was the County Surveyor of Lancashire and it may be no coincidence that the first section of motorway, the Preston bypass, was in Lancashire. All the organisations in the lobby made a point of developing worthwhile relationships with senior civil servants upon whose advice and knowledge ministers of transport depended. Altogether this was a formidable network.

The big players in the road lobby took advantage of the growing perceived desirability of private motoring and the rundown nature of the railways after the war to increase their criticism regarding the inadequacy of the road system and the seeming reluctance of governments to do anything about it. Just two months after the announcement of the 1955 Modernisation Plan for the railways, the government announced plans for a huge motorway-building programme only for the BRF to grumble that it was not enough. The BRF, the Institute of Highway Engineers, the SMMT and the RHA were all well-off and highly professional in the way in which they influenced the political agenda. Through the Roads Campaign Council they produced propaganda aimed at influencing popular opinion in favour of increased government spending to create a better road system.

Discussing the influence of motorists and the road lobby on governments in *The Motor Car and Politics*, Plowden (1971) says: '… the history of the motor car disproves conclusively any idea that close relationships between government and organised interests are a feature peculiar to mid-century politics. From the very beginning policy-makers – both Ministers and civil servants – relied heavily on the advice of the organisations composing the road lobby. They developed detailed knowledge and expertise on matters related to every aspect of road usage that ministers and their civil servants came to rely on in the development of transport policy. Consequently these organisations became firmly entrenched in the decision-making apparatus'.

By the mid-twentieth century, ownership of motor cars had become so widespread that politicians knew it made eminent sense to court the approval of motorists. After all, they constituted an increasingly large part of the electorate. However this did not always stop governments and local authorities taking actions which were deeply unpopular with motorists, simply to tackle the problems that growing road usage created.

In 1956 the BRF organised a conference around the theme of urban motorways. It demanded that the government embark on an urgent programme of building such roads to speed traffic up in the larger towns and cities. Many schemes were mooted and as might be expected London had more than its fair share. Over the following decades, parts of London, Glasgow and Birmingham, for example, had their topography and physical integrity radically altered and, some would say, irreparably damaged, by schemes that created new roads or greatly increased the amount of land given over to motor vehicles and their ancillary requirements. Far more projects were proposed than ever saw the light of day, however, as objections from various quarters or simple common sense were brought to bear. An example was at Nottingham where a direct fast approach to the city centre from the west was suggested. This road would have cut a swathe through the district known as The Park which was a planned suburb of superior residences built in the nineteenth century. Many of its residents were affluent and, possessing influence, were able to see off this threat. The Park was, and remains, one of the country's most delectable Victorian suburbs. This was a case of nimbyism but also of the realities of politics and power. At Oxford an inner relief road was proposed, part of which would have crossed the historic Christ Church Meadow, but for similar reasons to Nottingham failed to succeed. While the road lobby did not always have things its own way in such particularly sensitive localities, the residents of many other, less fashionable districts had their quality of life or their actual homes destroyed by road-building schemes where officialdom clearly pandered to the pressure of the road lobby. Considerable numbers of highly intrusive new urban roads, some elevated, were to be built in the mid-1960s in Chester and Manchester, for example, and, even better-known, parts of the A40 in West London. Early in 1965 feathers were severely ruffled with the publication of plans for what became known as a 'motorway box' – a box-shaped ring motorway elongated in an east-west direction and running about four miles from London's central core. As projected this was to run close to some highly affluent residential areas. The scheme was not proceeded with, the road lobby proving to be not all-conquering when faced with the kind of opposition such districts could marshal. Another factor in curtailing road improvement and schemes for new roads and motorways was the cuts in public spending brought about by Britain's economic travails later, in the 1970s.

The road lobby regarded railways as a financial black hole into which ever-increasing amounts of taxpayers' money was being poured without any apparent benefit, in effect money going to waste. The dice was loaded against the railways in the sense that road users did not pay the full cost of road infrastructure and services while the railways were expected to finance their own maintenance from receipts rather than taxation. Motorways were extremely expensive to build and the cost of their construction and maintenance meant less money available for the railways. As the motorway-building programme really got under way in the 1960s it was clear that governments saw roads as the predominant inland transport mode of the future.

In government circles the received wisdom was that the income generated by roads greatly exceeded the cost of road building and maintenance. Coyly omitted from public consideration was the almost unquantifiable cost of the pollution, congestion, policing, accident damage, litigation and medical bills that were inescapable as road traffic increased year by year. Yet the juggernaut rolled on, literally. The venom directed at railways was evident in an article in the April 1960 edition of the RHA's journal: 'We should build more roads, and we should have fewer railways. This would merely be following the lessons of history which show a continued and continuing expansion of road transport and a corresponding contraction in the volume of business handled by the railways … A streamlined railway system could surely be had for half the money that is now made available … We must exchange the "permanent way" of life for the "motorway of life" … road transport is the future, the railways are the past.'

Stark evidence of this mindset was the revelation that at one stage the Greater London Council (GLC) was almost clandestinely engaged in planning road schemes which would have involved the demolition of 20,000 homes in a conurbation which already had a shortfall of half a million dwellings. The mania for pandering to the motor car by building new roads or widening existing ones, which masqueraded as 'urban renewal', was often accompanied by the removal of dwellings classed as 'unfit'. Frequently old slums were replaced by high rise blocks of flats which took up less ground space. These were often built as cheaply as possible and soon proved expensive to maintain, having all kinds of structural problems that councils could not always afford to fix and innumerable associated social issues which meant that many of them rapidly turned into the slums of the twentieth century. The social costs were enormous and it is not unfair to attribute some blame for this to the demands made by the phenomenal growth of road usage.

A growing crisis on Britain's roads

There is little doubt that a crisis was developing as Britain's roads were becoming woefully inadequate for the amount of traffic wanting to use them in the 1950s. John Boyd-Carpenter, a former Minister of Transport (1954–1955), wrote in his memoirs that in the mid-1950s: '… public anger was rising against the inadequacies of our road system and the inaction of the government in respect of it. The road haulage industry and the AA and RAC were conducting campaigns of agitation'. Governments seemed reluctant to face up to the challenges posed by the exponential growth of road traffic. Sometimes they appeared to believe that the problems would simply sort themselves out in the fullness of time. This ostrich-like attitude was voiced by one senior politician who said that eventually congestion on the roads would develop to such a level as to deter their users and eliminate the problem! Motoring offences rose from 540,000 in 1957 to 990,000 in 1962. The problem was in danger of spinning out of control.

Despite austerity in the early post-war years there was a threefold increase in private car ownership between 1950 and 1962. At the same time the number of road goods vehicles rose by 70 per cent and many of these had a much larger carrying capacity than earlier lorries. After the war, the road hauliers and bus operators campaigned hard to obtain legal authority for larger and faster vehicles. Although larger lorries are more expensive than smaller vehicles, requiring more fuel and tyres and costing more to buy and maintain, these costs rise slower than the vehicles' potential earning power as reflected in their carrying capacity. It is therefore not surprising that the road haulage interest was constantly agitating for bigger, faster vehicles. No sooner had they achieved one set of targets than they recommenced their campaigning for even bigger and more powerful vehicles. Thus in 1964 the maximum weight limit was increased to 32 tons and in 1966 the upper speed limit was raised to 40mph from 30. The success with which they achieved their aims was indicative of the growing power of their lobbyists. One of the lobby's biggest lies posed as a 'fact' was that the use of large, heavier vehicles would mean far fewer smaller lorries and thereby reduce the number of lorries on Britain's roads. Of course this never happened. The number of lorries, big and small, simply went on increasing. Counter arguments concerning the safety, environmental and other implications of these vehicles were largely swept aside. As their dimensions grew, these vehicles simply became too large for Britain's crowded and often narrow streets and roads. The road lobby argued that large vehicles were in the public interest because they reduced the cost of inland transport which was reflected in lower retail prices for the consumer. The various negative aspects their presence created were not allowed to influence the debate and no politicians were prepared really to challenge the road hauliers and say that enough was enough. To point to the often devastating results of a high speed collision, the damage to the roads and to buildings or the chaos caused by huge lorries in crowded urban streets was, we were told, to stand in the way of 'progress'. Prosecutions of lorry operators for excessive speed or for being overloaded were not always pursued with much energy.

Organisations like the SMMT argued in favour of higher performance cars. Many of these cars, so it was claimed, could be exported to countries which allowed faster speeds. This would be good for the economy. A whole macho culture developed around boastings such as '0 to 80 in … seconds'. We were assured that any further restrictions on private motorists and road hauliers would reduce sales and lead to jobs being lost. Buoyant demand from the home market was essential, apparently, for the automotive industry to be successful in marketing overseas. Growth of the export trade was in the 'national interest'. This weasel phrase is sheer hypocrisy. The automotive industry was in business to make profits not to meet the needs of some indefinable national interest. In a parliamentary debate in June 1964 Tony Benn memorably described the motorists' lobby as 'the most hideous of all'.

The politicians and planners could not keep up with the apparently inexorable growth of road transport. In 1945 the Ministry of Transport estimated that there would be a 75 per cent increase in vehicles by 1965 over pre-war figures, but the number had doubled by 1950. In 1959 it forecast 12.5 million vehicles by 1969 but that number was exceeded in 1964. When planning new towns in the early post-war period, it was clear that the belief still prevailed that the motor car was a luxury for the minority and it was customary to allocate just one garage space for every four houses. There was an assumption in official circles that the existing road network with a few improvements and modifications could cope with likely levels of traffic. If traffic continued to grow it was believed that there was some metaphysical 'saturation point' at which congestion would prove so frustrating that the demand for motoring would simply level off. Of course it was not to be. Road usage kept on growing, highlighting the callowness of the planners. Road casualties rose by 1960 to exceed the worst figures of the 1930s. The Royal Society for the Prevention of Accidents produced figures that put the cost to the community of road accidents as having risen from £136 million in 1950 to £267 million in 1966. While this was a matter of major importance it was apparently not in the 'national interest' to take it into account when policy for road transport was being made.

Tackling road congestion in towns

In the 1950s, government measures to tackle the problems caused by road usage largely took the form of palliatives: a modest road improvement and building programme combined with various measures to manage and improve the flow of traffic in the towns. These included increasing numbers of traffic lights, zebra crossings, one-way streets, parking restrictions and, in 1956, an even greater source of resentment to motorists, the authorisation of the first parking meters. This aroused howls of outrage from motorists. The then Transport Minister, Boyd-Carpenter, assured the motoring organisations that net revenue from meters would be used to provide off-street parking facilities. Meters first came into use in 1958 in Mayfair in London's West End. Also in 1956 the compulsory testing of vehicles more than ten years old was introduced. Well-intentioned officially-sponsored road safety campaigns exhorted drivers to exercise more care and consideration but, as might have been expected, these fell largely on deaf ears. Governments found themselves in a cleft stick. If they introduced effective measures to control traffic, they knew that they would be assailed by the motoring lobby on the grounds that such measures would deter motorists and reduce the sales of new British vehicles. It was claimed that healthy home sales were essential for the British automotive industry to have the robust export sales regarded as an absolute necessity for a healthy balance of payments.

Tony Benn, then Anthony Wedgewood Benn, Opposition speaker on transport, told the Commons on 10 December 1959 that a crisis had been reached because of the growing gap between private sector involvement in road vehicles and the level of public sector investment in roads. If vehicles were simply allowed to continue increasing in uncontrolled numbers, a point would be reached where life in many urban areas could become intolerable.

There seemed to be many road builders and vehicle manufacturers who saw towns and cities as bastions to be conquered. Buildings impeded the flow of traffic and this deterred motoring. Some people believed that it was entirely justified to build major roads and urban motorways through large towns and cities in order to maximise the free flow of motorised transport and encourage the sales of vehicles because people would be able to enjoy the freedom of driving without inconvenient obstacles such as buildings getting in the way. Unless something drastic was done, urban road congestion would become sufficiently severe to deter sales of motor vehicles which, we were continually told, would be disastrous for the national economy.

Ernest Marples had only been in office a short time when on 10 December 1959 he told Parliament that a working party of architects and town planners was to be commissioned to examine the challenges posed by the seemingly unstoppable growth in the numbers of motor cars. Recognition of the extent of the problem came with the publication in 1958 of Colin Buchanan's *Mixed Blessing: the Motor in Britain*. It was clear that Marples had been impressed by this work. Buchanan was a pro-motor vehicle town planner who recognised that the traditional division between town planning and transport planning was outdated and had to be replaced by a holistic approach to the planning of towns and the traffic their existence created. Bypasses and motorways (of which 700 miles were authorised in the same year) could certainly relieve congestion in small towns by removing much through traffic but larger towns attracted and generated traffic on a scale that required radical measures to deal not only with existing usage but also to manage likely continuing growth. Essential, in Buchanan's view, was the need to separate the flows of vehicular and pedestrian movement. This separation needed to be taken into account when new developments were being planned in large towns and cities. Referring to Buchanan's work, Bagwell and Lyth, in *Transport in Britain* (2002) commented: '… it is hardly an exaggeration to describe it as a road builders' mandate'.

Within weeks of assuming office, Marples, with his usual flair for publicity, launched an 'emergency plan' known as the 'Pink Zone' in central London which was intended to ensure much stricter enforcement of the existing parking regulations over the Christmas period. This proved to be something of a flop. For the first few days traffic did seem to be moving more smoothly but it soon became clear that many motorists reckoned that the chance of having their cars towed away was small enough for them to risk illegal parking. They did this in the knowledge that there were not enough police to enforce the new regulations. It was clear from this episode that effective tackling of street congestion and inconsiderate or illegal parking would need expensive enforcement procedures if it was to be effective. In 1960 the Roads and Road Improvement Act extended the fixed penalty system for parking offences and created the hate figure of the traffic warden acting under the direction of the police.

Buchanan's book had attracted widespread interest including that of many in the road lobby and influenced the Ministry of Transport to appoint him to chair the working party which produced the report *Traffic in Towns* in November 1963. 'The Buchanan Report', as it was commonly known, had the brief of examining '… the long-term development of roads and traffic in urban areas and their influence on the urban environment'. It made clear that humans had created a machine which had become a necessity but with demands that threatened the shape and the very integrity of Britain's towns as well as the quality of life of those who lived and worked in them. Buchanan firmly believed that the continued growth of private transport was not only inevitable but desirable. The issue was how to plan for the growth of road traffic including the provision of new roads while minimising the impact of road traffic on the urban environment. He was well aware of the capacity of road vehicles to have a negative social effect but he would not agree that the requirements of cars should be subordinated to those of people. Town planning needed to adapt to the concept of generalised mass car usage and to do so urgently. At the same time that the committee headed by Buchanan was established, another committee, nominally independent of the Ministry and described as a 'steering group', was established under Sir Geoffrey Crowther. Its membership consisted of people with experience of town planning, municipal finance, civil engineering and land development. When introducing the Buchanan Report Crowther had remarked: 'We are nourishing a monster of great potential destructiveness. And yet we love him dearly. Regarded as "the traffic problem" the motor car is clearly a menace that can spoil our civilisation. But translated in terms of the particular vehicle that stands outside the door, we regard it as one of our most treasured possessions or greatest ambitions, an immense convenience, an expander of the dimensions of life, an instrument of emancipation, a symbol of the modern age. To refuse to accept the challenge it presents is an act of defeatism.'

Buchanan acknowledged the American experience that simply building more roads, widening others and creating more parking spaces did not solve the problems created by road usage but actually tended to encourage even more traffic in urban areas. Case studies showed that in many towns serious damage was being inflicted on the quality of the environment and on people's lives by allowing uncontrolled access by motor vehicles. Particularly the buildings, ancient layout, street pattern and general amenity value and integrity of old, historic towns were being blighted. Wholesale demolition was unthinkable and therefore ways had to be found to manage traffic by delineating areas as having restricted access. Less sensitive areas could perhaps be given over to car parks and some new roads. This was to prove only a partial solution to the impact made by motor vehicles on places like Chester, York and Canterbury. The centres of such places had historical and architectural features which had to be respected even in the face of those who would happily see everything bulldozed to accommodate cars and other motor vehicles. Would motorists accept greatly restricted access to the historic core of such places?

When *Traffic in Towns* was being debated in the House of Commons on 10 February 1964, Marples said that the government accepted the report in principle and that modernising and reshaping towns must proceed in a way that kept urban areas compact, or as Marples himself put it, 'keeping towns as towns' and 'country as country'. Marples told a BRF conference shortly after *Traffic in Towns* was published: 'All it says is that we must use our motor cars to the maximum and yet be sensible and keep some good environmental areas. We have to face the fact, whether we like it or not, that the way we have built our towns is entirely wrong for motor traffic. We want an entirely different type of town.'

The challenge of the motor vehicle would arguably be met more easily if new towns were built which from their inception recognised the incompatibility of pedestrians and motor vehicles in close proximity but took into account their symbiotic relationship. Buchanan was particularly keen on segregating them on vertical principles. This was described as 'traffic architecture' but it never really became established practice. Cumbernauld of the second generation of new towns displays some degree of vertical integration in its central area. Some new towns like Milton Keynes have been designed around motor vehicles and their needs and have largely segregated them from pedestrians, but often only by forcing pedestrians into lonely footpaths, footbridges and underpasses where they can be very vulnerable and which are easily blighted by vandalism. Being designed primarily for motorists' needs can mean such towns having minimal public transport. The road lobby largely dismissed public transport. Door-to-door transport by private car was the concept they wanted to embed, arguing that it was a person's right, a road to freedom. They equated the use of private transport with maximising freedom for the largest possible number of people.

The early 1960s was an era of optimism. What appeared to be sustainable continued economic growth led to a widespread belief in a better future. In particular there was the belief that technology and planning between them could bring about a better world – that of the 'White-hot Technological Revolution'. It was even suggested that the motor car could be an agent of slum clearance and social engineering as inner-city areas would be cleared of housing and the space turned over to parking and the other needs of motor vehicles. Sir Keith Joseph, then Minister of Housing and Local Government, told the Commons on 10 February 1964 that: '… urban renewal is wider than tackling the growth of traffic, but both can, to some extent, and in some cases, with the right policies, be tackled simultaneously'. Private motoring brought freedom and convenience and as long as it was planned, increased expenditure on road building and improvement was for the greater good. This was the optimism of good times. Within twelve months of the Buchanan Report being published, Britain went into one of its periodic downturns and retrenchment rather than expansion became the watchword. The number of road vehicles and the problems they brought with them continued to grow.

The priority given by the Ministry of Transport to road affairs over railway matters was exemplified in 1966 by the fact that about 80 per cent of its staff dealt with road business while the railways' share of staffing was less than 1 per cent. At senior level, roads were allocated eleven under-secretaries while railways enjoyed the services of just one. An employee of the Ministry who wanted career advancement had to display pro-road colours.

By the 1960s there was talk about motorists needing to pay a realistic fee for their use of urban space. It had become clear that there was a considerable price attached to road congestion which raised the issues about who was to pay and how was payment to be resourced. This brought debate about road pricing onto the political agenda. In 1962 the Ministry set up the Smeed Committee to examine all aspects of road pricing. It concluded, among other things, that considerable financial savings would accrue if traffic could move faster and more freely in urban areas. The Committee's report was published in 1964 as *Road Pricing: The Economic and Technical Possibilities*. It recognised that action was needed but it was also clear that the question of how payment was to be made was a political hot potato. Motorists would not want their movements to be restricted nor would they want to pay for the privilege of using urban roads.

Marples told the Commons on 10 February 1964 that in large towns and cities and in the conurbations it was impossible to permit unrestricted access for all the cars that wanted to get into them. He accepted the conclusions of the Buchanan and Crowther Reports that some means of limiting traffic in those areas was necessary. He declared that he had not yet made up his mind what action should be taken and that further in-depth study of the issues involved was needed. With typical brio he was reported in *The Times* of 11 June 1964 as saying: 'But I shall not funk it – any more than I have funked anything else.' Marples was a politician and this was politician-speak because a general election was pending and he had to be guarded on a subject which could be a vote-loser. Labour was ahead in the polls and Marples needed to be circumspect. In the event his verbal assurance that he was going to do something about cars in urban areas was untested as he went out of office with Labour's election victory.

Back in April 1963 Marples had shown a shrewd appreciation of the role of the motor car in modern Britain: 'We all have two distinct views of the motor car. It is liked by some people and hated by others … Collectively, motor cars are regarded as traffic problems which pollutes and kills and maims [*sic*] many people and so on; but individually, the one particular vehicle which we own, and which is in our garage or outside our house in the road, or generally outside someone else's house, is a status symbol, a very desirable object which opens up our lives. Our car is precious; the rest are traffic problems.'

In the 1930s one insidious result of the spread of motor vehicles had been identified as 'ribbon development' where houses were built bordering roads through countryside often on the periphery of towns. Ribbon development created areas which were neither quite urban nor exactly rural. Additionally, since the war motor vehicles, especially the private car, were having the effect of spreading residential development in low-density housing further and further from the traditional town and city centres. Everywhere central urban areas were losing population as people moved out to the suburbs. This accelerated inner-city blight as those who could afford to get out of the declining districts did so and thereby caused problems for those people who stayed. Public transport provision was always financially problematical in areas of low population density such as the leafy suburbs and villages which became so desirable and reachable by car. As passenger numbers fell, bus fares went up and services were pared down, becoming expensive and inconvenient. Even those with an aversion to cars were often forced to buy their own private transport.

The spread of private motoring was seemingly unstoppable. The number of buses entering central London in the morning peak fell by 1,900 between 1955 and 1965. The place of those vanished buses was taken by 29,000 private cars carrying a total of 39,000 people but occupying five times as much road space and producing infinitely more pollution, congestion and general wear and tear. In country areas between 1956 and 1960 car traffic increased by 22 per cent while bus usage declined by 13 per cent.

It was ironic but no coincidence that the Beeching Report appeared about the same time as the Buchanan Report. They were both clear indications that crisis points had been reached in road and rail transport and that urgent and drastic action was needed to tackle both crises which were closely interrelated and interdependent. Neither set of 'solutions' approached the issues holistically and being compartmentalised were consequently seriously flawed. Road transport and its proponents were in the ascendency and the idea that limitations could or even should be imposed on road vehicles and their users was widely seen as almost heretical. The pro–railway lobby had much less influence given little or no support from big business and it contained some who could not and would not accept that circumstances had moved on and rendered some of the railway's activities totally out of date and irrelevant to the needs of the 1960s.

The motorway 'solution'

In 1958 the first short stretch of motorway, the Preston bypass, was opened and in 1959 the first seventy-two miles of the M1. This was an event of national importance, clear evidence of the adoption of the car as the preferred mode of individual transport. It demonstrated the great acceleration of long-distance road traffic that a national network of motorways would provide. The 'Midland Red' bus company introduced the first motorway express coach capable of achieving 80mph on the M1 during its runs from Birmingham to London and vice versa. The clock was not for turning back. Henceforth the railways would have to fight for every penny of investment against an extremely powerful coalition of car manufacturers, fuel, tyre and component producers, road haulier organisations and lorry drivers' unions, bodies representing motorists and politicians and senior civil servants, large numbers of whom were unsympathetic to public transport, particularly the railways.

The case for a large programme of motorway building was encouraged with the publication of a government-sponsored report titled *The London-Birmingham Motorway: Traffic and Economics*. It contained a cost-benefit analysis of the M1 and argued that on this basis the case was clear for the creation of a motorway system. This report was highly influential and seems to have influenced the Exchequer towards favourable consideration of proposals for motorway projects from the Ministry of Transport. A programme was agreed for the completion of 1,000 miles of motorway and 1,700 miles of new or upgraded dual carriageway trunk roads.

Opposition to traffic management measures

Motorists, encouraged by the RAC and perhaps to a lesser extent the AA, were highly vocal in their opposition to all attempts to regulate driving and the practices associated with it as if these were an infringement of drivers' personal liberty and the prelude to a police state. One-way systems, for example, introduced during Marples' term of office, incurred criticism from MPs of all parties who were anxious to do nothing to offend the motorist. Shortly before Marples left office he told the House of Commons on 10 February 1964 that the tranche of measures implemented in London had succeeded in handling more traffic while allowing increased speeds accompanied by fewer accidents. While, for a time at least, Marples showed that comprehensive measures of traffic management could improve the flow of traffic, such was the exponential increase in traffic that the effect was like putting a finger in a fragmenting dam. The best efforts of town planners, road engineers and other experts and politicians did not then and have not since led to any significant success in managing the growth of motorised traffic and its impact on town and country. No politicians have been prepared to face up to the full implications of changing the face of Britain in order to maximise the ideal conditions for the motor vehicle. In the 1960s the precedent was established of simply muddling through.

In 1964 Marples said: 'Just as towns of the future must be rebuilt to come to terms with the motor vehicle, so the motor vehicle must be designed to come to terms with those towns. For example can't we design vehicles whose size, power and manoeuvrability make them more suitable for town use?' A report commissioned by Marples called *Cars for Cities*, not published until

1967, recommended greater uniformity of size in cars and faster accelerating capacity. While governments steered clear of directing manufacturers there was a definite move to design vehicles more similar in size and often faster and more manoeuvrable which enabled them to make better use of the available road space. On 10 February 1964 Marples told the Commons that it was the job of each road-administering authority to decide how it was going to achieve a workable compromise between providing accessibility for the motor car and handling the environmental and other issues created by motor vehicles, especially private cars. Such a denial of government responsibility for handling traffic and its problems hardly accords with the proactive and radical image which Marples wished to project. By this time Marples was being criticised in some quarters for being anti-motorist when he made statements declaring that motorists must be prepared to accept restrictions on the use of cars in the larger towns and cities. He introduced yellow lines to restrict street parking and also seat belts, although their use was not at this time compulsory. These worthy measures attracted loud criticism from many road users. A 'Marples must go' campaign was launched.

The interests of private motorists did not necessarily accord with those of the organisations who operated heavy goods vehicles but, like them, they were in favour of more motorways, dual carriageways and urban bypasses. Although it was affiliated to the BRF, the AA saw itself very much as the champion of the private car driver. In 1967 it launched a new magazine called *Drive* and, when introducing it to the membership, the AA's director general was unequivocal about the benefits he believed came with the growth of private motoring: 'Motoring … is the life blood of the nation's economy and perhaps the most significant explanation for the great advance in living standards in the last decade … All these are reasons why the AA is speaking out strongly against any attempt to thrust inferior, inconvenient and inflexible mass transport on a society which is so obviously determined to use the superior, flexible, transport of the motor car. This magazine, posted free to 3,750,000 AA members will be in itself a powerful weapon to influence transport policy, car design and town planning and to create a positive attitude to the problem of accommodating the motor vehicle for the betterment of the community.'

The same writer, a few editions later, takes on a more hysterical tone when he describes threats to prohibit drivers using their cars in the centres of towns and cities as 'sinister' and evidence of 'dangerous thinking'. They would compel people to use public transport which, according to him was 'an outmoded system that they have so plainly rejected'.

Labour, by contrast, argued in 1966 in the White Paper *Transport Policy* that the problems created by road vehicles could not be solved other than with an integrated policy for transport as a whole: 'The rapid development and mass production of the motor vehicle over the past twenty years has brought immense benefits to millions of people: increased mobility, a fuller social life, family enjoyment, new experiences. It has also produced new, quick, and convenient means of moving goods. But at the same time it has brought severe discomforts: congestion in the streets of our towns; the misery of the journey to work for commuters; noise, fumes and danger as the setting of our lives; a rising trend of casualties on our roads and a threat to our environment which, if it continues unchecked, will ensure the pleasure and benefit for which we use the car will increasingly elude us. The aim of a national transport policy must be to solve this paradox.'

Central to such a national transport policy was the improvement and expansion of public transport. If some parts of an enhanced public transport system were unprofitable but 'socially necessary' then Labour argued that they should be paid for out of taxes just as the cost of other essential but non-profit-making services are publicly subsidised.

As far as road transport was concerned, a programme of new roads and the upgrading of existing roads would be accelerated and it was intended to create 700 miles of motorway by the early 1970s. Urban motorways would be built but the watchword was now judicious measures to plan for road vehicles but set against the aim of promoting public transport usage. Grants became available covering 25 per cent of the cost of new buses as long as they conformed to certain specifications. This was intended to assist the bus industry by allowing it to buy modern vehicles capable of being one-person operated. Efficient public transport systems in the conurbations would be placed under passenger transport authorities. Freight haulage by road and rail would be coordinated to offer customers door-to-door transit.

These ambitious plans were implemented in the Transport Act 1968. This reorganised the nationalised transport undertakings and created passenger transport authorities in the conurbations to coordinate and operate integrated transport policies. There were also new systems for regulating and licensing road haulage which had the negative effect of creating probably the least regulated road haulage industry in western Europe. Local authorities were given new powers to regulate traffic in the towns. The National Freight Corporation was set up to take over the Transport Holding Company's and that part of British Rail's freight interests consisting of small consignments.

Out of control?

Attempts to control the continued growth of road freight transport were
largely unsuccessful. In 1951 the maximum permitted length of an articulated
lorry was 33 feet. In 1968 the operation of articulated lorries of over 49 feet
was authorised. The road lobby continued with almost unremitting pressure
to demand larger and faster vehicles. For their part, as cars proliferated, they
destroyed the very advantages of flexible travel freedom for which people
bought them in the first place. Politicians of all major parties were wary of
offending the feelings of road users and consequently no systematic measures
were taken effectively to tackle the problems caused by the intensive use of
road vehicles.

It had been intended in the Transport Bill of 1968 to place an additional
tax on goods vehicles of over 3 tons unladen weight so that they could make a
more realistic contribution to the cost of mending the damage they inflicted.
This proposal raised a storm of protest and was dropped in favour of variations
in the licensing fee levied on lorries. The lightest vehicles were exempted
from carrier licensing altogether. Even this was not enough for the BRF
which launched a ferocious attack on the Bill. Whole-page advertisements
were placed in the national press. Peter Walker, the Opposition front bench
spokesman on Transport, paid £10,000 of his own money to assist in the
funding of a research group to provide arguments against those parts of the
Bill thought to be threatening to the road interest.

The 1960s saw the beginning of the container revolution. Very few ports
in the early part of the decade had the facilities to handle containers and
unitised cargo. By 1970, however, the spread of containerisation was having
an enormous impact on road haulage and therefore on the roads and the
environment generally. To make optimum use of containers there was growing
pressure to modify the official regulations that specified the maximum size
and weight of the vehicles to carry them. In the 1960s alone there was a 45 per
cent increase in the carrying capacity of the average road haulage vehicle and
not surprisingly there was a similar rise in the size of the loads conveyed.

Barbara Castle was a non-driver when she became minister and made
herself highly unpopular by introducing the breathalyser in 1967. There was
a huge price to pay for drunken driving. There were howls of protest at the
breathalyser from the many who saw this eminently sensible and overdue
measure as intruding on the freedom of the individual and evidence of
the emergence of a potential police state. The fitting of seat belts in cars

became mandatory and the 70mph upper speed limit was made permanent, something which predictably enraged the motorists' lobbies. The testing of cars and other small vehicles over ten years old which had been introduced in 1956 was extended to three-year-old ones by 1967. Significantly, not one of these measures was repealed. Castle was nothing if not proactive and had made a study of measures taken in New York City to deal with congestion including methods of penalising the motorists who wanted to use the streets of the central zone. Road pricing was perhaps too much of a hot potato even for Barbara Castle and it was to be much later before this issue was faced up to. She became the *bête noire* of the road lobby and Edward du Cann, chairman of the Conservative Party, indignantly told *The Times* on 11 December 1965 that the Labour government was 'anti-motorist'. The AA, RAC and the BRF made it clear that they would oppose any move to restrict local usage. Such were the problems caused by ill-considered parking, however, that by 1965 twelve British cities were operating parking meters. Others that wanted to be seen as progressive were building underground or multistorey car parks. While Castle made it clear that she was no King Canute attempting to turn the clock back by forcing people to use the railways, she managed not only to upset motorists but also to alienate supporters of the railways. They thought that she should have stopped all station and line closures and curtailed the building of new roads and motorways. This was a hopelessly unrealistic attitude. The private car continued to take usage away from public transport, particularly buses.

The 1960s through to the mid-1970s epitomised the new age of road transport. These years saw a massive road-building programme which created 11,500 miles of new road including 1,100 miles of motorway. During this period the number of road vehicles increased by 149 per cent. Whereas in 1958 77 per cent of households were without a car, in 1975 only 43 per cent had no car. Lorries became heavier, faster and far more numerous. Between 1962 and 1975 freight-ton mileage conveyed by road rose by over 70 per cent. The weight of four-axle lorries rose 25 per cent between 1955 and 1972.

It was into the 1970s before widening and increasingly vehement concerns were being raised about the environmental costs of the growth of motor traffic. The oil crisis of 1974 was a wake-up call but by then the genie had long escaped from the bottle and it was too late to regain control and put it back. In 1973 7,407 people were killed and 346,325 injured in road accidents. These figures take no account of the air pollution created by motor vehicles as a cause of illness and premature death or the economic cost and sheer misery, even then, of road gridlock. There were many places where life had been rendered almost intolerable by the quantity of traffic and the noise it created. Historic buildings had been torn down and some of the most beautiful parts of the British Isles ravaged. Yet it has to be understood that the apparently unstoppable growth of road traffic was largely the consequence of choices by those who wanted to run their own cars and enjoy the seeming freedom bestowed by this choice even if it meant misery for others. Powerful messages from the media emphasised how much more convenient, congenial and desirable it was to use prestigious and flexible personal transport rather than inflexible and often inconvenient public transport.

Overall, living standards and expectations were rising in the 1950s and 1960s. The material growth of the period also provided the impulse that led consumers to reject the miserable weather and seemingly tawdry facilities of the British seaside for wall-to-wall sunny weather in Spain or other exotic destinations courtesy of air fares which were declining in real terms. This reduced the demand for much leisure travel by rail as did the attractions of centrally-heated homes and watching television in the front room. This was the modern world which most people wanted. It came with a price but it was the ideal of the time and it was unstoppable.

Chapter 9

Railways, 1918–1939

From their earliest days, questions have been asked about the nature of the relationship between the railways and the State. By 1914, over 200 general statutes had been passed pertaining to almost every aspect of railway activity. The railway companies considered themselves grievously over-regulated. Why, the private companies argued, could they not simply be left alone to get on with their business the way they alone best knew how?

Accepting reluctantly the fact that governments would subject them to regulatory measures, railway companies set out to enlist the interest and active support of MPs. A distinctive group of MPs associated with the railways emerged and became known as the 'Railway Interest'. This consisted of a varying number of MPs who held directorships or senior administrative posts in the railway companies or had other close connections with railways as engineers or architects, for example. They acted as an interest group with the purpose of generally defending and promoting the cause of the railway companies or, more particularly, those with which they were associated. They were expected to make common cause in attempting to prevent or minimise government measures that would cost railway companies money.

As the railways expanded, so did the number of MPs with their fingers in the railway pie. In 1866 the Railway Interest consisted of 161 members of the Commons and forty-nine of the Lords. Many other MPs had family or business ties with the railway members and might be generally supportive of the cause of the railways. Some large railway companies had four or more MPs on their boards. *Bradshaw's Railway Manual Shareholders' Guide and Official Directory* appeared annually from 1847 to 1922 and listed the recognised members of the Railway Interest. However, the Grouping of the railways, enacted in 1923, reduced the power of the railway lobby. Now there were just four major companies. While these had some MPs on their boards, previously there had been many companies with one or more board members who were also sitting MPs. The Grouping itself was clear evidence of the declining bargaining power of the railway lobby because it was implemented very much against the wishes of the railway companies and their lobbyists in Parliament.

Before 1914 we can see ominous signs for the railways given the threats posed by serious competition from the roads, the troubled economic conditions of the inter-war years and organic changes in Britain's manufacturing and industrial base and in international trade in the years up to the Second World War. The profits being generated made funding on the scale needed for necessary renewals and upgrading highly problematical. The railway network was over-extended, there simply being too many lines with resultant duplication while costs, especially those of labour, were rising rapidly. Most railway companies were not making sufficient profit to pay the interest on loans they needed to take out to finance necessary renewals and improvements.

During the First World War the railways quickly came under direct government control through the Railway Executive Committee, implying that normal private ownership could not be entrusted with the stewardship of the railways at such a critical time. They remained in private ownership but with unprecedented levels of government direction. Their income was guaranteed for the duration, this option being preferred to outright nationalisation. The economic benefits of the planned use of pooled resources were clearly demonstrated. The railways' vital contribution to the war effort was widely applauded. Many thought that a more permanent arrangement involving the State through nationalisation might be the best way to ensure that the railways met the challenges that the post-war era were likely to produce. When the war ended, Sir Eric Geddes, in turn the first Minister of Ways and Means and then the first Minister of Transport, drew up a plan in 1919 to nationalise the railway system but this was rejected in 1920 in favour of the consolidation of the railways into the 'Big Four' under the Railways Act of 1921. The railways remained in private hands and nationalisation, anathema to the railway companies and others favouring private enterprise, was avoided. The 'Grouping' as it came to be known, was also seen as a way to ensure there would be no return to the wasteful competition of the period before 1914. However, the disposition of the four companies' respective areas of operation was shaped by the irrational manner in which the network had developed in the nineteenth century. This meant that there were places and situations where two companies might in effect continue to be in competition.

In the immediate aftermath of the war, a pro-road group of MPs and a growing extra-parliamentary pro-road lobby emerged determined to ensure that a national plan for coordinating all inland transport was a non-starter. It was perhaps a straw in the wind that Geddes, who was formerly a senior railway manager, in 1922 jumped ship and joined the board of Dunlop, the major tyre producer. In 1924 he became part-time chairman of the new Imperial Airways. He abandoned railways for what would prove to be the up and coming modes of transport in the following decades.

The Big Four were saddled with a number of statutory duties originating in the nineteenth century. They had to publish their fares and charges for all the types of traffic conveyed and to carry all goods offered them because of their 'common carrier' obligation. They were required to offer what were imprecisely called 'reasonable facilities' and not permitted to exercise 'undue' preference for any customer. They had to provide facilities for through traffic and reduced rates for workmen and members of the armed forces. Additionally they had to observe statutory regulation of wages and working conditions and submit their financial accounts in a manner laid down by the government. This legacy of nineteenth-century regulation became an increasing burden as road transport, which had no such legal responsibilities, began extracting from the railways large amounts of freight traffic for which it could provide a better service. The railways were left with a residue of freight traffic that could not be charged at commercial rates but which they were legally required to handle.

Even before 1914 there were signs that Britain's economy might be based on insecure foundations. She was finding it extremely difficult to adjust to being one advanced industrial country among many others and not necessarily the most robust. Her staple industries faced great challenges after the First World War. That war had intensified tendencies towards self-sufficiency as Britain's customers were cut off from their normal sources of supply. It was clear that some of the products of her industries were being replaced by substitute materials; oil, for example, was a growing competitor for coal and rayon was offering an alternative to textiles. The UK found itself in the unenviable position of trying to find outlets for products for which demand was declining. An unfortunate coincidence was that many primary producers were experiencing falling prices and were unable to buy the same quantities of British manufactured goods as before. British industry was dangerously dependent on her staple industries. What had once been a trail-blazing economy was now finding it very difficult to diversify and conduct necessary innovation. Britain's main export industries were struggling in a much more competitive market. The inter-war stagnation of world trade affected Britain more than any other great trading nation because her additional income from invisible exports of shipping, banking and insurance also suffered in the worldwide trade depression.

These cumulative changes inevitably impacted on Britain's transport system. The railways had developed primarily to serve the needs of a rapidly expanding economy based on staple industries such as heavy engineering, iron and steel-making, ship-building and textiles. Their operations and services had been geared to the requirements of those industries and when they contracted, the railways were bound to be adversely affected. As if this was not enough, the railways began to experience strong competition from road transport which proved to be much better suited to meeting the needs of those sectors of industry which *were* expanding after 1918. The rising light industries were mostly in the South and the Midlands and located away from the coalfields. Being road-orientated and not necessarily dependent on coal as a fuel, these industries were often located closer to their markets. The development of such industries was not propitious for the railways but very favourable for road haulage. The railways lost considerable coal and mineral traffic which ironically was largely immune from road competition and this was partly due to the generally depressed economic conditions of these years. After a brief post-war boom, prices fell and the economy slumped. By June 1921 there were over 2 million unemployed and the figure never fell below a million in the 1920s and 1930s.

Roads therefore were able to abstract traffic from the railways and to seize new business from the developing light industries which the railways were often ill-suited to serve. As a legacy of their previous dominance of inland transport and the element of complacency that went with it, many of the railway companies' practices were wholly inappropriate in the face of road competition. Steam-hauled passenger trains often ran to timings which were abysmally slow. There were many examples of trains being timetabled to halt at a wayside station for twenty or more minutes for no apparent reason except that this had always happened in living memory. Such practices, which totally frustrated passengers who wanted to reach their destinations quickly, existed for reasons probably lost in the mists of time but they had no place when buses and cars were providing a vigorous challenge. Railway managers, however, seemed either unaware or these deterrents to rail travel or complacent when attention was drawn to them.

The challenging economic conditions of the inter-war years hit the railways hard. Although the demand for transport actually increased, the railways won only a frugal share of new traffic. With straitened income, the resources for investment in measures that might counteract the growing influence of road transport were simply not available. Even replacing life-expired infrastructure, rolling stock and other assets proved problematical.

Between the wars the railways remained the most important conveyors of non-passenger traffic but their revenue from this aspect of their business (which had always dominated their activity and generated a large share of their income) fell, which helps to explain the increasingly parlous state of the railways' finances and the lack of resources available for much-needed investment. Given the very real threats posed by growing road usage, it seems mistaken or simply vainglorious to have produced so much publicity for a few glamorous high speed services such as the streamlined expresses on the East and West Coast Main Lines. Likewise, it could be questioned whether it made good commercial sense to pursue the world speed record for steam locomotives at a time when the railways faced severe threats to major parts of their business. The glamour surrounding stunts of this sort disguised the reality of the fragile state of the Big Four's finances.

The costs of maintaining a railway system are high and relatively inflexible. If traffic declines, revenue is likely to fall faster than operating expenses. This is precisely what happened in the inter-war years with the result that the railways' operating ratio, that is, working expenses as a proportion of receipts, rose from 60 per cent pre-war to 80 per cent in the 1930s. Again, any attempt by the railways to reduce their charges adversely affected net revenue since comparable reductions could not easily be made in essential expenditure. A few closures took place although not in a systematic way. In 1930, admittedly a troubled time economically, no fewer than 903 route miles of passenger services were withdrawn, a sizeable figure forgotten in the furore around the Beeching Plan of the 1960s. Between 1923 and 1938 over 1,250 route miles lost their passenger services. No serious attempt was made to identify the real financial basket cases and cull them systematically. Where the railway companies bought out bus operators, they often left both rail and bus services intact even when they were directly competitive.

The railway companies seem to have been somewhat slow in recognising and attempting to deal with the very real challenges presented by the rise of road haulage. Efficiency improvements were instituted but perhaps rather too little and tending to consist of investment in existing rather than new forms of technology. For example, while containers were introduced which could be transhipped from railway wagons to lorries and vice versa to provide a door-to-door service, most freight handling remained antiquated, labour-intensive and extremely inefficient. Freight and mineral trains mostly moved slowly because few wagons had brakes controlled by the locomotive. Goods handling was inefficient because most wagons had a limited carrying capacity. A lengthy journey might involve a wagon being shunted time and time again in various yards along the route as it made its tortuous journey across Britain in the consist of one freight train after another. Wagons and their consignments sometimes literally got lost and the authorities might spend days trying to locate them. Lorries may not have been able to travel very fast at this time but their door-to-door capability often meant that consignments could be moved more quickly by road. As mentioned above, the railways were plagued by having to operate huge numbers of privately-owned wagons not fitted with brakes controlled by the locomotive. Many of these belonged to collieries, for example. These wagons had to be returned empty to their owners which involved considerable expense as they were unlikely to generate any income when being moved for this purpose. The continued existence of such primitive wagons acted as a blight on the railways right into the mid-twentieth century. Great skill was required from the men driving the engines hauling trains of unbraked wagons to keep them under control and in most cases they necessarily travelled slowly, their payload taking a long time to reach its destination while they got in the way of faster trains which in many cases had greater earning potential.

In 1929, Winston Churchill, not the most competent of Britain's Chancellors of the Exchequer, ended Railway Passenger Duty which had been introduced in 1832. By this time it was being levied mostly on first class passenger fares. This move may have benefited the railways, the Duty's abolition being based on the condition that the windfall created would be used for modernisation projects. However, Churchill had little interest in or sympathy with the railways but saw this as a ploy to pump-prime the economy and to create jobs and increase demand in the adverse economic conditions of the time. Under the Guarantees and Loans Act of 1934 the government provided money for the railway companies to undertake modernisation projects, again as an attempt to stimulate economic growth and create jobs. The Southern Railway (SR) was probably the most energetic in the use of these resources and much of its passenger network in the south-east of England was converted to third-rail electrification at this time, a venture which met with considerable success.

As road competition bit harder and harder, the railways lobbied governments to do something about what they, the railways, regarded as undue favours enjoyed by the road interest. The motorist, they argued, once he had paid his licence fee and bought his petrol, could travel freely anywhere he wished on Britain's roads whereas the railways had to pay rent for much of the land they used as well as rates to the local authorities. Sometimes the rates they paid to local authorities were used, among other things, to fund competing municipally-owned tram and bus systems. This was a somewhat negative approach based on the idea that because the railways were heavily regulated, road transport should be dealt with similarly. The railways were rightly subject to comprehensive safety rules and wide-ranging regulations. They were aggrieved that these rules were expensive to implement while road users had no similar obligations. The railways had their 'common carrier' obligations, meaning they must take any traffic offered, no matter how loss-making, whereas road hauliers could pick those assignments which were most lucrative. As noted, railways had legal duties to convey workmen and members of the armed forces at cheap rates but no such requirements were imposed on bus operators. Another unfair burden which the railways complained about was the requirement for them to publish their freight charges. Road hauliers laboured under no such obligation which gave them the great advantage of being able to look up the price the railways would offer for a job and then simply undercut that price. As Terry Gourvish, in *British Railways 1948–1973* (1986) has said: '… the continued obligation to accept traffic, publish charges, provide a reasonable level of service, avoid "undue preference", in the treatment of customers and submit to government regulation of wages and conditions, left the railways vulnerable to their more flexible and less constrained competitors'.

Although there was no longer any recognised 'Railway Interest' as such, the railway companies still had economic, political and personal connections which meant that they could exert some influence in places where it mattered.

The wishes of the railway companies could not be ignored. They still played a major role in the economy. In 1935 the Post Office was the largest employer with the LMS (London, Midland and Scottish Railway) in second place, the LNER (London and North Eastern Railway) in third and the Great Western Railway (GWR) in fourth. The SR was sixth. At least partly due to the lobbying of the companies, a Royal Commission on Transport was set up in 1928. It produced three reports between 1929 and 1931, the last of which was the first comprehensive survey of inland transport. Largely as a result of its deliberations, road haulage and the bus industry were brought under an extensive code of regulations in the early 1930s.

London Transport was formed in 1933. It gained an almost total monopoly of London's internal transport services and was designed to plan and provide an efficient coordinated public transport system in the capital and its environs. Its success was quickly evident and was a great fillip for those people who argued for the benefits of systematic transport coordination and integration. There was talk of establishing similar schemes in the provincial conurbations but it was probably the intervention of the war which prevented this happening.

In 1938 the Big Four launched a 'Square Deal' campaign for better treatment from the government and more equity when it came to competing with road hauliers, bus operators and private motorists. This campaign was the culmination of fifteen or more years of lobbying but it was clear that the then Department of Transport was largely unsympathetic to the idea of ridding the railways of the various statutory regulations and restrictions under which they operated their rates and charges. The railways wanted what would now be called 'a level playing field'. The road lobby launched its own campaign to discredit the arguments of the Big Four. The Department of Transport was aware that the current system acted to the disadvantage of the railways but it did not feel the time was right to bring about any meaningful concessions favourable to them. The Second World War intervened to put the issue into abeyance for the duration.

The railway companies were slow to react to the changing conditions of the inter-war years. They seemed reluctant to engage in systematic closures. Where modernisation of traction was concerned, limited schemes of electrification took place outside the south-east and there was a rather tentative use of small diesels for shunting purposes. The GWR invested in diesel railcars which proved very successful, but only to the extent of a fleet of about forty units. Britain's railways stayed firmly dominated by steam traction and traditional practices.

The Big Four were all financially enfeebled by 1939. The SR's electrification programme had generated much new business and its finances were in the healthiest state but the GWR was paying less than 1 per cent on ordinary shares in 1938, the LNER had paid no dividend from 1935 to 1938 and the

LMS dividend fell from 1.5 per cent in 1937 to nothing in 1938. When the Second World War ended, the long term issues facing the railways and the various demanding challenges created by the war effort meant that the railways were facing a crisis, and one at least of the Big Four companies was virtually bankrupt.

Chapter 10

Railways, 1945–1955

The Impact of War

Lessons had been learned from the experience of the First World War and were quickly applied at the outbreak of the Second. The railways came under state control on 1 September 1939. Already suffering from lack of investment, they were now required to cope with the huge extra burden thrust on them by the demands of war. A Railway Executive Committee under the direction of the Minister of Transport was established including the managers of the Big Four and London Transport. The feeling among senior railway managers was that although the government guaranteed them an acceptable level of income, it had no appreciation of or sympathy for the extra problems that wartime demand added to the existing generally difficult financial situation. If 1944 is compared with 1938, railway freight traffic rose by nearly 50 per cent and passenger traffic by 68 per cent. The railways were in a parlous state in 1939 and they emerged from the war in a considerably worse one. They were so run down that many of the services they were providing immediately after the war were markedly inferior to those on offer in the 1930s.

During the war, the railways suffered innumerable aerial attacks seriously damaging their infrastructure. Locomotives and rolling stock were commandeered for war service overseas or run into the ground through over-intensive use and skilled men had been conscripted or volunteered for active service. Many of their replacements, and there were not enough of them, frequently lacked necessary skills. Some railway workshops had gone over to armaments and other war production. The railways ended the war greatly over-extended, with a huge backlog of repairs and maintenance and shortage of materials. The LMS alone estimated that it needed £14 million to catch up with its arrears of maintenance on track and signalling and £26 million to restore its permanent way to pre-war standards. The private railway companies simply did not have the funds to put right the damage wreaked by the war and the huge backlog of repairs, maintenance and renewal. They were worn out from meeting wartime demand, inadequately compensated for the expenses they had incurred and were then prevented by the government from raising their rates and charges to help to meet the costs of getting the system back into something approaching decent shape.

It was this situation which led Hugh Dalton, the Chancellor, to tell the House of Commons on 17 December 1946 that: 'This railway system is a very poor bag of assets. The permanent way is badly worn. The rolling stock is in a state of great dilapidation. The railways are a disgrace to the country. The railway stations and their equipment are a disgrace to the country.' In the post-war world with shortages of vital materials and low levels of investment, no government was prepared to give the railways the resources they desperately needed. They were so seriously run down that the Royal Statistical Society estimated that there had been a net disinvestment in Britain's railway assets between 1937 and 1953 of £440 million at 1948 prices. Somehow the network, as the nationalised 'British Railways' (BR), managed to keep going but it was not well-placed to face the interconnected challenges posed by a huge post-war increase in road transport, wide-ranging economic and social changes and an era of unprecedented and destabilising government interference in its activities.

Whether or not the railways were Dalton's 'very poor bag of assets', they were still big business. With a route mileage of nearly 20,000, there were 8,294 stations, 973 freight sorting or marshalling yards, 20,148 locomotives, 56,425 carriages and 1,260,185 wagons. Staff employed numbered around 650,000.

Nationalisation in the air

The Labour Party gained an overwhelming, if unexpected, victory in the general election of 1945. It had an overall majority of 146 seats. It had gone to the country with the most radical manifesto in its history and prominent among its commitments was the taking of inland transport into public ownership and the welding of road, rail, air and waterways into one unified and integrated system. 'Integration' was a key concept in Labour's plans.

When it became clear that nationalisation was inevitable, the top brass of the Big Four devoted much of their attention to trying to obtain the most favourable possible compensation for their shareholders. It is not surprising therefore that in the period of uncertainty between the end of hostilities and formal nationalisation, little priority was given to projects involving medium- or long-term planning and expenditure. Many essential repairs and renewals went on hold. This was compounded by the end of American Lend-Lease in September 1945 which forced the government to restrict domestic consumption and promote exports at the expense of other calls on resources including investment in the railways.

The idea of nationalising such a vital utility as the railways had a long history. William Gladstone had considered the issue when President of the Board of Trade in the 1840s. In 1865 William Galt in *Railway Reform* compared the waste of virtually unbridled competition between railway companies in Britain with the benefits that were accruing from the operation of a planned state-owned system in the Netherlands. The question of whether the pursuit of railway business for private profit was compatible with the provision of services that best met public need constantly hovered around the political agenda in the first two decades of the twentieth century. Many workers in the industry thought that nationalisation would bring about improvements in pay and working conditions and the unions of course were supportive not only for that practical reason but because nationalisation accorded with the collectivist ideas of socialism to which many subscribed, at least in words. The MPs in the nascent Labour Party favoured nationalisation. Private Members' Bills for nationalisation were introduced each year from 1906 to 1909 and again in 1911 but none obtained a second reading. The issue was thrust into the limelight because of the vital role played by the railways in the First World War. As we have seen, governments after 1918 saw outright nationalisation as a step too far but the issue did not go away. The Labour Party Conference in 1932 passed a motion for the nationalisation of all the principle means of transport and the creation of a National Transport Board tasked with coordinating and integrating the various transport services. Coordination was seen as, for example, linking the arrival and departure of buses and trains at the same location as closely as possible. Integration involved bringing all the principal means of transport together under unified direction and control. The creation of the London Passenger Transport Board in 1933 was widely applauded as evidence of the benefits of comprehensive consolidation of transport and that effective integration and coordination of public transport was only likely to take place within the public sector. The Labour Party saw a State-controlled internal transport system as central to its plans for a brave new post-war Britain. Quite how such a system was going to be created and maintained was another matter.

The railways, basically under the direction of the State, had unquestionably made a heroic contribution to the war effort. It was not surprising that there were sustained calls for nationalisation, even among some Conservatives. Many people, not necessarily on the left, thought that an industry so vital for the economy should be run by the State. Even Churchill at one time had advocated nationalisation. It was also thought that a unified State-owned system would succeed in obtaining more resources for investment and modernisation. At long last historically conditioned legal strictures might be relaxed and the railways could gain much-needed commercial freedom. It was not to be. The Big Four were very alarmed about the possibility of nationalisation and from 1943 they began to publish propaganda concerning the improvements they intended to make once peace returned. There were grandiose promises but no explanation as to how the companies were going to pay for them. The chairman of the LMS declared that nationalisation would be opposed by all legal means. A campaign was launched against the alleged foolishness of nationalisation but it was somewhat toothless since little common ground appeared to exist between the four companies other than opposition to a state takeover. In the event, there was little effective opposition to nationalisation, perhaps because the railway companies knew that they did not actually have the resources to implement the improvements they loftily talked about introducing once things returned to normality. Their opposition may also have been muted because they had intimations concerning the generous compensation terms that would be offered to their shareholders.

In 1946 the Big Four joined their traditional enemy, the RHA, many of whose members were also concerned about the threat to their businesses posed by nationalisation, to challenge the threat of State ownership. They even talked about coordinating their haulage and freight-carrying activities, an idea which only seems to have occurred to them as an argument against nationalisation and had never previously been advanced as a means of providing the country with the best possible means of moving goods and minerals. They argued that the Labour government was driven by 'socialist dogma'. The government did indeed consider itself socialist and it had decisive electoral support for policies intended to bring about wide-ranging economic and social change. However, the use of the word 'socialism' was a jibe suggesting similarities with a collectivist state like Russia. Labour's horizons in reality did not extend beyond the idea of a 'mixed economy' where private enterprise remained dominant but certain key industries would be brought under state control to ensure that they operated in the best possible way to serve the needs of the majority private sector.

Some people demanded nationalisation because they were hostile to private enterprise and others because they thought that the war had proved that the railways could operate more efficiently under state direction. Some railway workers hoped that if the railways were nationalised, then there might be a place for workers' control. When nationalisation was enacted and much was being made of the fact that the railways now 'belonged' to the nation, it quickly became clear that appointments to the governing bodies of the railways and the other transport industries were to be made by the Minister of Transport alone and that employees were not going to be appointed to such bodies or have any say in the decision-making process. This very much accorded with the ideas of Herbert Morrison who had been Minister of Transport in the Labour government of 1929–1931. He had had a considerable input into what became the London Passenger Transport Board and was still a figure of considerable influence in the Labour Party. London Transport was an independent body but under public control and it provided a template for the management structure of the transport industries nationalised by the Attlee government of 1945. This favoured the use of men with what was considered to be a proven track record in commerce and industry. Fresh blood in senior positions in the railway industry was no bad thing in itself but here the practice brought with it outsiders, many of whom had cut their teeth in private industry and were permeated with the ethos of capitalism. Many had little sympathy with the concept of state-owned industry. Worse, some former senior figures from the Big Four who were known for their antipathy to nationalisation also obtained key roles in the new nationalised structure and were less than enthusiastic about attempting to make a success of the new order. Consequently railway workers did not feel that much had changed from the days of private ownership; that it was not their railway or the people's railway. The senior bosses were still considered often as much out of touch with the travelling public and the rank-and-file workers as they had ever been.

There was a mood in Britain after the war that rejected the idea of returning to the worst aspects of the 1930s and supported the concept of a more egalitarian society. Back in 1937 Attlee had told the Labour Party that when Labour next gained office, it would embark on an unprecedented programme of enlarging the public sector. The Labour Party made clear in its manifesto for the 1945 general election that, if elected, it intended to carry out policies that would considerably extend the involvement of the state in the lives of the people. Indeed, the party had received an overwhelming endorsement from the electorate for the idea of the welfare state, the NHS and the nationalisation of a range of industries which were vital to the workings of what was, however, to remain an economy dominated by private enterprise.

Although nationalisation was controversial, it is difficult to see how the privately owned railway companies, in the dire situation in which they emerged from the war, could have avoided approaching the government for substantial financial support over the succeeding years. It is even more difficult to envisage how, had they stayed in the private sector, they would have been able to face up to the threats posed by the rise of road transport and other economic and social changes in the 1950s and 1960s without receiving large elements of State support. The advocates of private enterprise had seemingly forgotten the economic problems of the railways in the inter-war years and the fact that they had received State financial support for various projects as part of government 'pump-priming' policy during the economic difficulties of the 1930s. Even before the war, the railways had been making puny profits and the advocates of free market economics had happily accepted financial support from the public purse for private railways on the grounds that they provided a vital public service. Labour on the other hand disapproved of the idea on the basis that it would mean taxpayers effectively subsidising railway shareholders. The tables turned after the war. With the railways in the public sector, it was now the Conservatives who tended to oppose governments providing public funding support for the railways while making sure that private investors in the railways received generous compensation from public funds when the Big Four were nationalised.

Transport nationalisation

Under the terms of the Transport Act of 1947 the British Transport Commission (BTC) was established, coming into existence on 1 January 1948. It was answerable to the Minister of Transport and delegated its powers to five executives: London Transport, Docks and Inland Waterways; Hotels, Road Transport and Railways. The BTC was intended to be the policymaking and directing body of the five executives. The day-to-day operation of the transport businesses was in the hands of these executives. From the start there were tensions between the BTC and the various executives. The railway system itself was organised in six regions designated as Eastern, London Midland, North Eastern, Scottish, Southern and Western. With the exception of the Scottish Region and perhaps the North Eastern, these names gave a somewhat inexact idea of the geographical area for which they had responsibility. The division into regions never sat entirely happily within the BTC structure. An example was the Great Central Main Line south from Sheffield to London Marylebone. Three regions, the London Midland, the Eastern and the Western had administrative inputs at various times. The sense of being nobody's baby must have contributed to its eventual demise.

The actual transfer of the assets of the previously privately-owned companies into the State sector took place on 1 January 1948. The BTC was intended to be a small, policymaking organisation. The executives were to deal with technical questions and detailed management. It seems that there was always some doubt about who was really in charge of the railways. Was it the Railway Executive or the BTC? The Railway Executive was the largest of the executives and, in terms of turnover, was bigger than the other five collectively. The BTC exercised strict financial control over all the executives, yet the lack of clarity in the division of power was typified by the fact that the senior officers in the Railway Executive were appointed by the Minister of Transport and not by the BTC. This called into question the integrity of the BTC's role and reduced its authority when it came to attempts to integrate the various transport media. It seems evidence of the muddled thinking of the time that one of the most outspoken critics of transport nationalisation and integration, Henry Dutfield, chairman of the RHA, took a post on the executive responsible for road transport.

The BTC was legally required to 'provide, or secure or promote the provision of an efficient, adequate, economical and properly integrated system of public inland transport and port facilities within Great Britain for passengers and goods ...'. With the emphasis on integration, road and rail were expected to work closely together which is why many haulage operators and bus companies also came under the auspices of the BTC. The desired integration and coordination never took place.

In *British Railways 1948–1973*, Terry Gourvish (1986) was very critical of the organisational structure around the Railway Executive and the BTC. He argued that the criterion underpinning the organisation of nationalised transport was 'political and administrative expediency rather than economic efficiency'. It was never really clear whether the BTC's task was to be a supervisory or an executive one. He was also critical of the nature of the newly-created Transport Users' Consultative Committees. These were ostensibly designed to take account of rail users' concerns when closures were being proposed. Gourvish found it anomalous that road operators were appointed as members: they might influence decisions for closures from which their own businesses could benefit.

The situation was made more complicated because of the complexity of the activities the nationalised railway inherited from the Big Four. Unlike the railways in most other countries, the pre-nationalisation companies had invested heavily in what could be described as 'ancillary' businesses. This included their own factories for building and maintaining rolling stock and many of the innumerable other artefacts needed to keep the railways going. They ran fleets of road vehicles for goods collection and delivery, hotels, refreshment rooms and on-board train catering, shipping and ferry services, ports and harbours and even canals. They had sizeable investments in bus operators, road haulage, travel agencies, airlines and the Pullman Car Company. They were also involved in property development and the letting of sites for commercial advertising.

Nationalisation involved compensating those who had investments in the private railway companies. The financial difficulties of these companies in the 1930s had prevented them rewarding their shareholders very generously. The senior directors of the Big Four and many of those possessing large railway shareholdings were, however, people with considerable influence. The chairman of the LNER argued that the terms of the compensation 'would bring a blush of shame to the leathery cheeks of a Barbary pirate'. The outcome of the compensation provided – a figure of over £1,065 million – was to saddle the BTC and the railways in particular with a very large interest burden which they had to service irrespective of their own income and outgoings. The resources spent in this way were not available for improving the services the railway could offer, which seriously hurt their business particularly at a time when they were faced with the rapid growth of both passenger and freight road transport.

In December 1946 when the Transport Bill was being debated in the House of Commons, the then Chancellor, Hugh Dalton, was accused by the Conservatives of offering miserly terms of compensation to railway shareholders. Obviously the Conservatives saw themselves as champions of the shareholders' cause but the latter really had little cause to complain. The terms they were offered were based on a stock market valuation in the period immediately after the war and well before it became clear what damage was going to be done to the income of the railways by the rapid growth of road transport. Those who invested in the Big Four were taking a risk in the hope of personal gain. The financial treatment, confiscatory according to some and over-generous in the view of others, received by the shareholders created a millstone around the neck of the railways until most of the debt was written off in the 1960s. This obligation, often referred to as the 'historic debt', was a factor inhibiting British Railways' (BR) response to the challenges of the 1950s and early 1960s. Whatever their trading position, they were required to make large debt repayments. Those hostile to the railways pointed to their deteriorating financial state and claimed that it was the natural concomitant of state ownership. In the Conservative Party there were influential people who had been directors of the Big Four or major shareholders and they never missed an opportunity to deride and debunk every aspect of the nationalised railways. They found it expedient to forget the extent of this debt burden while encouraging governments to provide the optimum conditions for the expansion of road haulage and private motoring.

Another factor inhibiting the ability of the railways to respond effectively to the challenges they had to face was that under the Transport Act of 1947 they were required to buy up most of the vast numbers of private owner wagons. Many were of ancient design and of low-capacity as well as being loose-coupled, i.e. not fitted with continuous brakes controlled by the locomotive. Many were poorly maintained. Trains composed of such wagons generally moved very slowly. Ideally they would have been consigned to the scrap heap with immediate effect. They numbered well over half a million and the compensation paid to their previous owners for what was often an artefact worth little more than its scrap value was another financial burden the BTC was obliged to meet.

Battling austerity

The enforced requirements of austerity harmed the attempts of the BTC to move forward with replacements and renewals. In 1949, for example, it needed a million tons of steel, much of it to replace wooden-bodied wagons, but only received 810,000 tons. After the devaluation of sterling in 1949, the reduction in funding from the government meant significant cuts in the number of new locomotives and carriages that were brought into service. Various military commitments around the world meant often giving priority to 'guns over butter'. Consequently the BTC was not given the funding necessary to obtain the materials needed to create a modern and efficient system out of the severely debilitated assets it had taken over in 1948.

The sudden ending of American Lend-Lease on 21 August 1945 and the economic crisis this precipitated forced the Labour government to strive for a 50 per cent growth in exports by 1950 in an attempt to obtain a more favourable balance of payments. In late 1950 BR was instructed to reduce its weekly coal consumption by 10,000 tons. The purpose of this was so that the National Coal Board (NCB) could prioritise the allocation of high quality coal to export markets. Such political interference inevitably created problems for BR.

Large-scale investment in the motor industry met with considerable success in exports but also in the domestic market where it appeared as if the government was actively encouraging the growth in private motoring. The number of motor vehicles in the UK rose from 3 million in 1946 to nearly 4.5 million in 1950 despite the continuance of petrol rationing. The cost of using rail and other forms of public transport rose more steeply in the post-war years than did the cost of buying and running motor vehicles of all kinds. A vicious circle was created whereby the railway was forced to raise fares to offset the lost income from passengers who had bought and were using their own cars. Increased fares then led to the loss of further passengers especially if cuts were made in services at the same time.

BR gained a not wholly deserved reputation for bureaucratic inefficiency once the initial enthusiasm for a more collective society had waned. It became a target for cheap gibes often launched by journalists whose ignorance concerning railways was bottomless. The railways and other nationalised industries were a small island of State control in an ocean of private enterprise and the political culture quickly moved to the right and against the concept of nationalisation. In such a situation no calumny concerning the State-controlled industries and the railways in particular was too ridiculous to be promulgated as a fact rather than as an opinion based on flimsy evidence or simple prejudice.

In April 1963 Harold Wilson was interviewed about his early days in politics and, turning to the railways, he vindicated the record of the 1945 Labour government when he made clear that the way in which nationalisation had been negotiated put a great financial burden on the railways. Despite this, state sector public transport as a whole remained viable until the Conservatives, elected to office in 1951, began to implement policies opposed to integration and public transport in general. Even then, the legacy of Labour meant that BR was still paying its way until 1953. This, Wilson claimed, was all the more remarkable bearing in mind the growth of road traffic and the dire financial state of the privately-owned railway companies before the Second World War. It was also an achievement given the chronic shortage of vital materials from which the railways suffered and early post-war government policy which tried rigorously to control domestic investment and direct efforts towards the export industries. Despite all the restrictions imposed by the government, in 1952 with 40,000 fewer staff, 1,500 fewer locomotives and 100,000 fewer wagons the railways were carrying 12 million tons more merchandise than in 1948 and 19 million tons more than in 1938. In the first six years of the BTC, that is, 1948 to 1953, a working surplus was achieved after deducting central charges, the main element of which was interest on money raised to compensate former private shareholders. As the 1950s unfolded, however, the question of what to do with a nationalised business that was making increasing losses forced itself increasingly onto the public agenda. The BTC had the legal responsibility to balance its books but it operated under conditions which rendered that achievement virtually impossible.

The BTC was charged with the requirement that its finances should break even 'taking one year with another'. Servicing the debt made this into a Sisyphean labour. However, the most crucial factor harming the finances of BR was the growth of road transport. On 1 January 1948 when the BTC began operations, there were 3,700,000 motor vehicles on the country's roads. In 1953 this had grown to 5,300,000 and by the time the BTC was abolished in 1962 there were approaching 11,000,000. The inevitable result was that the Railway Executive ceased covering its working costs by 1954 and plunged into ever-increasing debt. The future was to show that no organisational changes such as the Modernisation Plan of 1955 or the Beeching Plan of 1963 could arrest the decline in the overall economic fortunes of the railways.

The BTC dabbled very half-heartedly with the idea of replacing steam traction in the immediate post-war period but then embarked on a programme of introducing 999 so-called 'standard' steam locomotives across twelve classes. One 'standard' class consisted of just one member; one of ten; one of twenty and another of thirty. Such locomotives could hardly be described as standard and there was very little that they could do that was not already being done satisfactorily by similar pre-nationalisation locomotives, although they did incorporate a number of welcome labour-saving devices. Only one class, the '9F' 2-10-0, was truly innovative and it was arguably the most successful, with 251 being built. All these standard class locomotives had scandalously short lives and an argument could be advanced that they should not have been built at all. Perhaps even more ridiculous was the continued building of steam locomotives of pre-nationalisation design right into the 1950s. It almost beggared belief that twenty-eight small shunting tank engines of class 'J72' were built under BR auspices to a design of the North Eastern Railway introduced as far back as 1898! There were already diesel shunting locomotives in operation that could have done their job considerably more efficiently and economically. The disdain clearly felt for more modern forms of traction indicated outdated and hidebound attitudes in many influential railway managers, although the excuse was made that with new motive power urgently needed, steam locomotives were cheaper and could be brought into service more quickly than alternative forms of traction. While the new standard steam locomotives were easier to maintain than many older types, the fact remained that steam locomotives were thermally inefficient, labour-intensive in their operation and maintenance and an environmentally unfriendly form of traction. Diesel and electric traction were more expensive to build than steam but usually required less servicing, could work almost 'round the clock' and was infinitely cleaner. The infrastructure needed for electric traction was expensive and so some expressed a preference for diesels, not least on cost grounds. The USA had widespread experience of diesel traction and a large locomotive-manufacturing capacity but the government's determination to boost British exports rendered the purchase of proven American diesel locomotives a non-starter at this time.

Effective modernisation of passenger and freight traffic was not possible while steam power remained dominant. Railway enthusiasts may have delighted in watching ancient steam locomotives pottering about, but the years to come were a time of massive economic and social change and emphasis on the new. Steam engines, musty old carriages, sooty, dirty and ill-lit stations were redolent of times past. Railway usage continued at very high levels but the railways were becoming unfashionable. The motor car, the luxury coach and the eight-wheel lorry encapsulated the clean, the new and the exciting; the way forward. 'Image' was becoming all-important. The railways looked increasingly tired and caught in a time-warp. It was a positive achievement of the BTC that by 1952, with a substantial reduction in locomotives and wagons, the railways were carrying far more merchandise than in 1938 and advances had been made in productivity and standardisation of equipment. However, the predominant impression given was of nineteenth-century infrastructure and methods of operation looking increasingly incapable of dealing with a variety of serious challenges.

Britain's railways in the 1950s were still dominated by steam. This may have gladdened the hearts of many, particularly those who did not have to work with steam locomotives but with the benefit of hindsight it can be seen that systematic trials should have been conducted after the war to identify diesel and electric traction units that were efficient and mechanically reliable. This might have avoided some of the expensive experiences from 1955 with hopeless designs of diesel and, to a lesser extent, electric locomotives. Diesel shunting locomotives of 350hp were entering service in some numbers from 1953 and proving efficient and economical and yet it is scarcely credible that the Western Region, which already had numbers of these locomotives, was also introducing into service 210 members of the '94XX' class. They were introduced in 1947, of totally obsolescent design and offering no advantage over the existing highly successful '57XX' locomotives which performed similar duties and had a wider operating range. It was rumoured that some managers liked them because they looked rather more modern than the '57XX' locomotives. The '94XX' locomotives continued to be built until 1956 at least partly as a political gesture to provide work for struggling companies in the private locomotive building industry. There was little work for many of these locomotives and some spent much of their disgracefully short lives in store. As an example, No. 9499 entered traffic on 1 April 1955 and was stored out of use from 28 March 1956 until 19 January 1957. It was stored again from 25 May 1957 until withdrawn on 14 September 1959.

The position facing a railway system still dominated by steam in the mid-1950s was critical. The quality of suitable coal was deteriorating and there were chronic staff shortages because it was becoming hard to find workers prepared to service and operate such dirty and physically demanding machines for relatively poor pay, often slow promotion and distinctly antisocial hours. Looking after and operating steam locomotives was highly labour-intensive. Steam maintenance facilities were generally starved of investment and many engine sheds had staff facilities and working conditions that were an absolute disgrace. Some engine sheds were literally falling down while still in use. Morale suffered as conditions worsened, traffic levels dropped and jobs were lost. It was a wonder that morale and pride in the job remained as high as it did. Additionally, growing environmental awareness was critical of the filthy pollution that working steam locomotives inevitably created. Railway systems elsewhere in Europe were also replacing the steam locomotive but did so while maintaining much higher standards of servicing and accommodation for their declining numbers. All those BR employees still working with steam could have been excused for thinking that the management and their political masters held them in total contempt.

Nationalised railways: a political football

The railways back in the nineteenth century had complained about political interference in their activities but on a nationalised basis they were far more subject to the short-term whims of party political expediency. Vast amounts of time, energy and money were spent responding to government directives, some possibly vacuous and others simply capricious, which would have been better spent implementing modernisation and improving efficiency. Labour and Tory governments both seemed to regard railways as being in decline, even if they did not always say so publicly. Evidence of the scant regard and knowledge extended to the railways was clear in the debate in May 1952 on the Transport Bill. Winston Churchill, a man around whom a web of myths has been created, was Prime Minister and he told the Commons that he would like the railway regions to have greater autonomy so that they could enjoy what he described as a 'healthy rivalry'. A Labour MP retorted by asking how the Southern Region, for example, could compete with the North Eastern Region when the districts they served were at opposite ends of the country.

   Issues around transport generally received low priority in British political circles. The Transport portfolio was sometimes awarded to an up-and-coming politician as an apprenticeship before advancing to higher office. However it was also offered as something of a sop to a politician whose ministerial career was unlikely to go much further. Between 1947 and 1979 there were no fewer than fifteen Transport ministers. With Transport being such a political shuttlecock and given the short tenure of office of the relevant ministers, there were frequent changes and reversals in transport policy. Sir Stanley Raymond, when chairman of the BR board commented in the *Sunday Times* on 7 January 1968 that half of his twenty-one years of service in the railway industry had been taken up with 'organisation, reorganisation, denationalisation, centralisation and decentralisation'. He commented bitterly that there had been little time to get on with running the industry and trying to improve its viability and the quality of its services.

   As always, politicians had their own purposes and priorities, frequently the advancement of their own careers. Parties want to form governments and then implement those policies most likely to bring about their re-election. Such procedures do not necessarily accord with what is best for the economy, the electorate in general or for the railways in particular. Ministers of State may come and go very quickly, taking on the portfolio at short notice and often being moved elsewhere without becoming fully conversant with the specific requirements of the job. As Harris (2016) pointed out in *The Railway Dilemma*: '… it was virtually impossible for a Minister, however dedicated, to gain the same level of knowledge and understanding as a senior manager within the industry involved, particularly when the Minister was always at the mercy of the next Cabinet reshuffle …' This observation can be reinforced because some ministers had not even wanted the Transport portfolio, it by no means being among the more coveted jobs. In the generally anti-railway culture of post-war Britain, few politicians felt it was in their career interests to be seen as fervently pro-railway. Chancellors of the Exchequer, in reviewing public expenditure, looked askance at the losses being made by the railways and sought to restrict the resources available for their support. When consent was given to BR for increased fares and charges, the process of applying the increases was often protracted. In their attempts to counter inflation and court electoral popularity, governments used fare, freight rates and railway workers' wage increases as tools of national economic policy, delaying their implementation if it was thought expedient. This clearly had a disruptive and damaging impact on BR's finances. Nationalised industries such as the railways always sat uncomfortably in a so-called 'free market' economy.

Coordination and integration of inland transport had been one of the aims of Labour's plans as outlined in the 1945 election manifesto. The concept did not appeal to the Conservatives. Having won the general election in 1951 they were determined to return the bulk of the nationalised BRS to private hands, remove what they saw as a number of restrictions on road haulage and re-establish a situation in which road and rail freight haulage were in direct competition. Any notions of coordination were nullified by these initiatives. One Tory backbencher openly declared that the government's intention was to 'hurl against the railways the competition of the road'. The Transport Act of 1952/1953 embedded these objectives.

The Railway Executive, condemned for its alleged gross centralisation, went out of existence in 1954 to be replaced in 1955 by six Area Railways Boards. This was not a serious devolution of power because the power of the BTC increased as did the volume of business it had to get through. It became a massive bureaucratic monolith with a convoluted structure that seriously impaired decision-making. During its short existence the Railway Executive had presided over an increase in both passenger and freight traffic and this despite the conditions of austerity under which it and much of the nation had laboured at this time. Yet the railway industry continued to make substantial losses.

The Railway Executive set up two committees to review loss-making lines and, after due consideration and where appropriate, make recommendations for closure but the Executive seemed lukewarm about actually implementing closures even where some lines and services were basket cases. In the six years of the Executive's operation, route mileage fell by only just over 2 per cent. Systematic identification of loss-making activity and the will to do anything about it was largely absent. Some loss-making branch lines which were heavily used only at holiday times, such as those to Swanage and Hayling Island, when proposed for closure generated such vigorous opposition that the threat was withdrawn. Meanwhile railway finances went into free fall, with income from fares and freight charges lagging behind rising costs, partly because it was government policy to keep inflation and wage demands under control. Given that a nationalised railway system was subject to the self-serving whims of politicians and taking account of the understandable public hostility to price rises, it is not surprising that successive governments were concerned about the electoral implications of fare increases. The Tory government in 1952, for example, intervened to prevent fare increases in the provinces. While this may have been a balm for voters it was described by *The Times* as a recipe for continuing deficits. It took an unconscionably long time for all concerned to realise that the railways of post-war Britain were not going to break even unless a highly uncomfortable process of rationalisation took place. Even in the early 1950s a systematic and comprehensive survey of both passenger and freight operations should have been made in order to identify the traffics that were, respectively, profitable and loss-making. On that basis, a 1950s predecessor of the Beeching Plan would almost certainly have closed down a sizeable part of the network. There was no will to proceed in such a direction at this time but the crisis in railway finances meant that drastic action would have to be taken sooner or later. The time-bomb was ticking.

The failure of the BTC to obtain sufficient funding was not necessarily its own fault but was strongly influenced by successive governments who did not see railway investment as a priority among many other calls on public expenditure. The proportion of UK capital investment given to railways fell from just over 4 per cent in 1948 to 3.3 per cent in 1951. In 1952, just over £300 million was invested in road transport and around £950 million in 1960, whereas railways received about £40 million in 1952 and £175 million in 1960.

The railways were still required by law to accept all reasonable traffic offered, to refrain from discrimination between customers where circumstances were similar and to publish their charges and rates. These obligations dated back to the times when the railways had enjoyed a virtual monopoly of inland transport. Adherence to these requirements had become a shibboleth.

Despite such burdens, many in the industry at all levels seemed to assume that the railways would go on in the same old way for ever. Large numbers of senior railway managers were career railwaymen. While continuity and experience are very valuable, in the case of the railways it seems that they created certain inbred attitudes and some inflexibility in the management. Evidence of this was the priority often given to volume of traffic carried rather than the more useful criterion of profit made from traffic carried. It was this rather blinkered attitude that led Gerard Fiennes, a senior railway manager and author of *I Tried to Run a Railway*, to write in 1967: 'It is one of the disasters about British Railways that in the years between 1947 and 1955 no one had done the basic work on what we were there for at all; what traffic should be carried by what methods in what quantities, where from and to, at what rates'. BTC members, including those brought in from industry and commerce, were underpaid by contemporary standards if full-time and poorly-paid when part-time. Those without a railway background often mixed unhappily with senior professional railway managers many of whom they thought of as lacklustre and inward-looking. Both had a tendency to be suspicious of the motives of their political masters. There were always tensions within the nationalised railway industry. The chain of command and responsibility was not always clear, which could make the formulation and implementation of policy a slow and tortuous process.

Changing economic and social trends

In the early 1950s it was becoming very clear that road traffic was increasingly taking business from the railways and that there needed to be a serious appraisal of the role of the railway in a rapidly and radically changing Britain. The spread of television was reducing the demand for off-peak travel on public transport. People did not have to leave their homes for entertainment purposes. When the

1950s began, BR still enjoyed a working surplus before meeting interest and other central charges. In 1960 BR had an operating deficit of over £67 million. Crisis measures were urgently needed. Although roads were giving railways robust competition throughout Europe, no other country was experiencing such a loss of freight tonnage and indeed some national systems were actually gaining freight traffic in the generally buoyant economic conditions of the time. Many European railway systems were losing passenger traffic to the roads; indeed some to a greater extent than BR but others, notably those in the Netherlands, France and West Germany, were seeing increased passenger usage. Since the conveyance of freight and mineral traffic generated almost twice as much income as passenger traffic, it was the losses in this part of the business which were having a particularly harmful impact.

Britain was falling behind other countries in the priority governments gave to public transport by rail and road. By the mid-1950s the notion that supplies of cheap and abundant oil were available and would continue to be available into the foreseeable future had developed deep roots. This idea interacted with another notion which also proved mistaken and transient, which was that the classic cycle of boom and slump in capitalist-dominated economies had been overcome. The mood of optimism induced by these perceptions generated a belief in the inevitability of road vehicles largely replacing railways as the dominant form of internal transport in an increasingly affluent society, and that this was the best way forward. The UK proceeded further around this set of ideas than countries on the Continent where many had a longer and more firmly established tradition of the public ownership of transport undertakings which were seen as providing an infrastructure essential for vigorous economic growth. In Europe most political parties believed that financial support should be provided for rail operators if they were successfully to meet the challenges presented by road hauliers and private motoring. By contrast, British transport policy was a veritable political shuttlecock. The Labour administrations of 1945–1951 and 1964–1970 tended to favour public ownership of transport undertakings, although they found it difficult to resolve the conflict between the push for commercial viability and the need to provide services that met public demand but were intrinsically loss-making. Conservative governments generally sought to minimise the role of public transport and to encourage the growth of privately-owned transport of all kinds.

The frequent changes of ministers of transport and their under-secretaries provided abundant opportunities for the permanent civil servants to influence the decision-making processes to a greater extent than in many departments. Their political 'masters', knowing their tenure at the Ministry was likely to be short, tended to rely heavily on the research, advice and briefing of their supposed underlings, many of whom had little time for the railways or public transport in general. Close relations developed between the Ministry, its staff and the road transport industry. Organisations around the road interest employed personnel with impressive technical knowledge and operational research findings who could, and did, provide the Ministry with information it found very useful. Common practice involved the Ministry recruiting from the road lobby and those selected in this way brought their pro-road preferences with them. By the middle of the 1950s it was not unusual for critics to argue that the Ministry was biased to the extent that it was simply the mouthpiece of the road lobby (see Hamer 1987, *Wheels Within Wheels*).

It was this insidious influence that Barbara Castle was referring to in Parliament on 4 July 1973: 'When I took over as the Minister of Transport the most vociferous lobby in the country was that represented by road interests. The propaganda and pressure groups led by the British Road Federation said that we must concentrate all our resources on building the first 1,000 miles of motorway. The environment lobby had barely been born, and when I tried to suggest there were other considerations we should bear in mind I had an uphill task because about the whole of public opinion and the then opposition were against me.'

The BRF and its affiliates such the SMMT, the FTA and the RHA were wealthy enough to employ professional lobbyists and produce copious and effective propaganda aimed at holders of positions of serious power, and to create and embed a significant anti-rail and pro-road public culture. With this they set out create what was purported to be a 'common sense' view of the economic and social necessity of creating those conditions most favourable for the road haulage industry and the private motorist. The pro-railway forces then, and the environmentalists who appeared on the scene later, simply did not have the resources necessary to provide similar access to such methods of influencing public opinion.

Back in 1952 the Railway Executive had drawn up a plan for the modernisation of BR which envisaged a large programme of electrification and also the introduction of substantial numbers of diesel multiple units (DMUs). This plan, put together by professionals in the railway industry, proposed that the projected electric trains would use supplies generated in power stations via low-grade coal which would enable the release of better supplies of the fuel for export. Interestingly, no mention was made of the use of main line diesel locomotives. Such locomotives were, however, to be a major but extremely expensive and somewhat flawed component of the subsequent Modernisation Plan of 1955. It was clear that steam power was intended to continue to play a sizeable role in the future. These ideas were pigeonholed but are interesting for being a reflection of the views of railway industry insiders. They were right about the desirability of electrification. The problem was that the resources would never have been available for electrification on the scale needed to obviate the requirement for large numbers of expensive and frequently troublesome main line diesel locomotives and to eliminate steam power at the earliest possible opportunity.

Modernisation

In 1954 the BTC was required to draw up a plan to make the railways more financially viable. The 'Plan', officially *Modernisation and Re-equipment of British Railways*, was the product of deliberations over several months and was published in January 1955. It partly reflected the 'feel-good factor' engendered by the recent Festival of Britain and the Coronation of Elizabeth II. In the introduction it was stated: 'British Railways today are not working at full efficiency mainly due to their past inability to attract enough capital investment to keep their physical equipment up to date. The Plan aims to produce a thoroughly modern system, able fully to meet both current traffic requirements and those of the foreseeable future.' It was intended that the Plan would be fully implemented within fifteen years. There were several main strands. Steam locomotives were to be eliminated and replaced by diesels and a limited programme of electric traction, new passenger rolling stock would be introduced and stations would be upgraded, more long-welded rails would be installed and signalling would be modernised to allow higher speeds on trunk lines. Freight services were to be remodelled, particularly with a view to eliminating loose-coupled, hand-braked wagons. A number of new automated marshalling yards at key locations would eliminate much of the expensive and inefficient trip working of wagons from one small yard to another. It all sounded good but a senior industry insider who was clearly dubious of its merits described the subsequent Modernisation Plan as 'the greatest shopping spree in history'.

The emphasis on large modern marshalling yards was clear evidence of outdated thinking. Road haulage was already taking increasing amounts of the kind of wagonload traffic for which these yards were designed. It should have been evident that wagonload traffic would have little place in any modernised railway system of the future. Goods trains consisting of wagons whose braking systems were not controlled by the locomotive trundled slowly around the system and may even have looked as if they were paying their way when they were made up into trains of considerable length. The wagons themselves often had a capacity of no more than 12 tons but frequently they contained payloads of only, say, 3 tons, the kind of operation which could be handled so much more efficiently by a road haulage contractor and was intrinsically unprofitable for the railways. Some trains were composed largely or entirely of empty wagons, earning no revenue and costing money to be moved while cluttering up the system and getting in the way of faster traffic with greater revenue-earning potential.

A plan for modernising Britain's railways was desperately needed but the actual timing of the publication of the Modernisation Plan owed much to the requirements of political expediency. In late 1954 a major industrial dispute around pay issues was threatening on the railways and the government was anxious to avert what was likely to be an economically and politically disruptive and damaging dispute. A settlement that met the workers' demands would increase the BR deficit and would jeopardise the legal requirement of the BTC to pay its way. Major figures in the Conservative government including Prime Minister Churchill were far from convinced about the viability of an expensive programme of railway modernisation but in a masterpiece of political legerdemain they were prepared to offer the prospect of at least partial funding for such a programme. This programme was already largely drafted and was used as a bribe to the unions to agree to a 'reasonable' settlement and thereby avoid a strike. In the event, this cynical manoeuvre did not prevent a harmful stoppage but it did provide the go-ahead for a much-needed overdue but arguably flawed fillip for the railways. The politicians of course did not acquaint the public about the real reasons for their apparent Damascene conversion to an updating of Britain's railway system.

The Plan contained ideas which were repeated later by Dr Beeching and which made eminent sense at the time. For example, it wanted to shed some freight operations for which road haulage was more suited. Likewise long-distance stopping and branch line passenger services needed to be closely scrutinised and those that were hopelessly uneconomic should be abandoned. Where lightly-used stations remained open, savings could

The advert stretches the Morris Minor somewhat but even then the presence of adults, dog and luggage would prevent social distancing. Clearly the aim is at the middle class but this was precisely the kind of affordable car that would take passenger traffic away from the railways. (Authors' collection)

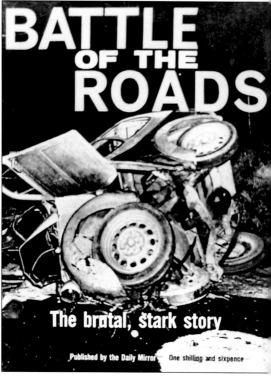

Above left: Barbara Castle was a feisty female who made her way in the man's world of politics. Minister of Transport from 1965–1969, she closed many lines but initiated a period of reversing the negative image of public transport. She went on to greater controversy at the Department of Employment when she proposed measures to limit the power of the trade unions. (Authors' collection)

Above right: Marples was concerned about the prevalence of careless and bad driving and contributed to this booklet published by the *Daily Mirror* which was full of horrifying images of road accidents. (Authors' collection)

Cartoonists found a rich seam in juxtaposing the lean Marples and the generously-proportioned Beeching. (Authors' collection)

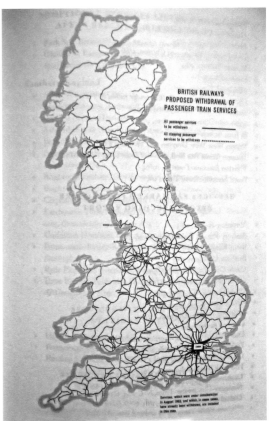

Above left: The map in the Beeching Report showing the extent of the UK's bus services. If it was intended to reassure the public that a comprehensive bus network was available, but it was highly misleading because it gave absolutely no idea of the frequency of the routes indicated.

Above right: The map that struck fear into the heart of millions, showing the lines and passenger services proposed for withdrawal.

Right: The harmless-looking booklet with the explosive content.

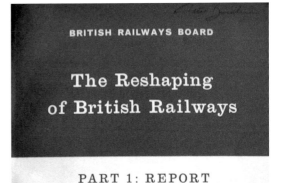

BRITISH RAILWAYS BOARD

The Reshaping of British Railways

PART 1: REPORT

LONDON

British Rail runs out of steam

Last steam train makes historic special farewell journey Sunday August 11th

Liverpool/Manchester to Carlisle & back

This will be the very last train to operate on standard gauge track headed by a B.R. steam locomotive. 314 nostalgic miles, 10½ happy hours, with luncheon, high tea, other refreshments, souvenir ticket and souvenir scroll. 15 guineas.
Liverpool Lime Street Dep 09.10 – Arr 19.50
Manchester Victoria Dep 11.06 – Arr 18.48
For Tickets. Write quickly to Passenger Marketing Manager, British Rail, London Midland Region, Euston House, London NW1. Mark your envelope Personal and enclose £15.15 per ticket required. Money immediately refunded if the 470 seats have already been sold.

≥≤ | British Rail

Above: Blackpool Central station was indeed central to its town. Many were critical of its closure and conversion into a car park in 1964 and saw it as evidence of the road interest ruthlessly shouldering the railways aside. (Authors' collection)

Left: Poster advertising the '15 Guinea Special'. This ran to mark the end of standard gauge steam traction on BR. BR was widely criticised for exploiting the occasion and pricing so many people out of the market. The trip of 314 miles left from and returned to Liverpool Lime Street via Carlisle and was steam-hauled throughout. (Authors' collection)

Right: Cartoon suggesting that Marples generously bribed Beeching to do a job which was bound to make him unpopular. (Authors' collection)

Below: Poster advertising the completion of the Manchester to Sheffield and Wath overhead electrification scheme in the autumn of 1954. Ironically much of the intense traffic flow on this route declined drastically within a few years because of the fall-off in the use of coal. The scheme was a ground-breaker and was highly impressive but many of the operating methods and equipment remained firmly in the steam age. (Authors' collection)

Is there any secret understanding between Mr. Marples and Dr. Beeching about the railway policy Dr Beeching is to pursue?
—Mr. George Strauss (Lab. Vauxhall)

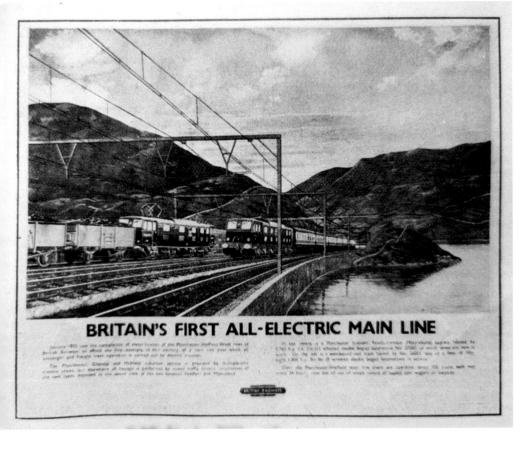

BRITAIN'S FIRST ALL-ELECTRIC MAIN LINE

Leyland was one of Britain's most successful automotive companies and here in 1950 it advertises its associations with a prestigious company of cider-makers. It has to be admitted that the use of such vehicles provided Bulmer's with a more flexible means of transport than the railways could provide at that time. (Authors' collection)

Official poster showing early moves in the use of rail-carried containers. The Freightliner concept was to prove a great success for which Beeching must take some credit. (Authors' collection)

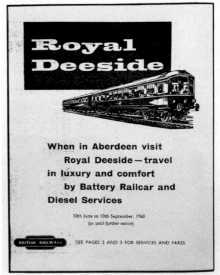

Above left: The early symbol applied by the newly-formed BR to locomotives and tenders, for example. Heraldically dubious, it was widely derided as 'The Cycling Lion'. (Authors' collection)

Above right: BR advert for the experimental battery railcar which was tried out on the Aberdeen to Ballater Deeside Line in 1958. It proved quiet and reliable but had not been replicated by the time it went out of service in 1962. It was evidence that BR was prepared to consider interesting new initiatives. (Authors' collection)

Deltic is seen approaching Preston with a test train from the north. Even many diehard steam enthusiasts had to admit that *Deltic* had some charisma. It presented a brash image which was just what was needed when so much of what BR did looked tired and out of date. It acted as the prototype for the very successful fleet of 'Deltics' that took over front-line duties on the East Coast Main Line. (Authors' collection)

Above left: Dr Richard Beeching in 1962. If he was put out by the unfavourable attention he attracted, he did not show it in public. (Authors' collection)

Above right: Ernest Marples when Minister of Transport. It is impossible to escape the sense that Marples never achieved the level of political eminence to which he aspired. (Authors' collection)

"First ticket I've sold since the train stopped halting here."

Closures, especially of obscure and little-used rural branch lines, had been going on well before the Beeching era. Such lines provided a rich field of inspiration for gently mocking cartoonists. (Authors' collection)

Cartoon of 1939 from *Motor Transport* suggesting that the railways were a massive lion equipped with sharp claws greedily eying up and about to consume a poor little defenceless road transport lamb. Even at this time the road interest was consolidating with friends in high places and after the Second World war came to constitute one of the most powerful lobbies in Britain. (Authors' collection)

Above left: Ernest Marples familiarising himself with the Post Office postcode training machine, 1957. Marples had an eye for every publicity opportunity. (Courtesy of Churchill College Archive, Cambridge)

Above right: Ernest Marples when engaged to his second wife, Ruth, 1956. (Courtesy of Churchill College Archive, Cambridge)

Marples cycling at the New Brighton Milk Race in 1966. New Brighton was in Marples' constituency and so this was good publicity but also emphasised the priority he gave to his own physical fitness. (Courtesy of Churchill College Archive, Cambridge)

Above left: Ernest Marples in Switzerland, 1934. Marples was a keen walker and climber, loving the outdoor life and finding it a way of working off some of his great reserves of energy. (Courtesy of Churchill College Archive)

Above right: Marples as a junior army officer in the Second World War. (Courtesy of Churchill College Archive, Cambridge)

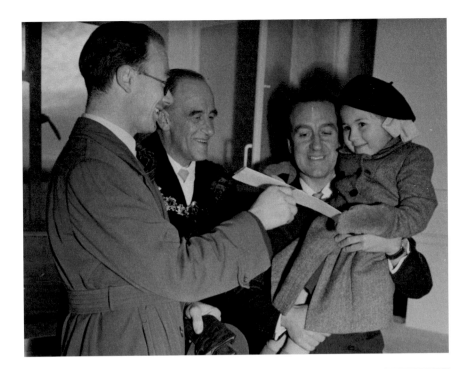

Above: Ernest Marples with dignitaries and fortunate family when they moved into their new house in Wallasey, 1953. (Courtesy of Churchill College Archive, Cambridge)

Right: Ernest Marples with his first wife, Edna, in Austria, 1934. (Courtesy of Churchill College, Cambridge)

Marples with royalty at the launching of the STD system in 1958. (Courtesy of Churchill College, Cambridge)

A sophisticated tramcar operating on Leeds City's system. Such vehicles provided the railways with strong competition in terms of fares and convenience on many urban routes. This one advertises a long-extinct local brew. (Authors' collection)

'Emett' was a popular, prolific and quirky cartoonist in post-Second World War Britain. Here is his take on the nationalisation of the railways. (Authors' collection)

An example of the ancient steam locomotives still chugging around Britain's railways in the 1950s. This is a 0-6-0 of the former Lancashire & Yorkshire Railway from a class introduced in 1887. The simplicity, reliability and ease of maintenance of such steam locomotives contrasted with the complexity and temperamental nature of their diesel replacements. (Authors' collection)

A standard 2-6-4T No. 80094 on a Bangor to Afon Wen or Pwllheli local train at Port Dinorwic in the 1950s. The locomotive is nearly new and the carriages are reasonably modern but the method of operating the line and its infrastructure remained strictly Victorian. By this time buses and then cars had creamed off most of the regular traffic. Unfortunately such services had a very limited future. The line closed in 1960. (Authors' collection)

A typical private owner wagon. The newly formed BR had to absorb huge numbers of such archaic vehicles and compensate their former owners. Eliminating these unbraked abominations was essential if the railways were to have any future in the haulage of non-passenger traffic. (Authors' collection)

The famous semaphore signal gantry on the southern approaches to Rugby Midland. This may be a posed official photograph but it provides some evidence of the labour-intensive nature of many railway operations into the 1950s which had to be addressed if the railways were to be modernised and to survive. (Authors' collection)

A rural bus in the 1950s. Simple and cheap to operate although not necessarily very comfortable, such vehicles could undercut railway fares and often provide a more flexible and convenient service. (Authors' collection)

Satirical cartoonists have found a rich source of material in railways. Especially in the major urban areas the existence of morning and evening peak travel periods caused many expensive operating problems. Campaigns were launched to encourage those who were not commuters to travel outside the rush hour and here fun is made of the possible results. (Authors' collection)

"Aye, Sir; there's always this rush to get home before the rush hour."

Above left: Sir Brian Robertson who chaired the BTC with considerable dignity through many difficult years but who was seen by Marples and Beeching as having no place in the modernised and slimmed-down railway system of the 1960s. (Authors' collection)

Above right: Britain's railways until the 1950s and 1960s generated a great deal of business from serving the country's seaside resorts. They invested heavily in advertising and promotion and produced much fine commercial art. Here it is the attractions of Whitley Bay which are being advertised and with flagrant political incorrectness it is the young woman who is the eye-catcher here. (Authors' collection) be made by de-staffing, this being a nod in the direction of pay trains. Improvements in efficiency and productivity were envisaged. It was believed that a modernised railway would gain and retain enough new traffic to pay for itself. This did not happen. The finances of the railways worsened. The Plan laid insufficient emphasis on attempting to identify and develop the kinds of traffic for which the railways were best suited.

Eye-catching elements in the Plan included the overhead electrification of the East Coast Main Line to Leeds and possibly York, of the West Coast Main Line to Birmingham, Manchester and Liverpool, the lines to Clacton and Ipswich and shorter lines from London Liverpool Street into the north-eastern suburbs. Other short-haul largely urban lines were London Fenchurch Street to Southend and Shoeburyness and much of the network around Glasgow north of the Clyde. The intention was also to convert most Southern Region non-electrified lines east of Reading and Portsmouth to the third rail system.

R.A. Butler, the Chancellor of the Exchequer, described the Modernisation Plan as 'a courageous and imaginative conception'. The press was largely enthusiastic. The *Manchester Guardian* cooed with pleasure: 'The plan for the railways is what we have all been waiting for … At last the Commission seems to have thrown off its defeatism and begun to think in a large way of how it can revivify a transport system that had slipped much behind that of other countries … The prospect is exciting.' Even *The Economist,* joining in the plaudits, declared that it was a praiseworthy attempt to rectify the long-term lack of investment in the industry. Fiennes, on the other hand, was scathing about the Plan: '… the Modernisation Plan produced in 1953–55 with the support of the Government to the extent of £1,500 million was little more than a change from steam traction plus a host of mouldering schemes which the BTC and the Regions had found after a hurried search in their pigeon holes. We made the basic error of buying our tools before doing our homework on defining the job'.

Basically, elements of modernisation were grafted on to a largely ageing, creaking infrastructure. An example of hidebound thinking among the policymakers was the electrification of the Manchester to Sheffield and Wath route. This scheme, which had been a very long time in the gestation, had been undertaken before the Modernisation Plan with fanfares declaring it to be 'Britain's first all-electric main line'. While it did indeed employ electric traction, its methods of working and much of its equipment were still largely rooted in practices dating back many decades.

Insufficient consideration was given to developing means to deal with the growing impact of road transport and the unpalatable fact that the door-to-door service provided by road haulage was simply more convenient, quicker and cheaper for many kinds of traffic. As Stewart Joy (1973) wrote in *The Train that Ran Away*, they were 'trying to solve yesterday's problems with tomorrow's money'. He argued that the whole exercise was based on the false premises that technical modernisation would regain lost traffic whereas what was really needed was the elimination of unprofitable business and the implementation of methods of increasing productivity. The stated aim of making the railways as a whole profitable again was simply unrealistic but a slimmed down modernised railway industry could concentrate on the types of business in which railways enjoyed intrinsic advantages over the roads.

The supportive initial response to the Plan was short-lived. *The Economist* became highly critical and opined that the Plan was likely to fail because of what it described as 'unimaginative' railway management, an unenthusiastic response from railway workers for demands for higher productivity, and competition from the roads. Supporters of roads just saw the Modernisation Plan as an example of throwing good money after bad. Some of them would probably have been happy to see the entire railway system closed but to a man they believed that the money put aside for the railways would have been better spent on improvement and enlargement of the country's road system.

The Plan was the product of the so-called 'post-war boom', a period of generalised economic growth. When compared with the difficult conditions in many parts of the country in the inter-war years, the sacrifices of wartime and the austerity of the immediate post-war years, an air of optimism was abroad and this was reflected in the Plan itself. The Plan made what proved to be over-enthusiastic assumptions of continued economic growth and consequent increases in traffic and receipts which were not borne out by events.

A White Paper of 1956 stated confidently that modernisation would make a major contribution to eliminating BR's financial deficit by 1962. The assumption incorporated in the Plan that, by modernising motive power parts of the business which were making consistent and growing losses could have their economic performance turned round, was muddled thinking. Simply putting a shiny new diesel locomotive at the head of an almost empty branch line passenger train was never going to transform a loss-making service into one generating healthy profits. Certainly a DMU, which was cheaper to run than a locomotive, might attract more passengers to a particular route but all too often steam power had to be retained to handle local freight traffic which was likely itself to be loss-making. On some lines, short steam-hauled parcels trains had to be run in order to move consignments too large for the guard's van of a multiple unit, thereby negating some of the multiple-unit's initial advantage. Also, even where the motive power was all diesel, little attempt was made to rationalise the *modus operandi* which frequently was based on Victorian railway practice and made little use of the diesel's far greater availability and reduced requirement for servicing. Sometimes steam-age timetables remained virtually unchanged which might involve the expensive units standing out of use and earning no money for substantial parts of the day.

Private motoring was seizing much of the passenger traffic and road haulage was gaining an increasing share of the conveyance of general merchandise. The car was in the process of becoming the transport of choice for an ever growing part of the population. Particularly in small towns and rural areas someone who had been enjoying the flexible travel options offered by the private car was not going to leave the vehicle in the garage simply because his local line was now diesel operated and the trains were cleaner and perhaps more frequent. The losses being made by many railway operations had become endemic and throwing new technology at them was not going to solve the problem. Even in a growing economy, the continuance of which seems to have been taken as read, it was naïve to suppose that modernising the railways ensured that they enjoyed a rising share of the increased demand for transport that would follow. For reasons generated largely in the nineteenth century, Britain was over-provided with railways and some parts of the system had always lost money or, at best, been marginal. One problem was that, almost incredibly, senior BR management had no clear idea which services were profitable and which made losses. Large parts of BR's activities, including many branch lines, longer-distance stopping services and wagonload goods were economic basket cases and it was mistaken to think that they could ever have a useful future.

The government defended the Plan partly because it believed that investment in the railways would be a generator of further economic growth, or at least that is what was said in public. With a new roads programme estimated at £410 million going ahead including the first motorway project, it might have appeared curmudgeonly to hold back on money for the railways given the general aura of economic optimism at that time.

Supporters of the railways thought that the positive measures outlined in the Modernisation Plan were wasted because the reappraisals to which it was subjected were imposed by governments that were predominantly pro-road. According to this argument, these measures destabilised an industry which otherwise was undergoing a much-needed reinvigoration. Governments were demanding profitability while refusing sufficient resources for the railways to achieve that goal, if it was actually attainable.

Even a better thought-out plan supported by adequate financial resources would have taken years to demonstrate any benefits. The scepticism with which the Plan was regarded in government circles is indicated by its being reappraised by the BTC in 1956 and 1959. With railways firmly on the political agenda, what had to be decided was whether governments could or should underwrite unprofitable operations on the basis that they met social need or whether BR should be allowed to operate without commercial restraint. A reluctance to commit major resources to thorough modernisation was shown by the shilly-shallying over electrification of the London to Manchester and Liverpool routes and the long-term postponement of the electrification of the East Coast Main Line.

As mentioned, the year in which the Modernisation Plan was announced was also the year of a major national railway strike. The footplate workers organised in the union the Associated Society of Locomotive Engineers and Firemen (ASLEF) struck in pursuit of a wage claim and the strike lasted from 28 May to 14 June. Other railway workers remained on duty and although some trains still ran, the strike forced many customers both in the goods and passenger spheres to make alternative arrangements and many of them never returned to the railway. This encouraged many politicians to argue that the strike 'proved' that the railways were no longer such a vital part of the country's transport system and that government transport policy should consolidate around road rather than rail.

Perhaps the Modernisation Plan deserved two cheers. It recognised that drastic action was needed to address the increasingly serious situation facing the nation's railways and, in one sense, it prepared the path, if only through its own shortcomings, for the Beeching Report of the next decade. The railways had always been undergoing change but they had arrived in the 1950s at perhaps the most critical stage in their history and their future was at stake. Flashes of modernity beamed out from what remained largely a rather tatty and outdated structure contrasting sharply with, for example, the increasing technical sophistication and stylishness of many cars. The year of the publication of the Modernisation Plan also saw the appearance of *Deltic*, the hugely impressive diesel locomotive built by English Electric (the whole class took its 'nickname' from this first locomotive). This went on to perform so impressively that its success led to orders for twenty-two further machines which revolutionised express passenger services on the East Coast Main Line. Above all, *Deltic* looked modern, confident and even brash. Dashing modernity had been combined with high quality performance, both almost entirely missing and yet so much needed on Britain's railways at this time.

There may be many reservations about the Modernisation Plan but it heralded an era of 'out with the old and in with the new' well before the Beeching Report hit the headlines in 1963. Particularly successful was extensive new electrification on the Southern Region, a new electric network on Clydeside and renewals of older electrified systems around provincial conurbations. The 'sparks effect' and the introduction of DMUs on more services frequently led to rising passenger usage. The increased use of long-welded rail and colour light signalling, plus the installation of the Automatic Warning System (AWS) improved speeds and enhanced safety on selected routes. The opening of the Railway Technical Centre at Derby was an earnest of determination to become involved in the technical research and development that was essential for the delivery of a modern railway system – if only the politicians would allow it. The latter did not, financial losses continuing, hence the reappraisals, road usage went on growing and the crisis meant that government was soon to require more radical measures for the railways. It is indicative of its priorities that the Modernisation Plan originally promised £1,240 million over fifteen years whereas in 1955 the government set aside £600 million to be spent on the roads in that year alone.

The 1950s through to the early 1960s was a period of electoral success for the Conservatives. They astutely presented themselves as the party which in government was the most able to manage the rising prosperity which so many people were enjoying and indeed coming to expect, delivering full employment and keeping the demands of the trade unions, powerful because of full employment, under control. The BTC was told to provide wage increases sufficient at least to mollify the unions' demands. This was playing games because the pay increases added to the wages and impacted negatively on the financial problems of the railways. However the politicians argued that swift settlement of the pay claims might produce a more supportive attitude from the unions for measures to increase productivity in the industry. A virtuous circle would be created because modernisation would increase productivity while generating the income that would allow for further wage increases. This all sounds very well but the governments of this period constantly intervened in the nationalised industries in pursuit of restraint on wage and price rises. In March 1956 the BTC was told to freeze many proposed fare increases and reduce a number of proposed freight charge rises. Small wonder that railway workers felt that they were the dupes in games being played by their political masters. They had every reason to feel aggrieved.

There seems to have been a degree of ambivalence among senior railway managers regarding closures. Some seemed locked into a catatonic state of refusal to recognise the economic and social changes taking place which were so greatly changing the nature of the demand for rail usage. Others seemed determined to get rid of the dead wood and were looking around for any excuse to do so. This seems particularly to have applied to the Scottish Region which from the mid-1950s began talking about the 'asset recovery' which would result from line closures. This referred particularly to the track and building materials which could be recovered for reuse or be sold for scrap. Closures were being advanced as a potential money-spinner and it was almost suggested that it would be a crime not to carry through certain closures. By example, such high figures were produced for the asset recovery that would supposedly result from the closure of the loss-making Hawthornden to Peebles and Galashiels line that it was made to appear as if there was no sensible alternative to closure. A figure of £3,400 per mile was mentioned which seemed questionable even at the time. It may have been an example of 'spin' before the age of spin because although the closure did indeed take place, substantial amounts of the infrastructure such as iron bridges were left intact which is unlikely to have happened if the redundant assets were actually as valuable as was claimed. Some of them are still in place.

Chapter 11

BTC Modernisation Fails

Difficult times

The Suez crisis of 1956 with its consequent oil and petrol shortage provided a fleeting opportunity for BR to regain traffic which had been lost to the roads. If BR could demonstrate that rail transport was efficient and economical, it might have been possible not only to retain this traffic when the crisis was over but also to win new customers. However, the result of long-term under-investment meant that BR could not respond quickly enough to meet the challenge. Once the crisis was over, regained passenger and freight business quickly returned to the roads.

The financial losses continued to grow after the announcement of the Modernisation Plan. A loss of £16.5 million in 1956 had become just over £48 million in 1958. A select committee convened in 1960 concluded that a major contribution to the losses lay with branch line and lightly used longer distance stopping trains. It was evidence of the opaque nature of railway accounting practices that the committee admitted that it could not identify the exact breakdown of 1959's loss of £42 million.

The railways were still burdened with high capital debt resulting from compensation paid to the previous private owners. Rising labour costs could not be avoided while staff shortages in many areas increased the reputation of the railways for unreliability. Revenue was jeopardised because of organic economic change, particularly the decline of the heavy industries which were traditionally the source of vast amounts of traffic, increasing competition from road haulage, the unprecedented growth of private motoring and changing social habits. BR seemed largely to lack a clear sense of purpose and direction at senior level and to be handicapped by ineffective management information systems.

During his years as chairman of the British Transport Commission from 1953, Sir Brian Robertson presided over a relative bonanza of funding for modernising and re-equipping the railways. The money was not always spent wisely and the predictions of trends in traffic and labour costs on which the expenditure was premised were frequently erroneous. Despite considerable money having been made available for modernisation, official attitudes towards the railways verged on the hostile. Harold Watkinson, then Minister of Transport, told Parliament on 23 July 1958 that: 'the railways are no longer a monopolistic organisation with an obligation to provide all sections of the community with a railway service'. With few avowed friends in the political parties, many critics in the Treasury, the Ministry of Transport, the media and the baleful existence of a powerful pro-road lobby, these were difficult times for the railways. The influence wielded by supporters of the railways was miniscule compared with that available to their opponents.

When the railways were nationalised, the political influence they exerted declined significantly. Many of the eminent figures in the Big Four had been men of great influence with the ear of senior politicians and civil servants. Now the leading figures in the BTC had much less power to shape events in favour of the railways let alone to stand up to the influence of the road lobby, which enjoyed close links, often personal and ideological, with the Ministry. It was not uncommon for retired senior officials in the Ministry to join one or other of the lobbying organisations. They brought much insider information with them.

Harold Macmillan, as a former director of the GWR, was generally thought to have a sentimental regard for railways but this was not apparent when union representatives met him on 22 April 1958 and he told them rather brusquely to increase their productivity before they could consider themselves eligible for wage rises. The issue of wages and salaries was particularly contentious as financial losses mounted and the remuneration of railway workers fell behind other industries and occupations. In some areas it was hard to recruit and equally hard then retain staff. Poor pay was a factor in low morale especially when it was obvious that the railway system was contracting. A national strike over wages was narrowly averted in 1958. A consequence of these concerns was the establishment of the Guillebaud Committee inquiry into pay in 1960. This was intended to establish job comparability with other industries, by no means an easy task. After the Committee's deliberations, many wage-earning grades won an 8 per cent increase and salaried staff one of 10 per cent. The BTC could not deny that railway workers deserved better wages but the settlement cost £33 million in 1960. With wage bills rising, more retrenchment of the system and cuts in manpower were seen as vital for reducing BR's financial losses.

In 1960 Macmillan told Parliament that the railway industry needed to be remodelled to meet the needs of a changing society. No other railway system in Europe was losing so much non-passenger business at this time. This needs to be seen in the context of wider economic and industrial changes some of which were unique to Britain and it cannot solely be blamed on factors intrinsic to the British way of operating its railways and the games played by the politicians who had become the railways' masters.

The travails of the diesels

Under the Modernisation Plan (*Modernisation and Re-equipment of British Railways*), around 170 main line diesel locomotives were ordered. Questions have been raised about whether the BTC had done its preliminary homework and was fully conversant with the technology of these complex machines let alone the implications of relying on an imported fuel and the minutiae of negotiating contracts for these locomotives with a large range of manufacturers. Reasoning that the products of several locomotive builders needed to be tried, BR ordered no fewer than fourteen different 'pilot' designs across three power groups. There were seven makes of power plant and eight types of transmission. The manufacturers, seven in number, were complicit in this scheme, wanting orders and arguing that a firm base in domestic sales was essential to provide the experience and proven hardware for robust overseas sales. Spreading orders for equipment across a range of manufacturers was a political move aimed at winning votes in constituencies benefiting from the resulting orders. It would have made more sense to develop a small number of classes of reliable locomotives, perhaps one class for each power group. A number of prototypes for each group could have been built and subjected to rigorous trials. The type that emerged as being by far the best in each power group could have then been chosen for being built in large numbers.

Huge waste of public money could have been avoided. As noted earlier, the government, despite being America's poodle in many ways, was opposed to buying from the USA despite its unquestionable world lead in the field of diesels. It wanted to encourage the British locomotive building industry, once dominating the world with the export of steam locomotives, to adapt effectively to building and selling this new form of traction globally. Even with this consideration, some of the power plants for the locomotives came from Europe. There were a few good designs but many of the others were absolutely wretched. The decisions of their political masters caused anger and frustration among the professional railway workers who had to try to make hopeless machines function effectively. The same dismal story could be applied to at least some of the varied fleet of shunting locomotives.

Railway managers would have preferred the new diesels to be built in-house by their own workshops and they probably saw the preference for private manufacturers as evidence that the politicians were intent on running down the capacity of BR's engineering workshops. Whether these workshops could have produced diesel locomotives at the rate at which BR required them to replace steam is questionable, but at least they might have been able to produce a smaller range of standard classes of greater merit. Although in-house locomotives would almost certainly have been cheaper and probably better in service, the government was strongly influenced by the Locomotive Manufacturers' Association. For example, sizeable orders of 'pilot' and production locomotives went to the North British Locomotive Company of Glasgow, which had been dominant in what until recently had been a British locomotive building industry exporting across the world. How were the mighty fallen! The company's impressive record with steam locomotives counted for little when it proved largely incapable of building satisfactory diesels. Those they built for BR were expensive, often delivered late and were notorious for their mechanical unreliability. An element in North British gaining its substantial orders was government concern to provide jobs in Glasgow's East End, which was an area of high unemployment. It was an expensive mistake. North British was not long for this world and typified a narrative of decline and failure that became all too common in British manufacturing industry.

Being charitable, perhaps six of the pilot scheme main line diesel classes proved satisfactory in service. For the 'Type A' locomotives in the lowest power group, much of the kind of traffic for which they were largely designed was ebbing away even before they entered service. Only one of these 'Type A' locomotive classes, the English Electric 1,000hp Bo-Bo, proved to be a very sound investment. Even then they made a fool of their power category by generally being used in pairs.

Little effort seems to have been made to maintain price control when batches of locomotives were being delivered. Initial estimates of the price to be paid were frequently exceeded. On occasions, where large numbers of a class were ordered, the price per locomotive doubled while they were in the process of delivery.

The six best of the designs were built in larger numbers, sometimes with various modifications, and went on to play a useful role. Of the others, the less said the better. Steam enthusiasts were treated to the sight of steam locomotives substituting for failed diesels or a steam locomotive hauling a failed diesel and perhaps its train as well. Locomotives under the Modernisation Plan were ordered from manufacturers with little or no experience of building diesels. It was a dog's breakfast. Lines of unserviceable and almost brand new diesel locomotives were stored at various locations, preferably out of public view. Any notion of standardisation and its benefits went by the board. BR, partly because of political considerations beyond its control, was burdened with classes of locomotives of dubious reliability, frequently unable to work in tandem with other types and few, if any, parts that were interchangeable. It was an engineering and operating nightmare.

The Western Region was even allowed to go its own way and order large numbers of locomotives with hydraulic as opposed to electric transmission. They frequently proved troublesome in service and were eventually replaced by diesel electrics well before their predicted life expectancy. It has to be said that across BR, the management of the various regions preferred to view developments through the prism of their own region rather than the region being considered as a component of a national system with a common purpose.

It added insult to injury in railway workers' minds that incompetent private manufacturers were being favoured with orders at the very time that closures and redundancies were being enacted in BR's own workshops, most of which had a proud history of steam locomotive manufacture. These workshops could have built the bodywork and frames even if the power units were manufactured elsewhere.

The BTC seemed obsessed with diesels, rushing large numbers of always expensive and complicated if not very competent locomotives into service to rid itself as quickly as possible of steam traction. This was happening despite new steam locomotives still being built until 1960 and having a life expectancy of decades. The writing was also on the wall for steam in Britain's European neighbours but they managed to maintain and operate the declining numbers of steam locomotives far more effectively. Great damage was done to BR's public image by the visible way in which the steam fleet was run down. Clanking, leaking and absolutely filthy steam locomotives created a very visible and unfavourable impression of the railway industry. It was a hugely demoralising experience for those still working with steam because they were insulted by the conditions under which they were expected to operate. Certainly there were many serious factors militating against any prolonged continuing use of steam but the BTC, in its determination to replace steam traction swiftly, badly mishandled this part of its function.

Diesel traction offered the economies associated with far greater availability but without changes to many existing working practices, such as timetables designed for steam operation, the advances offered by diesels were being partly nullified. The traction units of the future were unquestionably diesel and electric but the story of how steam traction was replaced on BR reflects little credit on those who made the decisions at this time.

The BTC was looking for a light and cheap-to-operate self-powered vehicle and came up with the idea of four-wheeled railbuses. Orders were placed for twenty-two such vehicles. The orders for such a small number of vehicles were spread across five manufacturers. The vehicles were intended for lightly-used branch lines and it was hoped that economies derived from their use might turn loss-making branches into marginally profitable ones. The idea went off at half-cock. Although service frequency was often enhanced on the lines involved and additional usage generated, partly because new basic wayside stopping places were opened on some lines such as that from Kemble to Tetbury, staffing and signalling were reduced to the absolute minimum and track maintenance costs were cut because of the lightness of the vehicles. The railbuses often rode badly, were mechanically unreliable and unable to carry bulky luggage, bicycles and prams. Occasionally they were victims of their own success and with their limited seating and standing capacity (between forty-four and fifty-six seated passengers, depending on type) there were occasions when would-be passengers were left behind. They were inflexible, having no drawgear and unable to be used in multiple. Even with such reservations a railway service with these vehicles was better than no service at all. However it could be argued that the entire concept was flawed. Even if these railbuses ran every journey with passengers packed like sardines, the fares generated would not turn loss-making services into profitable ones because of the unavoidable costs of providing the necessary infrastructure even of a basic sort for the lines on which they operated.

Away from tales of woe, the standard 350hp diesel electric shunting locomotives introduced in 1953 had been entering service in large numbers and proving to be an efficient and economical replacement for their steam equivalents. Efficient they were but with hindsight it can be seen that the work for which they were designed was already diminishing. It is doubtful whether a fleet of well over 1,000 of such machines was ever needed. Where smaller shunting locomotives were concerned, there was little attempt at standardisation. At least fifteen types were produced, some in very small numbers. Several types were notoriously unreliable and did very little work, being scrapped after just a few years.

The early years of modernisation with diesel and electric traction were highly chequered as the authorities wrestled with the challenges posed by these expensive and highly complex machines. Steam locomotives were relatively simple and rugged and could cope with considerable neglect. Staff were well versed in keeping them going on the 'if it won't work hit it with a hammer' basis. Diesels and electrics, however, were far more delicate and it was not unknown for them to fail when out in service and become totally immobilised. Frequently diesels had to share servicing accommodation with steam locomotives producing emanations which could result in very harmful effects to the delicate working parts of the diesels. The innumerable failures in service of the new traction were public relations disasters, giving the media just the kind of ammunition they could gorge on for their long-running saga ridiculing the nationalised railways.

Official practice was to spend as little money as possible on the care and maintenance of the declining fleet of steam locomotives. Some senior locomotive engineers such as Robert Riddles were not convinced of the worth particularly of main line diesel traction and argued that steam locomotives should continue to be produced and be used as an interim measure until such time as large-scale electrification could be carried out. Steam locomotives were cheaper to build and maintain and used indigenous fuel. As Riddles himself said, '… a pound spent [on steam power] will buy more tractive effort than is the case for other forms of traction'. Officialdom, however, would not be moved from looking askance at steam traction. Among many reasons for this aversion was the estimate that steam locomotives had produced 15 per cent of the 'pea-souper' smogs that had bedevilled London in particular in December 1952. The die was cast for BR steam power.

It was extremely demoralising for the enginemen working with increasingly decrepit locomotives, watching traffic ebb away and knowing that, for many of them, redundancy was looming. Sometimes steam locomotives went off for expensive overhauls, returned and were put straight into storage and never turned a wheel in revenue-earning service again, withdrawn at the whim of BR's accountants eager to meet targets for the reduction of the steam locomotive stock. An example of this almost criminal waste occurred with the Class 'O1' freight locomotives. A batch was thoroughly overhauled. No sooner were these overhauls completed than regional boundary changes occurred and the locomotives found themselves transferred on paper to the London Midland from the Eastern Region. They were withdrawn with immediate effect. Similar examples of scandalous waste of public resources could be given. With all the issues involved, steam's days were clearly numbered but the rundown of steam was badly managed and there was enormous waste. No fewer than 744 steam locomotives were delivered in the period 1954–1960, each of which had an estimated useful economic life of forty years. In 1968 the last standard gauge BR steam locomotives were withdrawn from service.

Although they experienced some teething problems, most types of the growing fleet of DMUs did the job required of them. Some mechanically reliable units when in motion had fittings that rattled irritatingly and there were passenger complaints about overheating in hot weather and insufficient heat in winter. For all that, they were cheaper to operate and maintain than steam trains, cleaner and often speedier, and they projected an attractive modern image. Particularly popular was the opportunity for passengers to sit behind the driver and watch the scene ahead unfolding. Some large increases in passenger traffic resulted from their introduction. For example, traffic on the lines in the West Riding scheme increased by over five times in the first four years of their use. The Birmingham to Sutton Coldfield and Lichfield service enjoyed a 210 per cent increase in usage in the first years of its conversion to diesel traction. Their introduction was no panacea, however. Sizeable increases in passenger numbers did not necessarily guarantee the long-term survival of many of the lines on which they ran as changing social habits and increased car usage took passengers away from the railways. The service between Banbury and Buckingham, for example, saw no less than a 300 per cent increase in passenger usage but it still made a loss and had not long to live. It was unhelpful that on some lines where multiple units replaced steam, the timetables did not change to reflect the greater speed, potential productivity and flexibility of the units. Expensive new units might stand idle for periods reflecting the time previously needed for servicing their steam predecessors. As with the railbuses and diesel locomotives, many builders were involved. Often units from one manufacturer could not be worked in multiple with those from a different maker, an inflexibility which eroded some of the advantages that these units offered.

A key part of the Modernisation Plan was the allocation of £105 million for what would now be called the 'infrastructure'. With a view to raising line speeds as well as replacing old equipment, money was set aside for track renewals. The use of multi-aspect electric signalling was extended and many manual signal boxes were replaced by a greatly reduced number of power-operated installations. Increasing amounts of continuously welded rails were laid down, cheaper to maintain and providing a quieter ride. Experiments with automated level crossings were sanctioned and laudable reductions in track and signalling costs went ahead, on the Central Wales Line, for example.

In 1959 the BTC's growing financial woes led to a reappraisal of the Modernisation Plan of 1955. During the parliamentary debates on the Reappraisal, the anomaly was starkly highlighted that the railways were required to compete in the marketplace like normal business concerns but at the same time to offer services which inevitably ran at a loss. The two approaches were clearly contradictory. Loss-making services might provide important social benefits but these were not shown as such in the railway's accounts and not generally perceived by the public who were encouraged to see railways in a negative light as a drain on taxpayers' money. The reappraisal argued that modernisation had, so far, been successful but needed to be speeded up as did a judicious rationalisation of time-expired or hopelessly loss-making facilities. Some progress was being made. The working deficit of BR was down from £48 million in 1958 to £42 million in 1959. Between 1958 and 1959 1,666 steam locomotives had been withdrawn, passenger carriage numbers decreased by 1,451 and freight wagons by 59,844. The process of rationalisation was in place before the more radical changes associated with the Beeching Plan.

Very upbeat predictions were made about likely working surpluses by 1963 but they proved to be based on mistaken estimates of how much traffic could be won back to the modernised railway. They also failed to take account of changing economic activity which reduced demand from the heavy industries from which the railways traditionally derived so much revenue. Rationalisation was planned to lead to the closure of several railway workshops, selective closures of individual passenger services and goods depots and complete closure of about 1,800 miles of the network. While the London to Manchester and Liverpool electrification and some suburban electrification schemes were to proceed, the financial losses continued to mount, however. Something had to be done but the auguries did not favour the railways.

A blunter axe

State ownership always sat uncomfortably as a small component in a so-called free enterprise economy. In the dominant political culture of the 1950s it was cheap and easy to characterise BR as outdated, inefficient, bureaucratic and a drain on taxpayers' money. This did not answer the hypothetical question of how much of the railway system would have remained in existence in the mid-1950s had it continued in private hands. The answer is probably not very much without massive subventions from the public purse. Those who stood up for the railways were mostly abused as wallowing in nostalgia or, in later terminology, as 'anoraks'. Operating as they did in hostile or, at best, unfavourable conditions, it is not unfair to say that the railways were the sick man of the nationalised industries. The 1959 general election campaign propaganda of the Conservative and Labour Parties made no mention of railways where transport issues were being discussed. Both the Treasury and the Ministry of Transport saw cutting the railway system as a means of saving money and, theoretically at least, putting the money saved to better use elsewhere. The Conservatives, in office for some time, were looking somewhat jaded yet were shrewd enough to portray themselves as being associated with symbols of 'modernity' such as motorways and air travel. Railways did not accord with this image. There were far fewer votes to be had from trying to promote the railways.

In 1961 a White Paper was published which pointed to the need for greater Treasury control of the nationalised industries. Given their losses it was clear that the railways were under close Treasury scrutiny which was likely to lead to large-scale, systematic curtailment of services. The massive growth in road haulage and private car use made a seemingly watertight case for major investment in motorways and improved roads. If roads were doing a better, more efficient job than loss-making railways, then the railways needed to be culled. Given rising road usage, it made no sense at all for there to be, for example, two lines providing services between Plymouth and Tavistock in Devon. They were the product of outdated nineteenth-century beliefs in the virtues of unrestricted competition and the self-regulation of the market. They provided striking evidence in the late 1950s of the limited scope of that element of rationalisation that had been implemented. Hard-liners at the

Treasury dismissed BTC utterances about its social obligations as nothing more than a smokescreen to cover waste and inertia. In the contemporary political climate it is easy to see how politicians and senior civil servants were questioning whether investment in the railways represented value for money. A climate of opinion was being created which flowed on naturally to Ernest Marples and Richard Beeching and the plan to bring about a radical retrenchment and reshaping of the railways. Government preferences were clear when, in November 1962, purchase tax on private cars was reduced from 45 per cent to 25 per cent, resulting in a leap in car sales and usage. It is hard to believe that the resulting fall in passenger traffic on the railways had not been the intended outcome. The railways stood damned in a culture where they were regarded with hostility by most of the power-brokers.

Back in 1954, BR had the Lewes to East Grinstead line in its sights for closure. This line, evocatively nicknamed the 'Bluebell Line', ran through sparsely populated but extremely attractive countryside, had few passengers, less goods traffic and made thumping losses. The line closed in June 1955 although not without protest and, as a harbinger of future acrimony around closures, rancour was caused by the steadfast refusal of the BTC or the Transport Users' Consultative Committees (TUCCs) to provide information about exactly how the alleged financial losses were computed. Opponents of closure proposed a number of measures to cut costs but these were dismissed by BR.

The story of this particular saga has often been told and suffice it to say that opponents of closure found that the Act of Parliament authorising the line back in the nineteenth century contained a clause requiring four passenger trains to be run daily in both directions. This clause had never been annulled and BR was breaking the law by not running this minimum statutory service. BR restored a service of the four required daily trains until such time as Parliament repealed the Act and legal closure could take place. It ran these trains with such ill grace that the operation gained opprobrious nicknames such as the 'sulky service'. BR employed decrepit rolling stock and ran the trains at times inconvenient for most travellers, the timetable now being designed to be completed within a single shift. The original Act did not apply to the stations that were opened later and now BR refused to restore the service at what had previously been the best-used station giving as its reason that this station had not existed when the original Act was passed. The trains now missed connections at Lewes and East Grinstead and this gave ammunition to opponents of this and other future closure proposals who asserted that BR manipulated the timetables of services they wanted to close in order to make them less attractive to travellers. Most through bookings to other lines were suspended. The service was withdrawn for the second and final time in March 1958. The fallout from this saga led to a future Conservative government changing the law. Under the 1962 Transport Act objections raised with the TUCCs to closure proposals were only valid if they were based on issues of hardship. No questioning or criticism of BR financial data concerning losses would be considered as relevant by any TUCC.

In 1958 proposals had been published to close completely most of the Midland & Great Northern (M&GN) system. The incredulity with which much of the railway-loving fraternity met this announcement showed that many of them dwelt in a cosy little bubble in which endearing but loss-making and inefficient railways would go on forever, come what may. For others, more realistic, this was a wake-up call. Patterns of travel and social habits were changing. Substantial parts of the railway network were losing money. Retrenchment was inevitable. Modernisation was never going to turn the economic prospects of such lines around. On a few Saturdays of the year, the M&GN, much of which was single track, operated at total saturation point, carrying holiday trains to and from the East Anglian seaside resorts and industrial towns primarily in the East Midlands. However, for most of the year the passenger service was sparse and little used and there was declining seasonal agricultural business. It was estimated that the M&GN was losing about £640,000 annually, a situation which could not be allowed to continue. A factor put forward for closure was that a major bridge on the system needed to be rebuilt and traffic receipts were insufficient to justify the expense involved. There was a huge storm of protest and objection to the proposals when they were announced in September 1958. The TUCCs worked with extraordinary speed and the forthcoming closure was confirmed on 25 November. Actual closure took place on 28 February 1959.

The closure process was stepped up from 1958. Between 1958 and 1962 the TUCCs approved twice as many branch line closures and more than double the amount of route mileage closure as they had from 1950 to 1957. Most of these closures were so clearly justified in commercial terms that opposition was largely muted. Some closure proposals went through literally without any objections, an example being the passenger service between Wellingborough and Higham Ferrers in 1959. Also in that year most of the former Hull & Barnsley Railway system was closed. In 1960 express passenger services on the ex-Great Central line from London Marylebone to Leicester, Nottingham, Sheffield and Manchester were withdrawn. These two were significant closures but in both cases it could be argued that they provided duplicate facilities and other routes could handle their traffic.

These examples show that significant closures did not start with the Beeching Plan of 1963. Some 300 route miles had closed between 1954 and 1958, a process the Beeching Plan only extended and systematised. The number of passenger service closures approved by TUCCs rose from twenty-eight in 1958 to forty-nine in 1959. What was emerging, however, was an awareness that closing a branch line might mean a loss of contributory revenue to the other lines with which it connected. In the anti-railway culture of the 1950s and 1960s branch lines were not seen as feeders but largely regarded as suckers.

A notorious case in 1960/1961 was that of the Dunton Green to Westerham branch in Kent. This line, a serious loss-maker, was proposed for closure. There was considerable opposition and protestors submitted a list of measures that could help to reduce the line's operating and running costs. The BTC was embarrassed when protestors revealed that substantial amounts of track had recently been relaid. Such activity was not unknown, a cynical ploy using the expenditure involved as part of the argument for closure. The London Area TUCC, which had first supported the closure proposal, reversed its decision claiming that the BTC had failed to provide all the necessary financial information. The Minister of Transport at the time was Ernest Marples, who had taken the post in 1959, and he consented to the closure which took place in October 1961. When the M25 was later built over some of the line's formation, critics were quick to blame Marples and his vested interest in building motorways. The company with which he had been associated had not tendered for the contract but such insinuations were inevitably going to follow Marples in his work at the Ministry.

In pre-Beeching days large numbers of small rural wayside stations on main lines had been closed. These stations often had a very limited service and the stops frequently saw little usage but impeded the passage of faster passenger and other traffic which generated greater income. The East Coast Main Line, for example, lost many such stations in the 1950s and early 1960s. These closures often aroused little protest but when such stopping services were withdrawn, the trains rushing through no more served the local community than a passenger aircraft flying overhead. Such closures acted as a disincentive to rail travel for local people who now, instead of driving to the nearest railhead, might decide that it was simply easier and more practical to use the car for the whole journey. These closures may have saved some money but contributed to a growing perception that railways were on their way out and that private transport was a more flexible, convenient and often quicker and cheaper means of getting from A to B.

Even before the Beeching Plan was published, proposed railway closures were becoming a political hot potato. For example, in Parliament on 1 August 1958, Stephen Davies, MP for Merthyr Tydfil, alleged that, in attempting to justify the closure of the line between Merthyr and Abergavenny, BR had (again) deliberately inflated the figure for the line's losses by substantial expenditure on improvements to the permanent way and the stations. This supported the conspiracy theory that unexpected renewal and renovation of track and other infrastructure often meant that closure was in the offing. On occasions genuine management ineptitude saw such work taking place on lines that were already scheduled for closure.

The BTC and BR were frequently accused of deliberately running down services they wished to close. This was being done, critics alleged, by modifying the timetable to deter potential users. Long gaps between trains might render a service unattractive or even virtually useless, or retiming might mean that branch trains now missed useful connections with main line services. In 1962 the Central Transport Users' Consultative Committee complained that during the previous year there were several instances when train services being considered for withdrawal were omitted from public timetables before closure proposals had been heard and adjudicated on by the appropriate area TUCCs. In one case, the omission was made before the proposal had even been submitted to a TUCC. Many thought that the TUCCs themselves were insufficiently sympathetic to the people whose needs they were supposed to represent.

In the 1950s it clearly became helpful for advancement within the Ministry of Transport that its civil servants should be pro-road. When James Dunnett became permanent secretary to the Ministry in 1959 he quickly stated that he wanted to move towards a smaller and more cost-efficient railway and a much more extensive road building programme. He promoted the future notorious David Serpell to be deputy secretary. This man was no lover of the railways.

Chapter 12

Superseding The British Transport Commission, 1959–1961

Ernest Marples at the Ministry of Transport

The general election of 9 October 1959 was Macmillan's greatest personal triumph. He had steered his party from the rapids that might have capsized it after Suez: now he had his own majority, a landslide promising five years of confident Conservative government. In Wallasey, Marples took 35,587 votes to 20,501 for his opponent C. Woodburn, confirming the 1950s pattern of a Conservative share of 63 to 64 per cent when in straight contests with Labour. He had demonstrated his worth locally, helping to secure a large new and modern Cadbury-Schweppes factory located in Moreton. This man who had proved himself a highly effective Postmaster General was now an obvious promotion candidate. James Dunnett, later permanent secretary at the Transport Ministry recalled Macmillan's determination to have in the Cabinet 'at least one person who was clearly not an old Etonian and who had not been to Oxford or Cambridge'.

Behind his studied avuncular manner, Macmillan was a shrewd, worldly and even ruthless politician. He knew that drastic modernisation was needed if the growing prosperity being enjoyed by much of the UK's population was to be maintained. He demanded decisive action to reduce the loss-making of the railways. He recognised the growing obsession with private motoring and the seemingly unquenchable desire of the public to enjoy the freedom of being behind the wheel; each their own personal wheel. As well as urgent action on railways, something had to be done to control the problems caused by the enormous growth of road traffic. What was to be done and who was to do it? Harold Watkinson had been the incumbent minister in 1959 but did he have the drive and fortitude to deliver policies that would bring brickbats a-plenty? Equally, was Sir Brian Robertson, as the chairman of the BTC, the man to implement a programme of what would inevitably be very controversial rationalisation on the railways?

On 18 October Macmillan offered Marples the Transport portfolio, moving the incumbent Watkinson (another self-made man) elsewhere. After fourteen years as an MP, Marples was now in the Cabinet, attending for the first time on 20 October 1959. Macmillan admired the energy and drive Marples brought to politics, seeing him as a man who got things done, a 'swordsman'. Despite little expertise in transport policy, he saw Marples as having the energy, flair and necessary thick skin to take responsibility for implementing the potentially contentious measures needed to rein back on the losses being made by the railways. If they were to survive, they had to be transformed into a modern, efficient self-sustaining industry. Marples bullishly promised a working surplus of between £50 and £100 million by the end of 1963. Equally urgent was the tackling of the problems caused by the exponential growth in usage of a completely inadequate road system.

Ernest Marples was to become a nationally-known figure and one whose name was excoriated by protagonists both of the railways and of the roads. The post was not seen as a useful stepping stone to higher office but Macmillan hoped Marples would think that making a success of it under difficult circumstances would be a springboard to further progress in his political career. Marples was to hold the post for five years, longer than any other post-war Conservative Minister of Transport.

In the 1950s there had been a marked ideological consensus between the two main political parties. Perhaps because of memories of troubled economic conditions in the 1920s and 1930s and the experience of two world wars there had been an agreed sense that State involvement in certain key economic and social activities was essential. It was the recognition of this feeling that contributed much to Labour's memorable election victory in 1945. In the 1950s the Conservatives were careful not to undertake any major reversal of the Statist measures undertaken by Labour in the immediate post-war years, notwithstanding their ideological belief in a 'small state'. By the 1960s, however, despite economic growth and a generalised rise in living standards and expectations, there were signs that not all was well with the British economy. Some on the right of the of the Conservative Party like the highly influential Enoch Powell thought that politicians had gone 'soft' in backing away from tackling contentious issues. Conservatives like Powell had always regarded nationalisation as anathema and they used the losses being made by the railways as evidence that state ownership was a fundamentally flawed concept and that railways in particular were parasitically drawing on the more vigorous and productive parts of the economy. They believed that the future lay with roads and motor vehicles and that substantial parts of the railway system should be closed down as loss-making, inefficient and obsolescent. A greatly scaled-down railway system might, just might, have a viable economic future. Those lines that could never be made to pay should simply cease to exist. A less extreme view argued that a core of services that were viable should be made as efficient as possible while others that were loss-making would have to be maintained because of the considerable hardship that would follow from their closure. Such intrinsically loss-making services would require government subsidy, underwritten by the taxpayer. For a party seeking to maintain a low tax regime, this was bound to be a problem and one which became more urgent as the level of loss-making by the railways seemingly spiralled out of control.

The interplay between these currents within the Tory Party and other conflicts of opinion regarding transport were part of the can of worms inherited by Marples with his new ministerial portfolio. He was regarded in some quarters as a self-seeking publicist and dedicated go-getter and his appointment as Minister of Transport immediately aroused controversy. He may have had little expertise regarding transport policy but as a successful civil engineering contractor he certainly knew about road building. Could such a man be an honest broker in his role as Minister of Transport? This question was to hound Marples in his years at the Ministry. His appointment continued to arouse controversy when he decided to employ Dr Richard Beeching to analyse the problems facing the railways and to prescribe a solution to their financial losses which involved implementing major cuts in Britain's railway system.

Even before the election month of October was over, Ministry of Transport officials were starting to fret about their new political chief. He still owned 64,350 of the 80,000 ordinary £1 shares in Marples Ridgeway. These were estimated to be worth £350,000 to £400,000 at the time. Marples, well aware of the rumour-mill at Westminster, seems to have taken the initiative himself, setting in motion the acquisition of his holding by Warburgs, for a fee. Temporarily, the Whitehall mandarins were appeased with understandings that he would receive no income while in office and no option to reacquire the holdings after leaving. The matter was still under internal review in the new year when it burst into the public domain, courtesy of a 'Londoner's Diary' piece in the *Evening Standard* of 22 January. The occasion was London County Council's award of the Hammersmith flyover (now part of the M40) to none other than Marples Ridgway!

Inevitably this reignited concerns at the Ministry, severely embarrassed that the new boss's old firm would receive nearly a million pounds for the contract. Marples had a private meeting with Home Secretary R.A. Butler who insisted that the matter be referred to the Attorney General. On 25 January 1960 the latter demanded a personal statement from Marples to the Commons in which he would have to explain and justify holding the controlling interest in Marples Ridgway while he had been junior Housing Minister and then Postmaster General. 'Nothing less,' the Attorney General grimly concluded, 'will avoid the risk of serious trouble.' Butler, managing the Cabinet in the absence of Macmillan who was on his celebrated African tour, confronted Marples with rumours that were circulating about contracts given to Kirk & Kirk while he was the junior Minister for Housing. This issue was being eagerly pursued by 'Mr Mellish and his friends'. Robert Mellish, Bermondsey's formidable Labour MP, was certainly after Marples. With Butler as acting Prime Minister overseeing the matter and keeping Macmillan appraised, Marples had no choice but to cooperate.

The statement, exhaustively redrafted by the Attorney General, was finally delivered on 28 January. This is what he said: 'I was at one time a director of a company called Kirk & Kirk. I entirely severed my connection with the company in 1950. Before I became a junior minister, I was managing director of Marples, Ridgway & Partners, and held a controlling interest in that company. As soon as I became a junior minister I resigned my directorship and ceased to take any active part in the business. When I became Minister of Transport last October, I realised that there was a risk of a conflict of interest appearing to arise in consequence of my holding a controlling interest in the company. I immediately took steps to effect a sale of my shares. It has taken some time to arrange this as the company is a private one engaged in long-term contracts in civil engineering, but I hope that it will be completed very soon. Then I shall have no financial interest in the company. But I think I should tell the House that the prospective purchasers have required me to undertake to buy the shares back from them at the price they are to pay if they ask me to do so after I have ceased to hold office. I myself have no option to buy the shares back. I have not, of course, had anything whatever to do with any tenders put in by the company while I have been a member of the Government.'

It cannot have been easy to stand up and explain the nature of his business interests to a rapt audience in the House of Commons, including some members who were clearly after his scalp. Marples was, at best, economical with the truth. Some commented that he did not sound totally convincing. The exact nature of how he had disposed of his shares only reached the public domain some time later. Alan Lennox-Boyd, when Transport Minister in the Conservative government of the early 1950s, once described transport ministers as 'rather unprincipled persons'. Throughout his political career there were many who thought that Marples fitted this description rather well.

The complaisant Butler reported to Macmillan that it had gone down 'reasonably well' even though 'Mellish & Company' were clearly still intent on hounding him (Butler to Macmillan telegram, 2 Feb. 1960, PREM 11/4543). Butler believed that revenge was the motive since Marples had 'led the hunt' against James Milner 'in the old days'. When his private secretary Tim Bligh showed Macmillan what Butler had written, the Prime Minister apparently said, 'no printable comment'.

On 1 March a relieved Marples reported to Butler that the sale was complete. A more prudent man might now have pulled back from any kind of business activity that was questionable given his role, but not so Marples. That autumn the influential Conservative backbencher Burke Trend recorded a private conversation in which Marples had revealed his ownership of a property company, all the shares of which were owned by his wife. While he had not directed the company for 'eight or nine' years, she now proposed to use the company to finance a replication of the recipes served by the Auberge du Pont restaurant of Paul Bocuse in an exclusive restaurant of her own, Le Beaujolais. Trend promised to mention it to the Prime Minister but did not; when the matter resurfaced four years later, the context was quite different ('Perhaps Mr M is looking to the future', mused the *Sunday Express*, 14 June 1964).

Marples gets to work

This climax to Marples' political career would in time make him a household name, even if one that was often reviled. At his new ministry Marples would eventually establish a grip over all aspects of the department's work rivalled by few of his predecessors or successors. Dunnett noted the revival of Marples' partnership with Lord (Percy) Mills, describing the later decision to set up the Stedeford Committee, for example, as a joint one. Their bond endured throughout Marples' time at the Ministry. Mills was now Paymaster General. Marples had three junior ministers. John Hay, MP for Henley since 1950, was a solicitor skilled at expounding briefs and Lord Chesham fronted for the Ministry of Transport in the House of Lords. Macmillan had refashioned the Ministry, replacing civil aviation with shipbuilding, so the Admiralty's Rear Admiral Hughes-Hallett became the third junior minister. Petersfield MP Joan Quennell became his parliamentary private secretary and J.R. Madge his private secretary. On 26 November 1959 he announced the 'Pink Zone', ('a colour not associated with the three principal political parties'), all his own work. This was a six-week plan intended to keep West End traffic moving over the Christmas period. It involved free temporary car parks for over 6,000 vehicles, more buses and longer Tube trains. While backbench Labour MPs welcomed the news, Anthony Wedgwood Benn, speaking for the official Opposition, was hostile. Interestingly, outside the Commons, Marples privately enjoyed cordial relations with Benn throughout his political life.

On 10 December 1959 came Marples' first major Commons speech as Minister of Transport, an assured performance that ranged boldly over his road responsibilities: it anticipated an explosion of road traffic and a large rise in accidents and congestion in the cities.

Marples and motorways

The first section of motorway in the UK, the eight-mile Preston bypass, envisaged as part of what was to become the M6, was opened on 5 December 1958. Macmillan not only carried out the opening ceremony but then drove his car at the head of a cavalcade along the route, a publicity initiative intended to demonstrate his conviction that the motorway age had begun. It was an astute political stunt because being seen to support motorway building was a way of stealing an advantage over Labour which was seen as lukewarm regarding the expansion of Britain's road network. A member of the Cabinet as early as June 1957 had said 'there are votes in roads'. Any party advocating measures to restrict road traffic risked offending the 750,000 workers in the automotive industry, car owners who were growing in numbers by the day, and aspiring car-owners of whom there were also more each day. Conservative thinking was more keenly attuned to the growing electoral significance of road users than that of Labour.

Britain lagged seriously behind parts of Europe because the first motorway building programme had begun in Italy as far back as the 1920s and, famously, Hitler had inaugurated a prestigious large-scale autobahn programme in Germany in the 1930s. The Labour government in 1949 had passed the Special Roads Act which authorised the building or roads available only to certain categories of vehicle but it was not until the 1950s and with the Conservatives in office that authority was given to proceed with a programme of road building that included motorways.

Marples was about to inaugurate a shift in transport policy arguably more significant even than the future Beeching Report. Having opened the Wetherby bypass he went on, with a great fanfare of publicity, to bring the London to Birmingham motorway (then the M1) into use. The initiative for this lay with his predecessor, Harold Watkinson. Work on this motorway began in March 1958 but it was Marples who presided at the opening ceremony on 2 November the following year. It took place at Slip End, the junction of the Tarmac and Laing road-building contracts. After Sir Owen Williams, for the county surveyors, formally handed over the motorway, Marples briefly responded and then used a police radio car to order the county police to open some seventy-one miles to traffic. He then drove to the Luton Spur roundabout to observe the arrival of the first cars. After this the 400 assembled dignitaries retired for a slap-up lunch at the Savoy. His speech extended the credit entirely to Watkinson. However he was already worried about speeds, making speeches into which he dropped homespun mottoes to motorway users: 'Take it easy motorist' and 'If in doubt – don't'. In an early sign that the expansion of the system would quickly become normalised, the remaining two-and-a-half miles were opened without ceremony just before Christmas.

Privately, Marples was studying road use. He supplied ideas to the Cabinet in March involving a root-and-branch assessment of the country's long-distance road network and he pulled no punches. Britain had the highest road use density in the world; vehicle growth was three times the rate of motorway and trunk road growth; a major programme of road building must be initiated, either of £550 million or £630 million, and it should be funded entirely from vehicle excise income. Inaction meant traffic would be 'chaotic in 1964 – a most inconvenient year' (it was likely to be the year of the next general election). The grit in the oyster was his bid to raise the share of road spending in excise income, an argument that took no account of the state of the national finances ('The Road Programme', 25 March 1960, CAB 129/101/8). Conspiracy theorists will enjoy Appendix A of *The Road Programme* which shows a motorway network for England and Wales remarkably similar to that in the UK today.

Though he took his Advanced Driving Test during 1960 Marples was no mere 'petrolhead', as the 'Marples Must Go' campaigners would discover.

To the House he would later confide '… with all these motor cars about, one thinks one is in bedlam. The Hon. Member … suggested that I cycled to get out of the traffic. I assure him that anybody who cycles in London gets into the traffic very quickly and knows more about diesel exhaust fumes than any car owner. It is getting a dangerous occupation' (HC Deb, 1 March 1961). His dominating concern was the 'dreadful carnage' on the roads where he had brought in compulsory ten-year vehicle fitness tests. He hoped one solution might be improved vehicle design.

The powerful RHA was sensing that this was a highly favourable time for sidelining the railways and persuading the government to embark on a huge programme of motorway and road building. Through formal and informal channels it went about the process of influencing the politicians and senior civil servants who made and executed high-level policy. John Hay, Marples' junior at the Ministry, sounded exactly the right note for his audience when he spoke at the RHA's annual dinner in May 1960. He flattered them when referring to the battle they had won back in the early 1950s in returning the bulk of road haulage to the private sector and he assured them that the government was on their side in its desire to ensure expansive prospects for the road haulage industry in particular and for road users in general. It was clear that many senior politicians and civil servants thought that railways were a largely loss-making and outmoded transport medium and that it made no sense to throw growing amounts of taxpayer's money at them when lorries and cars, in particular, and even buses, could do their job more effectively and less expensively for the taxpayer.

Report of the Commons Select Committee on Nationalised Industries

Very soon after the 1959 general election result, the government gave the Commons Select Committee on Nationalised Industries the urgent task of investigating how the modernisation programme was progressing and examining the financial situation of the railways. The Committee reported with admirable promptitude by July 1960. Much of the information scrutinised by it had been provided by representatives of the Treasury and the Ministry on the one hand and officials of the BTC on the other. This was by no means ideal since the former were opposed to expenditure on modernisation and the latter were determined that the process must continue. If anything, the Committee's conclusions clouded the issue, at least from the government's point of view.

The Committee recognised that increased efficiency, largely resulting from the implementation of parts of the Modernisation Plan, was having a beneficial effect on the finances of BR. Evidence of this lay with a reduction of track and movement costs, of manpower and locomotives and other rolling stock. It was clear that the very substantial interest repayments with which the railways were saddled were a major contributor to the losses being made. Another factor for which the railways could not be blamed was that governments had tightly controlled fares and charges and allowed them to lag behind the rate of inflation. These findings may not have been exactly what the government really wanted to hear. However, the Committee was critical of the BTC for what it regarded as the haphazard and ineffectual way in which it gathered and processed financial data when making forecasts of likely income and expenditure. These forecasts frequently bore little resemblance to what actually happened. The Committee made clear its belief that some services had to be maintained to meet social need even though they were inescapably unprofitable. Governments should meet the costs of these services from public funds but decisions regarding such services and the costs involved should be in the hands of the Minister of Transport, not the BTC. It recognised with some reluctance that public subsidies for such services were desirable because of the enormous cost of road building, maintenance and upgrading and the almost unquantifiable costs created by road congestion, accidents and policing, for example. Underwriting some unprofitable services might ultimately prove cheaper than escalating expenditure on the roads. There were aspects of the Committee's findings which the anti-railway, pro-road lobby did not welcome.

As railway losses continued to mount, the electrification project for the line from London Euston to Liverpool and Manchester came under scrutiny. Marples, with some reservations, allowed the project to continue but it was clear that other major electrification schemes mooted earlier were now definitely on the back burner.

Reorganisation of the British Transport Commission

At the Cabinet meeting of 23 February 1960 Macmillan proposed a major reorganisation of the BTC. Legislation would be required while it continued its statutory duties and negotiated with the railway unions before the findings of the Guillebaud Report on railway workers' pay were published. The Committee of Inquiry under Guillebaud had been set up by Watkinson in

1958 and had bought a truce in industrial relations. The report was imminent and Macmillan wished to honour its expected recommendation of 'fair and reasonable wages' for the workers in the industry.

Once that was done all railway modernisation proposals would be reviewed or reappraised in consultation with the Ministry of Transport. The government would decide broad policy lines with details left to a planning committee of BTC representatives, Treasury officials and the Ministry plus 'independent' advisers. It might be appropriate, thought Macmillan, to have another independent as chairman of the planning committee. He wanted the formation of a Transport Council holding all BTC assets in trust; the division of assets between the different undertakings before each separated under an independent board. The Transport Council might retain or dispose of its assets but not manage and the Minister would have direct access to each chairman. Macmillan's approach rested on these points: that modernisation was essential; that the public must accept some reduction of uneconomic services and increases in fares and that the BTC would be extensively restructured.

Macmillan followed up with a speech in the Commons, declaring that 'The life and trade of the nation require a railway system, but it must not be allowed to become an intolerable burden on the national economy' (HC Deb, 10 March 1960). He told the House that the amount of mineral traffic in particular, vital to the railways, had been declining whereas increased use was being made of road transport in all its forms. The public would need to accept a contraction of uneconomic railway operations. These thoughts were exactly those that the RHA wanted to hear and Macmillan's speech provided a foretaste, three years early, of the thought underpinning the Beeching Report.

It is important to stress that Macmillan's was a broader canvas. He was deeply concerned that Britain's whole economic performance was indifferent: growth was patchy and there were periodic crises in the balance of payments. It was clear that on the mainland of Europe, widening free trade was already promoting growth among the founding members of the European Economic Community (EEC). Macmillan was an astute politician and he desperately wanted to be remembered as a Prime Minister who presided over good times.

It was clear that a very considerable challenge was facing Marples: he must reorganise the railways on business principles and turn round their economic performance. Here was a man wedded to the concept of free enterprise who had inherited responsibility for a portfolio of nationalised transport undertakings of which BR was the dominant member. The existence of these undertakings was anathema to considerable numbers of his fellow Conservative MPs but there were many traditional Conservative voters who were opposed to the closure of railways in the rural constituencies so many of them represented. He was constantly being lobbied by groups, some with considerable clout, representing road users, vehicle manufacturers and other interests diametrically opposed to the railways. Other lobbyists warned him about the damage being done to the environment by road building and the seemingly inexorable rise in road traffic. There were other people who seemed to think that the railways should be allowed to chug along forever, immune to wider economic and social considerations. It helped Marples to know that most newspapers were critical of the losses being made by the BTC and the railways in particular. In this, they made their own contribution to a generally anti-railway culture.

Marples did not let the grass grow under his feet. During the long January 1960 parliamentary recess he visited the USA, primarily to study bridge building methods, but he could not fail to notice the enormous shift from public to private transport. Additionally he was already wondering about importing the breathalyser. Macmillan's press secretary pictured Marples at this time in *Downing Street Diary: the Macmillan Years*: 'It is easy to see why he impresses people despite his flashiness. He bubbles with enthusiasm … while at the same time leaving no doubt he has thoroughly mastered his brief' (Evans 1981).

The BTC had been established by Labour in 1948 to acquire the country's transport assets. Churchill, on his return to office, was disinclined to restore private ownership, and had installed General Sir Brian Robertson (1896–1974) as the BTC chairman. He had made a name for himself as a very effective administrator of the Occupied Zone in Germany. Clearly regarded as a 'safe pair of hands', he quickly became popular and respected in his new role. During the1950s, a substantial number of services and lines had been closed, a precursor of the cuts made during the much more controversial period of Beeching's chairmanship. Robertson was well aware of the many outdated and inefficient practises continuing on Britain's railways and, for example, he had referred disparagingly to the very common pick-up goods trains of loose-coupled wagons as 'Emett-like trains going clankety-clank through our countryside'. For Marples the question was whether the BTC, easily portrayed as a lumbering giant, was the appropriate vehicle to carry rationalisation and more drastic modernisation forward. Was Robertson, with his old-fashioned integrity and his military-style management structure, a man who could fit comfortably into the private sector business practices Marples believed had to be applied to a radically updated and, hopefully, revitalised railway system?

While the Modernisation Plan over which Robertson had presided had made steady, if unspectacular progress, the BTC's financial performance was discouraging. Its total deficit had risen to £350 million and would hit £80 million, including interest, in 1960. It anticipated a railway operating loss of £45 million, to which would have to be added the cost of a substantial pay award. Interest on the BTC's accumulated deficits ran at £15 million. Marples therefore would have to restructure the BTC, devise a viable modernisation plan and pay whatever formula the Guillebaud Committee came up with, but the wider context was not propitious. The shift to individual transport modes was proportionately just as pronounced in Britain as in the USA. Marples had to decide whether it was feasible to continue with the BTC in its present or even in an amended form. Modernisation of the railways was taking effect. Diesel and electric miles worked overtook steam early in 1960 and significant electrification projects were in progress. However, much work to create a modern railway system remained to be done.

There were other urgent matters to be addressed. For example, Marples thought it intolerable that the regions of BR could authorise costly schemes without even referring them upwards to the BTC. Four months into office Marples made his first move: the Ministry would scrutinise in detail all BTC rail projects and schemes in excess of £250,000. The days of the open chequebook were over. Two issues particularly irked him. One was the complicated and prolonged process of enacting passenger route and station closures. This he wanted to streamline. Second was the apparent difficulty of identifying loss-making activities and then accurately quantifying those losses. It was much the same with profitable activities. Swift action was urgently needed to address these matters. Action to control the way the BTC conducted its business was also urgently required.

Marples backed the railways at Cabinet. They stood to gain commercial freedom but they would be divided into autonomous groups, then coordinated by a central body of general managers. Higher rail freight charges would cover part of the BTC deficit. The Cabinet wanted to present pay rises as implementation of Guillebaud despite the BTC's parlous finances – a quid pro quo. Capital write-offs, reorganisation of the capital structure and subsidy payments would follow reorganisation. This, Marples claimed, had been intimated informally to Robertson who had promised cooperation: his support would certainly be needed. The BTC and the unions would negotiate Guillebaud but with the BTC current deficit unsustainable, its implementation must be carefully phased in. If the unions demanded immediate interim wage rises these should be conceded only in respect of differentials. The unions had acknowledged the need for a rationalised and smaller railway, provided redundancies occurred through natural wastage; now they must be convinced that the government would support rationalisation even if it meant subsidising unprofitable services. To the public however, modernisation meant the 1955 BTC plan. A 1959 White Paper still stood, claiming 'the Modernisation Plan drawn up four years ago, and the financial appreciation made in the White Paper of 1956, were soundly based'. As late as 9 May 1960 the BTC was still assuring the press its plan had reached the point where '… its more substantial and dramatic features will become increasingly apparent', promising its next phase would bring 'the rapid growth of practical achievements' (J.R. Dodson, 'Notes to Editors', 9 May 1960, AN 13/2739).

The publication of the Guillebaud Report implied that if railway workers were, quite rightly, to be paid a decent wage, then the costs of the railways and their losses would rise dramatically. How could widespread closures and job losses be avoided? It was almost a catch-22. Better wages for railway workers would lead to a smaller system with fewer jobs. Which course of action was preferable? Which was politically expedient? The continuance of poor pay in the railway industry would further weaken morale, cause personnel to leave the industry and exacerbate the unreliability of many services.

It could be argued that the railway unions were being duped. While they had accepted the need for a rationalised railway system and redundancies, the Ministry agenda was somewhat different. Yes, pay rises would be awarded but, secretly, far more draconian cuts were being planned. This was hardly a quid pro quo given the unions' willingness to concede job losses in return for improved pay.

Questions were being asked in a culture increasingly critical of the railways. Was the Modernisation Plan providing real value for money? Was the BTC spending its income in the most effective way? Were there new managerial and financial structures that could be employed to make the BTC better value for money? Indeed, was there a future for the BTC? Could it ever be made viable? It was being castigated as an expensive, inefficient and outdated body which needed radical reconstruction in order to reduce the massive losses it was making. These losses could no longer be tolerated. It must have been clear to Robertson that his role as chairman of the BTC was under scrutiny as indeed was the entire role of the BTC. Was he the man to take it or a replacement body into a new era of a slimmed down, modernised network supported by full financial accountability and modern managerial practices? In such a situation it was probably helpful that Robertson was approaching retirement age. Was this not the time for a clean break with the past to be made? Marples clearly saw no future for Robertson in his present role and wanted him out. He knew he would have to be circumspect because there were many influential people who admired Robertson and the values for which he stood. A new man was needed to head the BTC or any possible replacement body. This man would need to bring a radical new approach to the job and have the official status and support to cope with the criticism and unpopularity which would inevitably be directed at anyone tasked with masterminding major cuts to the railway system. Who should it be?

The Stedeford Committee

Marples did not want to hear that the Modernisation Plan was bearing some fruit, even if it was not exactly a bumper crop. Having introduced the investment review mechanism, he now took decisive action and established a Special Advisory Group under Ivor Stedeford, chairman of Tube Investments. This body advised delaying any new modernisation proposals which were not already planned for imminent detailed scrutiny. Both Macmillan and Marples clearly knew the thrust of thinking at the Select Committee on Nationalised Industries, due in July. Publicly, Macmillan blurred the differences, arguing 'what the Plan proposes is a continuation of a deliberate course of action' growing from several recent initiatives. The government accepted Guillebaud's principle of fair and reasonable pay, but knew that far fewer railwaymen would survive to receive it if Stedeford's recommendations were implemented. This clearly seems to pre-empt the Special Advisory Group's recommendations and does suggest a thinly-veiled plot to create an 'impartial' body which would come up with the findings the government wanted. The whole deceitful presentation projected a process of continuity when the actual aim was a clean break with the status quo. By 17 March the Cabinet had concluded that the BTC needed written instructions from the Minister, Chancellor, Paymaster General, the Minister of Labour and the Chancellor of the Duchy of Lancaster on its negotiations with the unions.

It had lost its final say on large investment projects; now it lost its autonomy in pay talks. This same Cabinet learned of the Special Advisory Group for the first time. Knowledge of this group had previously been highly restricted.

Macmillan first publicly described the new body as a 'planning board', declaring:

'The body will be impartial, and it will advise the Government. The chairman and the Commission have told me that they will do everything they can to help it. It will consult the trade unions. When it comes to the proposals, we shall have to take the full responsibility, but I say again, and I say it sincerely with real affection for the railways, that we must try to get the highest agreement that is possible. The detailed application of these principles to all the Commission's undertakings is a matter of urgency and will be worked out by a special planning board. Legislation, as well as administrative action, will certainly be required. This planning board will be appointed by the Government and will report both to the Government and to the Commission. Meanwhile, the Commission is securing expert advice on the question of regional accounting for the railways' (HC Deb, 10 March 1960).

In the Commons (HC Deb, 6 April) Marples had to correct the Prime Minister, redefining Stedeford as an 'advisory group'. He disclosed the membership: Frank Kearton (Joint MD of Courtaulds, the textile conglomerate); Dr Richard Beeching (ICI technical director); H.A. Benson (a senior figure in Cooper Brothers, the accountants); Matthew Stevenson from the Treasury; and the later to be notorious David Serpell from the Ministry of Transport. Beeching was perhaps the least known of these members. He was regarded as a bright up-and-coming analyst and problem solver schooled within ICI, which was then held up as a model of the best British business practice. The group was therefore composed of men perceived as having a successful record and proven managerial skills in big business or in government departments and agencies. Stedeford himself had been a member of the committee of inquiry into the BBC in 1949–1950 and the UK Atomic Energy Authority. Care was taken not to co-opt any professional railwaymen, members of the BTC or even an outsider with knowledge of and sympathy for the railways. The Central Transport Users' Consultative Committee, the RHAs and the Railway Conversion League were to be 'consulted' as and when necessary.

The Special Advisory Group's remit was to 'examine the structure, finance and working of the organisations at present controlled by the Commission' and '... advise the Minister of Transport and the British Transport Commission, as a matter of urgency, how effect can best be given to the Government's intentions as indicated in the Prime Minister's statement'. While 'BTC' was constantly being referred to, it was clear that it was particularly the railways on which the Ministry had set its sights. Nonplussed Opposition members seemed more interested in re-fighting the last war (in this case the 1953 Act) than anticipating the virtual blitzkrieg that would soon be launched. Railwayman Ernest Popplewell lamented the deterioration of the BTC: 'An efficient undertaking, which was developing a good organisation and management structure before the 1953 Act, has been converted from being a full-time Commission which was getting on with the job and which understood it into a Commission of fourteen members half of whom are part-time from outside industry.' He pointed out that Tube Investments was already well-represented on the BTC's area boards.

Introducing Dr Richard Beeching

Richard Beeching (1913–1985) grew up in Kent. From a solidly middle–class background, he was always academically able. He was educated at Maidstone Grammar School and the Imperial College in London where he read Physics, obtaining a First and staying on at Imperial College doing research which led to the award of a doctorate. He joined Mond Nickel Industries as a senior researcher in the areas of physics, metallurgy and mechanical engineering. He quickly gained recognition as a very able researcher and organiser with an incisive intellect.

During the War he was seconded to the Ministry of Supply where he worked in its Armaments Design and Research Departments. While there, he worked under Sir Frank Smith who was superintendent and chief engineer. Smith, who was greatly impressed by Beeching's capabilities, had formerly been chief engineer in what was then the mighty Imperial Chemical Industries (ICI). After the war, Smith returned to ICI as technical director. He was succeeded as chief engineer of Armaments Design by Sir Stuart Mitchell who was also impressed by Beeching and promoted him at the age of thirty-three to the post of deputy director with a rank equivalent to brigadier. Clearly, Beeching's star was in the ascendant when he rejoined ICI as personal assistant to Sir Frank. For about eighteen months he studied commodity manufacture with the brief, which he successfully fulfilled, of improving efficiency and reducing production costs. He was then appointed to the Terylene Council and later to the Board of Fibres Division. In 1953 he went to Canada as vice-president of ICI (Canada) and was given overall responsibility for bringing a Terylene plant in Ontario into full production. After two years he returned to become chairman of ICI Metals Division on the recommendation of Sir Frank. He carried through a successful reorganisation of this division. In 1957 he was appointed to the board of ICI as technical director and for a short time also as development director.

It was on his reputation for analytical and organisational ability that Beeching was recommended for membership of the Stedeford Group. Having decided that he wanted Beeching in the group Marples had to be at his most persuasive to get ICI to release Beeching which it did only reluctantly. As a member of the Stedeford Committee he quickly impressed Marples who became convinced that Beeching was exactly the right man to deliver what he wanted and to become chairman of the BTC. Although the nominal term of his office was five years, Beeching revealed privately that he and Marples had agreed that he would only serve three years if it was considered that real progress had been made in that time.

Beeching was very different from his predecessor Robertson. He gave the impression to most of those he met in his emerging role as relaxed and friendly although not of a naturally gregarious nature. In *British Railways 1948–1973*, Gourvish (1986) suggests he presented an image of 'avuncular geniality'. This view was not shared by Macmillan. His diaries reveal that he had misgivings about the appointment of Beeching who he thought of as 'difficult'. That Marples was allowed to go ahead with the appointment of Beeching therefore says much about the influence he was able to exert on the Prime Minister at that time.

Temptations to attribute the brusqueness of the Special Advisory Group's communications to Beeching alone should be resisted: a curt note from Stedeford himself to Robertson on the London-Midland electrification project, centrepiece of the BTC plan, read 'may I express the hope that … expenditure on this project will be slowed down and no new commitments entered into whilst it is under review' (Stedeford to Sir Brian Robertson, 10 June 1960 AN 13/2739). This tone showed that his group was confident of full political support. Yet it is the pantomime villain Beeching who was to attract most of the subsequent opprobrium. It is curious that even contemporary politicians were wary of challenging his judgements, preferring to lodge the blame for his sins with Marples. Historians likewise seem unsure. Where lay his expertise? Was he an accountant? (see Lamb, *The Macmillan Years*, 1995: 433). One Labour MP thought him 'a tycoon'. Really he was a scientist, something of a boffin.

The Special Advisory Group started meeting in early April. A week later Marples portrayed it rather ungrammatically as 'a small group of outside advisers with experience who would spend virtually most of their time on the job', seeing him every week or fortnight. While enjoying top civil servant status, they would have in-depth knowledge of industry but not be paid. He foresaw that the group would carry through two separate consultations with the unions. It was on this occasion that he told the House that Stedeford would not be published. Understandably there was a somewhat stunned response to this announcement. John Hay defended its members' 'extensive and detailed knowledge of the problems of organisation and management of large-scale business in modern, twentieth-century conditions'. In barely a month Beeching compiled a formidable questionnaire containing nine general questions followed by eighty-nine (!) detailed ones and providing a thorough investigation of the implications of BTC modernisation ('Questionnaire on Modernisation Scheme', 11 May 1960, AN13/2739). His view is confirmed by a seven-page memorandum, two months into the process, unsentimentally dismantling BTC complacency ('The Preparation and Presentation of Railway Modernisation Plans', R.B., 8 June 1960 AN 13/2739). By 18 May the Special Advisory Group had already met fourteen times: it sustained several business-like meetings weekly until disbanding that autumn. Labour's Philip Noel-Baker alleged its members were known jovially to railmen as the 'Marples's Gestapo' (HC Deb, 26 October 1960). The Stedeford Group continues to tantalise. After it was wound up the government still downplayed its significance. In Hay's words 'Hon. Members have spoken about the publication of the "Stedeford Report". There is no such thing ... advice has been tendered to my Right Hon. Friend and a number of recommendations have been made ...' (HC Deb, 26 October 1960). It did not report, yet it made recommendations! To Hay, Stedeford was essential for a realistic rail modernisation that did not break the bank. He even implied it would eventually look at all transport modes, and he didn't pull his punches, declaring 'the modernisation plan has to be adapted ... dead wood has got to be cut out and the outmoded restrictions and obligations – the common carrier obligation – the control over fares, the inability to use property in the most economic and effective way must all be re-examined'. The BTC, in other words, must be restructured in order to achieve financial viability. Neither the 1947 Act nor that of 1953 had set clear-cut objectives. If a public BR was to be judged by non-commercial criteria, then the government should set them and the BTC must force it to assume responsibility: this had been done by neither. The BTC demanded modernisation without curtailment; government accepted assurances that costly modernisation would work. Both shirked difficult choices.

In the summer Marples had established an additional railway 'study group', himself in the chair. Its existence emerged only in late October when he brought forward an anodyne resolution to the House, 'that this House takes note of the Annual Report and Accounts of the British Transport Commission for the year ended 31st December, 1959 (H.C. 226), and of the Report from the Select Committee on Nationalised Industries (H.C. 254) relating to British Railways'(HC Deb, 26 October 1960). Bracketing these reports (which did not wholly agree) was disingenuous. The House upheld the motion by fifty-six votes. Labour moved an amendment but did not oppose the substantive motion. The Prime Minister's press secretary thought Marples' performance in the debate 'deplorable' (Evans 1988, *Downing Street Diary*). He and Hay no longer dissembled. They intended to be radical, did not disguise their contempt for the BTC, and could count on press support ('A Minister is not Enough', *Time & Tide*, 3 September 1960).

Marples secured Macmillan's agreement to the Beeching appointment on 12 December, the Prime Minister grumbling that it was only the government that was keeping the railways going. Marples was, with Mills, due to see Robertson and sought agreement in principle that Beeching should replace him on a part-time basis with ICI making up his salary shortfall. Macmillan concurred, offering to placate Robertson if he were unhappy. Marples, privately viewing the BTC as 'incompetent, both technically and financially' believed Beeching would put this right along with a vice-chairman 'strong on the financial side'. He thought Beeching would need powerful government backing on manpower matters. The December 1960 White Paper *Reorganisation of the Nationalised Transport Undertakings* still did not refer to a smaller railway, specifying that managerial structures must first be rationalised. The press was sceptical. *Modern Transport* (31 December) spoke of 'illusory coordination'; the *Financial Times* thought it 'confused social obligations with commercial considerations' (21 December 1960).

Two days later a ministerial group on the chairmanship convened where the Chancellor, Paymaster General and others discussed the proposal.

Marples, an early protagonist of the argument that nationalised industries required competitive salaries to attract the best men, believed Beeching's calibre demanded a salary two and-a-half times his ICI package; Mills, a BTC defender and his long-time friend, was concerned, pointing to the glaring conflict of interest and fearing internal resistance to an outside appointment. Where, it was asked, was the railwayman who could bring the necessary reorganisational drive to the job? Fears of the likely public impact of a £25,000 salary provoked general dismay. Marples took a month to revise his proposal: he anticipated no progress under Robertson and now suggested Beeching be appointed part-time to the BTC in succession to Weir, a board member whose retirement was imminent: after two months on the board he would replace Robertson on a government-funded salary of £24,000. Selwyn Lloyd favoured generous compensation for Robertson on early retirement grounds but Mills restated his reservations about Beeching and opposed hustling Robertson out. Neither side favoured a long overlap. The matter reverted in mid-March to the Cabinet which determined the final plan. Robertson retired on 1 June, with Beeching now chairman-designate of the new BR board. Sir Brian must have felt affronted by the manner in which he was pushed aside but he went with the dignity that was only to be expected of the old soldier.

The next day Marples spoke to a House which was in uproar. Nor was it just from opposition parties because Robertson had Conservative friends and admirers. Macmillan's backing had been decisive so it is surprising he did not even meet Beeching until May. Beeching queried the White Paper's proposed relationship between the main and area boards but the two agreed over the need for high-calibre managers and a new structure to run the railways. Early Cabinet disquiet centred on Scottish Secretary Michael Noble, who Marples soothed with the argument that only 33 of the 740 miles proposed for closure were in Scotland. The Transport Bill also gave him 'ample powers in case of hardship to require the railways to keep open uneconomic passenger services or to provide and maintain alternative bus services' (Marples to Macmillan, 7 June 1962, PREM 11/4548). Noble did not give up without a fight: the Minister might intervene to forestall hardship from passenger line closures but no such provision existed for freight. Scotland had areas 'involving distances of up to 100 miles where the alternative roads are an inadequate substitute'. This worried Macmillan but the wily Marples had learned to feint. He fell back on the deceitful argument that Beeching's plan was as yet unknown. His greatest fear was Noble's call for prior road improvements, which would keep 'wholly uneconomic railway services going, possibly for some years ...' (Marples to Macmillan, 10 July 1962 PREM 11/4548).

Macmillan backed him up. At the 1961 Conservative Conference where he might have been deemed unpopular for not building enough roads, Marples achieved, in the words of *The Times,* 'one of today's outstanding successes', as a 'born raconteur'. Backbench opinion was, for now, more easily placated: Macmillan took comfort from Beeching's reception at 'our party committee' in early November, confiding to Marples that 'we must back him up, especially over the closing of unprofitable lines' (Prime Minister to Minister of Transport, 4 November 1961, PREM 11/4028). There would be no Switzerland before Christmas for in that era Ministers of Transport had to be seen to be on duty, alert against drink-driving. 'If you are going to drink, let the wife drive ...' Marples urged motorists in the revealing language of the day. By January 1962, however, they were at Davos where he and John Diamond led for Britain in the annual Anglo-Swiss parliamentary ski race. There were some signs of restiveness in an otherwise loyal press: the *Mail* detected a civil war in Marples' implied attacks on Watkinson's earlier BTC plan; in the *Sunday Express,* 'Cross-Bencher' believed Marples was 'finished'; by March Douglas Brown was telling *Daily Mail* readers 'why Ernest Marples will never be PM'; Aubrey Jones told the *Daily Herald* the government had wrongly opted for decentralisation when this was properly a matter for the putative new board. Such was the unfavourable press coverage of the phoney war preceding publication of Beeching's plans.

Marples, in bed with flu, was in no position to celebrate. In March 1961 he tabled his Road Traffic Bill introducing the breathalyser and blood tests for those suspected of drink-driving. Later that month the government comfortably saw off an Opposition censure motion 'That this House deplores the statement of the Minister of Transport on his appointment of a new chairman of the British Transport Commission.' Strauss, for Labour, complained that 'Dr Beeching knows nothing about transport matters other than what he gathered when, as a member of the Stedeford Committee, in the Minister's words, he ... saturated himself with railway matters.' He lamented the continued failure to publish Stedeford. He had read press reports of a 20 per cent cut in rail services, 'far heavier than any hitherto contemplated' and grumbled about Beeching's 'Himalayan' pay. Marples, he averred, had achieved 'a double folly – that of dealing a severe blow to the morale of all those who work in the railways, and of undermining the principles and tradition which have hitherto operated over the whole sphere of public service'.

Marples wanted Beeching in place as soon as possible: 'I attach great importance to his not being merely an inheritor of a fabric which others have built.' Beeching would 'look at the problem on its merits when he gets in the saddle'. If this was highly disingenuous, ensuing references to the 'high opinion held by ministers' of Robertson were downright dishonest. The press, in restive mood, deemed that Marples had had long enough to devise a plan. Scenting trouble, the government fielded the Chancellor of the Duchy, Charles Hill, to reply. He opted for higher ground, deploring the personal attacks on Beeching of backbenchers like Mellish. The Labour attack, anticipated *in extenso* at their Scarborough conference, was that the government refused to view transport as an integrated project. Marples (in a distorted version of the private feelings of many Conservative MPs) was a greedy self-publicist. A disgruntled Michael Foot told the *Daily Herald* 'he is Minister of Transport, not Minister for Marples Publicity Incorporated and Unlimited' (1 November 1960). In reality Labour's scattergun approach merely confused the issue. Was Beeching Marples' stooge or a desiccated calculating machine? They never really made up their minds at the time.

By May the transport focus had shifted to the seas. Marples had opted to subsidise home construction of the new Cunard liner. This stirred up bitterness on the Conservative back benches when the North Atlantic Shipping Bill reached the Commons, resurrecting ancient feelings that the Transport Minister was unsound. It may have been a relief for him to escape in September on a tour of European shipyards, taking in Italy, Germany, Holland, Sweden, Spain and Norway. On 20 October he returned to the House to announce a climb-down: abandonment of his plan to replace the *Queen Mary*. He received a battering. Unrepentant, he popped up on *Panorama* to insist that there was much to be learned from the Europeans – industrial unions for example. June brought the Ramblers' Association Festival of Rambling where he was guest of honour, and he had the same status at the Royal Variety Club annual dinner as well. This may have brought some relief in his somewhat embattled state.

In the saddle

Beeching was now in the saddle. He demanded detailed traffic-flow studies cross-matched with types and location of travel; consideration of the merits and demerits of rail in each case; study of rail's share in each category; an assessment of what feasible improvements could be identified and where costs could be cut; forecasts of probable future traffic flows; and, finally, the formulation of a plan that 'meets the requirements of adequacy, efficiency, and safety, in the optimum manner'. Further, he insisted that all future modernisation bids should be subjected to a similar detailed analysis. This was, indeed, the process he would follow as BR chairman over the next two years. It was, he explained, specialist work that must be directed by men of the right calibre. Neither the BTC, nor indeed the Ministry, had ever been subjected to such overdue and rigorous scrutiny. Beeching was beginning to make an impact.

Opening the Second Reading debate on the Transport Bill based on the White Paper, Marples created an unfavourable impression. He appeared not fully conversant with his subject and, contrary to custom and practice, it was clear that he was reading his speech. Referring to the speech, the editor of *Modern Railways* described him as 'one of Westminster's masters of suave sophistry'. Marples emphasised that for all of its length, the Bill contained three clear and fundamental principles: each element of the BTC must have a separate authority with clearly-defined responsibilities and be fully equipped to meet them; each must have its own assets and carry its own capital debt and financial performance; each must acquire commercial freedom including the freedom to fix prices and with more scope to exploit publicly-owned assets. While the role of the BTC was clearly under scrutiny, Marples' focus was on the financial state of the railways which he saw as the heart of the problem. He put it succinctly: 'Last year, their gross receipts were £478 million, but they spent £546 million, leaving a loss of almost £70 million on revenue account alone, which is fifteen per cent on turnover.'

The White Paper of 1960 had been unequivocal on the challenges facing the railways: 'Sweeping changes will be needed …The public will have to be prepared to face changes in the extent and nature of the services provided, and when necessary, in the prices charged for them. The taxpayer will have to face a major capital reorganisation as well as continue to carry a large part of the burden until the railways are paying their way again. Those working in these undertakings, if their livelihood is to be assured, will have to play their part in increasing productivity and enabling the labour force to be deployed so as to secure maximum efficiency.

'… The railways… are a great national enterprise and a vital basic industry. They employ half a million people and represent an investment of nearly £1,600 million. A railway system of the right size is an essential element in our transport network and will remain so for as long as can be foreseen. The development of other forms of transport now faces British Railways, like the railways in other countries, with problems of competition and adaptation to modern circumstances and public demand.

'The railways are now in a grave financial plight. They are a long way short ... of covering even their running costs. This is quite apart from the problem of meeting their interest charges, whether upon the price paid for the undertakings or upon the money since borrowed for modernisation and other purposes. These interest charges now total some £75 million a year.

'The practical test for the railways, as for other transport, is how far the users are prepared to pay economic prices for the services provided. Broadly, this will in the end settle the size and pattern of the railway system. It is already clear that the system must be made more compact. There must also be modernisation, not only of lay-out, equipment, and operating methods, but of organisation and management structure.'

Marples stated that the break-up of the BTC which he was proposing was because the tasks it was required to undertake were too much to be handled by a single body. The Opposition quickly pointed out that this excessive workload was the result of the government's Transport Act of 1953 which had abolished the Railway Executive and transferred its work to the BTC. Criticism was also voiced to the effect that the Bill's whole thrust seemed to contradict the aims of transport coordination. The MP for Derby South argued that the Bill, if passed, would stimulate a massive increase in motorised transport. It would add greatly to car usage and exacerbate existing road congestion to the extent that the reasons why people bought their own transport would be nullified.

Here was an impasse. The BTC still wanted the resources for modernisation in the belief that it could retain existing and gain new traffic. The government, however, wanted to ensure that the BTC fulfilled its obligation to break even. With these objectives being irreconcilable, one side was going to be the loser. Marples was determined that it was not going to be the government

The Transport Act 1962

The outcome of the White Paper and the determination of Macmillan and Marples to sort out the financial and organisational state of the railways had become clear. The consequence was the Transport Act of 1962. This major piece of legislation replaced the BTC and established four new public authorities: the British Railways Board (BRB) with Dr Beeching as its chairman; the London Transport Board; the British Transport Docks Board and the British Waterways Board. These boards were to be composed of members appointed by the Minister of Transport. The Transport Holding Company was set up to manage road passenger operations and British Road Services. All board members were to be appointed by the minister as were those of Thomas Cook and various other residual activities. The BRB was to run the railway hotels. All the boards, with the exception of the London Transport Board, were given the freedom to adjust their fares and charges on a commercial basis. Regional Railway Boards would replace the existing Area Boards. Financial targets were to be set for the railways which clearly could not be met without significant cuts in services. Ill-feeling was generated among railway workers when Marples decreed that none of the boards would be allowed to manufacture or repair equipment for outside customers. This threatened the future of the railway workshops.

Proposals in the earlier White Paper had already met widespread criticism by being unclear on the future size of the railway system, the fate of unprofitable services and the status of the Modernisation Plan. Now questions were being asked about the Act itself. What exactly was to be the role of the proposed new boards? How could a government, supposedly committed to decentralisation, be proposing a more centralised structure? Why had transport coordination and integration been dropped completely? Why were profitable parts of the BTC's activities being hived off within a publicly-owned holding company? Railway workers at all levels asked why they could not be left to get on with their jobs rather than having to undergo yet more reorganisation.

The BRB was inaugurated on 1 January 1963. Much of the outstanding debt of the railways was written off but on the understanding that the new BRB and all its component parts had to be run on commercial lines. No longer would profitable operations be permitted to cross-subsidise those making losses. The long-standing common carrier obligation of the railways was abolished and the BRB was given almost total freedom to fix passenger fares and choose the freight traffic it wished to handle based on commercial decisions. Sadly the new commercial freedom was implemented very slowly causing much potential income to be lost during the Beeching years.

The case of Lowestoft provided evidence of the burdensome nature of the common carrier obligation. Fish traffic from this port had once been lucrative but income declined as the industry turned to road haulage. However, BR was still obliged to accept and handle two trucks per day of exceptionally obnoxious fish offal. The line to the dockside had to be kept open just for this traffic. Thumping losses were made on such activities and their elimination was urgently needed.

The function of the TUCCs was modified to accelerate the procedure by which lines were considered for closure. The BRB had to give a minimum of six weeks' notice of intention to withdraw a specific service and publish details of its proposals in local newspapers over two successive weeks. The public was to be informed of the proposed closure dates and details of alternative public transport facilities including any new ones intended as rail replacement services. Objections were to be lodged within the six-week period and only those based on issues of personal hardship, the inability of the local roads to cope in adverse weather conditions or with extra traffic would be considered. Claims that official figures supporting a closure proposal were inaccurate, that the service could be operated more economically or that planned large-scale population growth in the area meant that the service should be retained, would not be considered. It was clear that questions from objectors concerning the verity of data submitted in support of closure proposals had been greatly irritating the mandarins.

Submissions could be made by letter or in person to be considered at an advertised public meeting of the relevant Area Transport Users' Consultative Committee and the Committee would consider the objections and submit a report to the minister for adjudication on whether the closure would cause hardship. The TUCC concerned was permitted to suggest measures to alleviate such potential hardship. The closure could not be implemented until the minister had given the go-ahead. The responsibility for a closure decision lay with the minister alone and he/she could legally proceed with a closure proposal even if it was evident that hardship would be caused. The issue here was: what was meant by 'hardship'? How was hardship to be defined? Who was to define it?

This all made it look as if the government was loading the dice in favour of closures. It was obvious that every time a line closed, some traffic was lost and went to the roads, usually permanently. The government knew that more votes were to be had from policies encouraging road usage than those which did the railways any favours and was determined to press ahead. Critics argued that the TUCCs were intended to give the impression that they were part of a genuine consultative process but in reality, with the Ministry not being required to take any account of their findings, their actual function was merely cosmetic.

In with the new

Time had run out for the BTC. Clearly neither Marples nor Beeching were impressed with the ex-army brass hats that Sir Brian Robertson had appointed to senior positions. Sir Brian, who had held the post since 1953, retired as chairman on 31 May 1961. He was respected for his integrity and, despite being shy, was no pushover. He had the ability to relate well with professional railway workers of all levels. It is difficult not feel some sympathy for Robertson in his last couple of years when he was in effect being required to work with political masters who were engaged in implementing the demise of the BTC of which he had been the conscientious steward for so long. He kept his own counsel in public but he must have been sensitive to the manner in which he was being undermined. He would probably have found very little to respect or admire in Marples and the way in which he operated.

Robertson's Old Guard gave way to Dr Richard Beeching. *The Economist* was unimpressed. On 16 March 1961 it said: 'Beeching was appointed to give effect to government intentions for its largest loss-maker by a Minister bent on redirecting resources into road transport.' The *Daily Mirror,* by way of contrast, deemed Beeching to be 'the right man in the right job'. The appointment of a man with no experience in the railway industry was evidence that the government was making a decisive change in direction. It was an appointment which, not surprisingly, was viewed unfavourably by large numbers of workers in the railway industry and at all levels.

Appointing a new chairman to oversee the breaking up of the BTC was no simple matter. The terms and conditions of this appointment were controversial. Marples believed that a man of Beeching's calibre required remuneration commensurate with his ICI package. Lord Mills, who had succeeded Marples as Postmaster General, did not share the latter's admiration for Beeching and disagreed. He saw moral hazard in Beeching belonging to the group recommending dissolution of the BTC and then assuming the chairmanship of that organisation, even temporarily. He also rightly warned that the appointment of a non-railwayman would provoke a storm of criticism among professionals in the railway industry. The problem for Mills was that no senior railwayman with the necessary analytical skills and organisational drive came readily to mind. Additionally it was obvious that the proposed £24,000 annual salary would enrage much public opinion. Marples, however, was convinced both that he had to buy the best brains for the job and that no progress towards his desired objectives would be made while Robertson still chaired the BTC. Chancellor Selwyn Lloyd favoured a generous buy-out to compensate Robertson for his involuntary early retirement. Mills again opposed, reiterating early reservations about Beeching and thought it unseemly to hustle him out.

Beeching's brief was to analyse the business being conducted by the railways, identify the profitable and unprofitable activities and recommend those measures he considered were needed in order to make the railways profitable, and to perform this task quickly. It was never in his power to close any line, ill-frequented passenger station or rusty, virtually disused wayside goods depot. It was tempting but mistaken to describe him as 'The Axeman'. For many that characterisation was taking root even before Beeching's findings were made public and it has continued to prevail down to the present time. Beeching had a job to do and although he had never shown any previous particular interest in railways it did not take him long to appreciate the historical reasons why his services had been sought after and secured.

Harold Wilson made a speech on 30 April 1963: '… we saddled the railways with an uneconomic interest burden, and made it a fixed charge on railway earnings. But basically, whatever mistakes we made, we achieved viability for the transport system, a viability which continued until the wreckers got at it after 1951. Of course British Railways were still paying their way until 1953. This was remarkable – it really was – because of the growth of road competition on a scale far exceeding pre-war, especially with "C" licences, because the House will recall that the privately-owned railway system was already facing financial disaster before the war'.

The period between 1945 and 1963 was a difficult one for the railways and Beeching knew this. The Doctor was gathering material for his diagnosis and would soon make his prescribed remedy known. Was his Report to be a continuation of an insidious, slow process of running them down or was it to be the precursor for a leaner, hungrier and revitalised railway system?

Chapter 13

Beeching Goes Public

The combination of a restless, energetic minister in Marples and the coldly analytical Beeching was provoking much public and trade union hostility even before the Beeching Report hit the headlines. Beeching was impressive when he gave his first press conference after appointment. He argued that modernisation was essential but would not alone lead to viability. That process must be continued but each scheme should be judged on its merits. He preferred diesel to electric traction but was overruled by Marples when the latter gave authority to complete electrification of the West Coast Main Line from Crewe to London Euston. Beeching conceded that partial modernisation had raised the productivity of the industry but that BR's financial situation continued to be dire. A far-reaching examination of the business would seek to establish exactly how much traffic was being handled at every passenger station and goods depot so as to identify clearly profitable and loss-making operations. Beeching believed that there was business the railways could handle better than any other transport mode and that efforts should be made to win such traffic where it was not already on the rail. He also believed that hopelessly uneconomic railway activities needed to be radically cut in order to reduce the wholly unacceptable level of losses they were generating. With a hint of the naivety that sometimes characterised his public utterances, Beeching speculated that it might not be necessary for him to argue the case for certain closures 'since the need would be self-evident'. If he thought that by presenting apparently incontrovertible evidence about loss-making services and then proposing their closure he would avoid opening up innumerable cans of worms, he was badly mistaken.

To his credit, Beeching never said that the railways were without a future. This distinguished him from the more rabid elements in the road lobby and numerous influential politicians and senior civil servants. However, he made it clear that the medicine he would prescribe for the railways' ailments would be unpalatable for those who wanted them to continue in the same old way forever. The losses continued to mount up. In 1960 BR had an operating deficit of over £67 million; in 1961 one of £87 million and a nadir reached in 1962 with £104 million. The pro-road lobby made much of this. Arguments that long-term underinvestment made it hard for the railways to compete with the roads cut no ice with taxpayers or users of their frequently rundown, slow and unreliable services. It was too easy to portray funding for the railways as good money being thrown after bad.

Beeching began implementing organisational and structural changes to ways of doing things that he despised. He despised them for being revered and perpetuated for no better reason than because they were familiar and long-established. He was putting into effect practices that would be central to the BRB in its role as successor to the BTC. His recommendation for three replacement new full-time members of the BTC was readily accepted by Marples. Three senior figures from commerce and industry replaced three with a background in transport. Beeching and Marples were bullish about such individuals arguing that they had the proven business and commercial experience which qualified them to run public transport, especially the railways, effectively. Not everyone agreed. For example, the appointment of Philip Shirley, chairman of Batchelor Foods and a man with a background in accountancy, incurred ridicule when he was nicknamed 'the frozen pea man'. He proved to be highly disruptive with his tendency to stray into areas outside his jurisdiction and to fall out with colleagues. Outside appointments had their supporters, however. The *Financial Times* on 18 August 1961 described them as 'The Men to put the Railways Right'. Improvements in management performance and the streamlining of administrative procedures were a vital and valuable part of Beeching's plans for the reshaping of the railways. Beeching was determined to gather around him people he was sure would break down what he saw as outdated and entrenched attitudes towards railway management and operation. He created a hand-picked clique, many from outside the industry, who were wedded to his own ideas. The drafting in of 'outsiders' from commerce and industry understandably generated anger among many with a lifetime in the railway industry. The maverick professional railwayman Gerard Fiennes, then of the Eastern Region, was supportive, however. As usual finding himself in a minority among his peers he described railwaymen as 'an enclosed order, far worse than the Benedictines ... inbred, inward-looking'. Even if not all Beeching's appointments were top-notch, the introduction of new people unsullied by the attitudes endemic to many career railway managers almost certainly transformed the railways' approach to business operations and management practices for the better.

Beeching's tidy mind could not tolerate the labyrinthine BTC structure and he quickly set about abolishing many of Robertson's committees and subcommittees. Typical of the practices which gave the impression that the BTC was a cosy gentleman's club was the booking each week of ninety first-class sleeping berths on overnight trains carrying Scottish Region managers to and from meetings in London. Such practices had to go and they did.

The auguries were not good for the BTC. Freight traffic was in sharp decline, the deficit was growing, the government was becoming increasingly sceptical about the Modernisation Plan and industrial relations were rancorous. These all made the BTC vulnerable. They came at a time when Conservative governments were increasingly questioning the performance of the nationalised industries and the railways in particular. The financial failings of the railways were grist to their mill. Egged on by the road lobby, they used them as 'proof' that nationalisation was a flawed concept.

The responsibilities handled by the BTC were to be allocated to new boards all of which would be expected to break even 'taking one year with another'. The creation of the BRB and abolition of the BTC allowed the former to concentrate on matters concerning the railways. The issue of unprofitable but socially necessary services was recognised but remained unresolved until Barbara Castle as Minister of Transport later officially instituted the notion of subsidies for 'socially necessary lines' in national transport policy.

The BRB was given powers to develop surplus land, an area of activity likely to grow where many valuable sites were now becoming surplus to railway requirements. Some saw this as defeatism, as recognition that rich pickings could be made out of the contraction of the railway system rather than seeking to win new traffic.

An early thrust of the Beeching era was a five-year plan to rationalise and modernise the railway workshops. There were twenty-nine workshops and their regional disposition reflected the fiefdoms of the Big Four companies of pre-nationalisation days and had no logicality in the conditions of the 1960s. There was over-capacity given the continuing reduction in locomotives and rolling stock but it angered railway employees that so many contracts for the building of new equipment were going to private sector manufacturers and that even those BR workshops thought to have a long-term future were not allowed to tender for contracts with outside business.

The BRB employed a new tougher and uncompromising policy towards job losses. Gone were the days when the BTC under Robertson seemed happy to get together with the unions to negotiate a gentlemanly agreement offering something to everyone involved. Now the BRB tone concerning redundancies and the terms and conditions involved became far more peremptory. This soured industrial relations in the industry as shown by the one-day strike called around the issue. The unions, realising that they were facing a far more hard-nosed employer consequently began to dig their heels in. Now the BRB's new initiatives all tended to be seen as threats.

Dr Beeching was not known for his sentimentality. It was typical of the problems facing him that the Western Region was probably the most popular, with large numbers of enthusiasts who were indeed sentimental. They liked the Western Region because as far as possible it had staunchly gone its own way since nationalisation, attempting to maintain continuities with the old GWR. This independent spirit was evident for example in its insistence on hydraulic transmission for its new main line diesel locomotives as opposed to the electric transmission of the locomotives being built for other regions. Many of these diesel-hydraulic locomotives had Great Western-style numberplates and nameplates. A highly attractive but retro chocolate-and-cream livery was introduced for the carriages on its crack expresses. Unfortunately this flamboyancy did not extend to the operating and commercial aspects of the region's business. Its trains were notorious for their unpunctuality and frequently for their slowness. Its account books were equally notorious for the losses they recorded. In the push for greater efficiency across the system as a whole, such quirks could have no future and Beeching was the man to unearth and uproot them.

In October 1962 Beeching, in an address to the Institute of Directors, alluded to railways developing at a time when the horse and cart were used as feeders and distributors to and from the railway. This necessarily meant that the consignments handled had generally been small. The railways of the mid-twentieth century inherited a legacy of fairly short-haul operations in wagons of low capacity usually needing to be expensively sorted and re-marshalled en route, often several times. Such operational practices conflicted with the natural advantages of rail in handling regular bulk flows of traffic over long distances with low unit costs. Road haulage had seized much of this small consignment business for which they were well suited and BR was left with a residue of loss-making traffic which road hauliers did not want to bother with but which the railways could not legally discard. This obligation, he made clear, was totally outdated. It greatly disadvantaged the railways and had to be abolished if their financial difficulties were to be tackled.

Initially the process facing Beeching seemed to be a simple one. Commission a nationwide comprehensive traffic study and process the data obtained. Next, present the findings to the public. However, it was obvious that many people would find these facts unpalatable. Recommendations to curtail unprofitable services would inevitably elicit criticism and opposition. Marples had the job of trying to make the railways financially viable. Beeching was answerable to Marples and was required to analyse the statistics on railway usage and recommend measures which, if implemented, would in his opinion make the railways pay their way. Both men would undoubtedly be seen as the villains of the piece but they were working to a brief agreed by Parliament which was the body ultimately responsible for whatever actions would be taken to try to bring the railway finances under control.

Macmillan, concerned about damage limitation on the incendiary issue of railway closures, had already expressed his opinion that Beeching was '… better at making plans than at getting them across'. He wanted quick action on railway losses but with his acute politician's radar he fretted about the possible electoral repercussions if his government was blamed for serious cutbacks in the railway system. He wanted the Conservative Party to be seen as the facilitator and guardian of the increasing general prosperity which was a feature of the so-called 'post-war boom'. A reduction in the size of the railway system would inevitably entail large-scale redundancies and was likely to be electorally damaging. Figures of 30,000 job losses among railway workshop employees within a year and a 100,000 operating staff over time were mentioned. It is clear that Marples was also well aware of the implications. Upbeat as ever, his response was that: 'It is going to be a time of crisis – but a time of crisis really is a time of opportunity.' In a scenario of sustained economic growth it would require transferring workers from a declining industry such as the railways to virile new industries. It was essential to portray proposed changes on the railways as playing a positive role in the process whereby what was old and outdated was replaced by new initiatives that encouraged economic growth and rising living standards. Marples expansively told Macmillan that his strategic plan for the next eighteen months would 'cover rail, road and the rebuilding of our cities'.

Handling the industrial relations dimension worried Macmillan especially when the National Union of Railwaymen (NUR) threatened a national strike over the workshop closure issue and he feared that the public might sympathise with the strikers. Marples took the offensive with an interview in the *News of the World* claiming that the new redundancy scheme for railway employees was five times more valuable than its predecessor. A continuously nervous Prime Minister wanted him to go further, using TV and that autumn's Conservative Party Conference to put his case across. He also urged Marples to consult Iain Macleod, the experienced, wily and ebullient Party Chairman and Leader of the House of Commons, as to the best way to proceed. Marples was clearly concerned to pour oil onto potentially troubled waters and he arranged three meetings with Beeching, even hosting a lunch for him and George Woodcock, the cerebral general secretary of the TUC. Faced with the very real threat of a one-day rail strike, Marples in October 1962 apparently attempted to solve the rail dispute live on television during a debate with Sydney Greene, the leader of the NUR. Macmillan privately deplored Marples' action but felt that he had to support his minister despite calls from the *Daily Mail* and the *Daily Express* for his resignation. On 27 June 1962 in an Opposition Day debate, Marples was in whimsical mood: 'The leader of the deputation said to me, "If they killed a man in 1830 for opening a railway, what are they likely to do to you in 1962 for closing railways"?'

Replying for the Opposition, George Strauss emphasised the difficulty of predicting the social consequences of closures and the danger of going ahead with a wide programme of closures unless these possibilities had been more fully investigated. He said: 'Neither the Labour Party, nor the railway unions, nor anybody else has opposed in principle the closing of stations or branch lines where there is a strong case for doing so. Obviously there is always local opposition, which should be heard … we recognise the necessity for closing many lines which are used by few people and which are wholly uneconomic. However Dr Beeching is contemplating something quite different. He has said – the same thing has been echoed in ministerial speeches – that everything that does not pay should be shut down – never mind the social consequences; they are not his responsibility; somebody else must take care of those. I do not know, any more than the Minister or anybody else knows, what the consequences will be.'

Macmillan was sensitive to the Strauss argument. He wanted to shape public perception regarding the future of the railways and he urged Marples privately that if, for example, the government deemed a line from Inverness to Wick to be needed on social grounds, Beeching should quote a price and the government should pay it.

Neither Macmillan nor Marples thought that pushing through an extensive programme of railway closures was going to be easy. The most rabid opponents of closures were those who were convinced that the government was totally hostile to railways and was hell-bent on going ahead with a massive cull of lines and services while peremptorily sweeping aside any opposition. It was never as simple as that. Politicians crave the gaining and retention of office and have to find ways to assuage public opinion or at least to make the electorate believe that their views are being taken into account. Marples was acutely aware of this and made much of the existence of the TUCCs. These were presented as neutral adjudicators, their job being disinterestedly to examine objections based solely on the possible hardship which would be caused by the implementation of a closure scheme. Where hardship was identified they would make proposals to the minister in question to alleviate it. This included the provision of adequate public transport alternatives.

Many people believed that the function and purpose of the TUCCs had been changed specifically to expedite the process of railway closures. During the 1950s they had received proposals for the withdrawal of passenger services from some 3,000 route miles. Many of these closures had been unopposed. At the time the questioning of closure proposals had generally been far less vehement and systematic. In the 1960s, however, faced with better informed opposition to the increasing number of closure proposals, the government had changed the rule book of the TUCCs to disallow many kinds of opposition and to speed up the whole closure process.

A major criticism of the system was that the ultimate decision on closure lay exclusively with the Minister of Transport. There were cases where assent to closure was given even when a very strong case had been made that hardship would result. Although under the Transport Act of 1962 questions regarding the financial case for closures were no longer allowed at TUCC hearings, Marples must have known that there were many determined and skilled objectors around always likely to pick embarrassing holes in the quantitative evidence put forward in support of closure proposals. To elucidate the arguments for closure based on statistics, or, some would say, to provide impressive obfuscation, Marples took on Sir Robert Hall, until recently the government's chief economic advisor.

Through the autumn of 1962 BTC press releases hammered home its principal point on the redundancy of large parts of the railway network. It also began presenting a new argument, wishing to be seen as positive – that some 90 million tons of freight carried annually in longer-haul road journeys might be winnable for the railways. Macmillan, however, continued to worry about the political fallout from railway closures and early in 1963 established a powerful ad hoc committee of the Cabinet chaired by R.A. Butler to oversee the Beeching proposals, now imminent. While Marples was naturally a member of the committee, its formation represented a significant curtailment of his influence. The Prime Minister's continued niggling anxiety over the public reception to the Beeching proposals had taken concrete form.

This setback brought out the best in Marples. He was determined to shape the thinking of the committee, leading with a detailed review of closure proposals that had come before TUCCs, published as *Summary of Past Referrals of Proposals for Closure of Rail Services to TUCCs*. An individual proposal for closure could take anything from four to ten months to be processed and the backlog was only likely to increase in 1963 and 1964. He sought to reassure Cabinet colleagues that after initial resistance to closures, people eventually realised that they could manage without a line or a particular station. 'This pattern,' he soothingly suggested, 'has been repeated over and over again.'

On New Year's Day 1963 the Transport Act passed into law vesting the assets and liabilities of all the nationalised industries in the newly-designated boards, previously mentioned. For all the anticipated collateral benefits, Marples' focus was firmly on the financial state of the railways. He saw them as the heart of the problem, pointing out that in the previous year their gross receipts were £478 million and their expenditure £546 million. This left a loss of almost £70 million on revenue account alone, representing 15 per cent of turnover.

By 26 February 1963 Marples had seen most of the Beeching draft, reassuring Macmillan that: 'It is the most comprehensive analysis ever made of the problems, weaknesses and potential strength of our railways.' In conjunction with modifications and improvements to the road system, he predicted that the way would be opened for a coordinated transport system. The ad hoc committee was less than impressed, noting that the text contained a large number of closure proposals for which no economic case had been made. Noble, as ever snapping at their heels, was determined to publish his own statement on the prospects for the railways in the Highlands.

On 14 March, Butler reported to Cabinet concerning the second meeting of the ad hoc committee. He told them that *The Reshaping of British Railways* meant substantial service closures but it also contained positive proposals and the prospect of eliminating the annual deficit of about £150 million. The government should endorse plans to make freight transport more efficient and seek to clarify the 'delicate question' of staff redundancy. Ministers commented that while there would inevitably be protests, the government should emphasise that the report was intended to make a positive contribution to the economic well-being of the country; that ending losses would facilitate modernisation for road and rail alike; that the extensive existing network of bus services should be energetically publicised; that the number of TUCCs might need to be increased to expedite the process; and that closure decisions should be announced in groups and not on a piecemeal basis. Marples was directed to bring a draft of his proposed parliamentary presentation to the following week's Cabinet.

Ever alert to the public impact of radical government announcements, Macmillan believed Beeching's report might be the moment to commission a complementary report on the roads. This, he felt, would create a sense of fairness that it was not just railways that were under official scrutiny. He urged this upon Marples, reminding him that he had previously seen the Beeching Plan as 'the first step towards an integrated plan for transport as a whole'. Cabinet met on 21 March to consider a new draft of Marples' statement, which now emphasised a general policy of coordinating all public transport. There would be coordination between the BRB and London Transport; no statutory hindrance to accelerating the TUCC process; closures would be considered and decisions announced on an area rather than an individual basis. This proved insufficient to avert a revolt; ministers insisted that adequate alternative transport should be available before rail services were cut – the very requirement Marples had tried to forestall. Ministers sought to make a clear distinction between an uneconomic line that was maintained for social reasons and those closures approved that were conditional on the provision of alternative public transport. It was clear that bus services needed improvement. Marples was directed to redraft his statement in collaboration with the Chancellor and to speed up the process for Scotland and Wales. His fifth attempt turned out to be the final one.

With publication of the Beeching Report looming, attention turned to public relations management. Anxiety was most acute over relations with the unions. Knowing Beeching's tin ear, Marples persuaded him not to give formal notice of any of the proposed passenger closures for four weeks after publication of the report, by which time the Commons debate would fall due. There would need to be consultations with local authority associations, bus and road haulage interests and associations representing major industrial concerns. The workings of the TUCCs would require streamlining and making more efficient.

For publicity purposes, the Ministry and the BRB proposed to work closely together, covering national and regional news outlets. A BRB film would be shown to railway employees and offered to the BBC. Copies of the Beeching Report would be distributed to staff down to district officers (about 4,000) but a proposal to provide every railway worker with an individual summary was abandoned. The Ministry of Transport produced a fact sheet for lobby journalists. Granada Television would network a programme on the railways and a panel of backbench MPs would be briefed and be available for appearance on regional television programmes. Marples himself, and the Chief Whip, would address backbenchers on the eve of publication and provide a brief for use in speeches. Even the Parliamentary Labour Party was offered facilities.

Finally, on 27 March 1963 Marples presented the Beeching proposals to the House of Commons. *Modern Railways* described his performance as 'abysmal'. He had earlier briefed six daily newspapers on what was to come. He told the House that the proposals offered a major contribution to the government's plan for providing an efficient, economic and well-balanced transport system. One observer waspishly noted that no such plan existed. On Macmillan's advice Marples proffered assurances on the security of freight services and to passengers and other interested parties on the robustness of the consultative processes. He assured the House that he would take account of important social considerations and changing industrial patterns. He was immediately criticised for making it appear as if the closure of a third of BR was a foregone conclusion. He also managed to make the Conservative government's approach to the railways appear as blindly dogmatic as Labour's stance on nationalisation, as described by the Conservatives back in 1948. To give Marples his due, he emphasised that Beeching had been brought in to do a *job*. The responsibility for the commissioning of the Beeching Report and the implementation of its recommendations lay with the government and him as appropriate minister.

For the Opposition, George Strauss was remarkably conciliatory. He congratulated Beeching on 'a very able Report ... lucid, comprehensive and well-argued'. He extended his 'whole-hearted support' while lamenting Beeching's scant attention to the results: road congestion, new road building as well as the possible social consequences which could be many and problematical. The new Opposition Leader Harold Wilson was far more robust and bullish, depicting Beeching as a tool of the government, one which had outstayed its welcome. He chose to trace Tory responsibility back to 1953 'when they started the disintegration of the transport system'.

To judge from the arguments advanced during the Commons debate by MPs against the proposals as a whole or closures in their own constituencies, even Marples found it hard to justify a number of the projected closures. There was the revelation, for example, that whereas the Ayr to Stranraer line was losing £66,000 a year, it would cost at least £530,000 to bring the local main roads up to the required standards to be an effective substitute. It emerged that in Devon the road bill to cope with the rail closures might be as high as £46 million. Critics of Marples were not slow to point out that this was likely to make much work for the road construction industry.

With that demanding occasion behind him, Marples visited the Prime Minister on the afternoon of 16 April. Their meeting was unusually long, lasting two hours. Macmillan recorded: 'He really is a remarkable figure and I only wish we had more ministers with his imagination and thoroughness.' Marples seems to have ranged over the whole field of transport policy, forecasting a figure of 18 million cars on British roads and predicting that the problem would not be so much on the roads between the towns but in the towns themselves.

Full debates in the House followed on 29 and 30 April when Marples welcomed the Beeching Report as the culmination of three years' work responding to a cultural shift which had witnessed a threefold increase in personal consumption on private travel by road. There had been an enormous and sustained swing to road transport, both freight and passenger. Even the most entrenched of Beeching's opponents should have been able to recognise this and accept that the government had to take some sort of action to deal with the situation.

He sought to put *The Reshaping of British Railways* into context: it would be followed by the Hall Report on the *Transport Needs of Great Britain in the Next Twenty Years*, the South-East Study, the London Traffic Survey and conurbation studies produced in cooperation with local authorities. Marples wished to rebuild cities to accommodate the car but recognised the thorny dilemma of how to reconcile people's individual desire for the freedom that cars brought with wider issues about pollution, congestion and road safety, for example. He stressed that wherever appropriate, bus services would replace withdrawn trains but he failed to mention that there was no statutory requirement for these services to continue if the bus operator could not make them pay. This accorded with his view expressed elsewhere that the problems caused by a passenger service closure were quickly forgotten. Marples had a manner which even irritated people in his own party when, for example, he derided the nature of some of the objections submitted to TUCCs regarding certain proposed closures. He pointed out that many objections were lodged by people who did not even live anywhere near the line under consideration. This rather cavalier attitude failed to take into account the fact that some of the objections might come from holidaymakers and day excursionists who made habitual use of lines to seaside resorts, for example.

For the Opposition, Strauss now urged delay, pending a comprehensive analysis of overall transport needs in the UK. He viewed the Beeching Report as: 'an accountant's report rather than an economist's one' dealing 'only cursorily' with the social problems involved. Political interference, he urged, had put the railways, already struggling to compete with roads, into the red, especially when a large profitable part of the nationalised BRS had been sold off. The 1962 Act, he argued, was folly for severing buses from trains, literally dis-integration. On Beeching himself, Strauss remained cautious – 'an expert, whom we all respect'. He even thought of him as an appropriate person to oversee Marples' other proposed transport studies. While the large government majority could see off Strauss and the Opposition, the ensuing debate featured a long sequence of Conservative 'Knights of the Shires' lamenting the likely impact of the Beeching Report on their own constituencies. Careful planting of points to placate backbenchers by Marples' civil servants had had little effect. Sir John Maitland (Horncastle) deplored the inadequate roads of Lincolnshire; Henry Clark (Antrim North) and John Brewis (Galloway) were concerned about Ulster and Scottish railway lines feeding the Larne-Stranraer ferry service; Sir David Robertson (Caithness and Sutherland) was appalled at the proposed loss of so many Highland railway services. Robert Matthew (Honiton) felt the same about Devon and the Member for Truro likewise for Cornwall. Robert Mellish (Labour, Bermondsey), who always enjoyed baiting Marples about Marples Ridgway, wanted a Roads Board, charged with taking over the company's road building contracts. Noble, who had his own more private doubts, replied on the first day but left many more questions for Marples on the morrow.

On 30 April Wilson opened for the Opposition in rumbustious form, though he exonerated Beeching: 'he was told to apply surgery in a situation where surgery was not the ... answer ... the surgery has preceded the diagnosis'. Closures there would have to be for 'no one wants to perpetuate the railway map of the 1860s, a map which shows the results of Tory private enterprise run mad'. But 'to close one sector of the railway system affects all the others' and 'it is totally wrong to base a decision on a narrow obsession with railway accountancy'. Wilson saw weakness in the consultative proposals, doubting the impartiality of a minister who repeatedly declared his intention of closing two-thirds of the railways. 'What will he do to solve this problem when he has closed one-third of our railways? Will he build more motorways?' This was the central flaw, for Beeching was merely doing what Marples and Macmillan had intended all along. Wilson portrayed Marples as an over-ambitious minister and echoed the call for a pause pending an economic assessment. He did not, however, offer any cogent alternative in the form of research into the true economics of all inland transport based on cost-benefit analyses which could have formed the basis of a flexible and efficient national transport policy.

The Chief Secretary to the Treasury, John Boyd-Carpenter, brought his department's traditional take to the debate, noting 'there are only 122 miles of track where the railway service is not already paralleled by an existing bus service'. Such a statement starkly revealed his lack of knowledge of the realities of the public transport situation in rural areas. He found no merit whatever in the 'public transport as necessary social service' argument. However, the Conservative complainants continued with F. Blackburn (Stalybridge and Hyde) lamenting road accidents, Sir Arthur Vere Harvey (Macclesfield) and Sir Alexander Spearman (Scarborough and Whitby) on northern deprivation, plus John Macleod (Ross and Cromarty) and David Webster (Weston-Super-Mare). The latter observed a double deprivation: 'The motor road service will finish at the south end of my constituency which is almost completely cut off by this report.' Julian Snow (Lichfield and Tamworth) and Bryant Godman Irvine (Rye) also weighed in, joined by the MPs for Dorset North, Dorset West, St Ives and Tiverton.

Rising to reply, Marples had a lot of ground to cover but opted for ebullience, embracing 'the heavy responsibility' of having to decide on closures'. He took encouragement from Monday's *Times* leader: 'What has been exposed is that, of several horses backed by the Minister of Transport, one has far outpaced the field. The London traffic survey, Buchanan on environment, Jack on rural transport, Rochdale on ports, Hall and Crowther on long-term transport – each has contributed or will do to new and necessary thinking on Britain's transport problems. Only Dr Beeching has produced a plan of action, ready to be carried out.' The House divided comfortably enough, defeating the Opposition amendment 323 to 248 and resolving 'That this House welcomes the Report of the British Railways Board on the Reshaping of British Railways as a major contribution to the development of a sound and well-balanced transport system for the country.' As yet no Conservatives were ready to break ranks.

The next day (1 May), the action moved to the Lords. Viscount Mills, a party to the creation of the Stedeford Committee, recalled that it was three years since the Prime Minister had announced the intention to remodel the railway system, lift the financial burden and raise the public esteem in which the railways were held. He thought that *Reshaping* was an excellent report and praised Marples for selecting Dr Beeching whose 'drive and energy' facilitated such a thorough examination of the problems confronting the railways. Lord Hailsham, like Mills, defended Marples against 'ungenerous attacks', praising 'his determination to reduce the casualties on the roads' and hailing him as 'one of the most valuable figures in our public life'. He declared: '... if we were to defer the implementation of the proposals in the Beeching plan until such time as we had completed a generalised inquiry into transport ... we should have to wait until Domesday'. He continued:'... the danger is the force of inertia behind our economy ... one of the greatest dangers from which we suffer at the present time'.

The Opposition's Lord Stonham had spotted discontinuity. He rebuked the government benches: 'But, if it is the same plan, why is it then that in 1955 it was accepted almost without demur but in 1963 it has occasioned anger – anger cutting across party barriers; anger deeper and more widespread, in my opinion, throughout the country than almost any domestic issue during the last twenty years? In fact, the only pleasant comment I have heard on the Plan is the advice to use Dr Beeching's face cream because it removes lines ...'

Debate raged in the papers, among the travelling public and doubtless among others whose ignorance concerning transport and railways in particular was boundless. The journalists who produced eye-catching headlines and wrote supporting articles did not necessarily know any more about the subject than the bulk of their readers. Some of the debate, however, was better-informed. For example, a correspondent to *The Times* pointed out that a 6-ton tare oil-engined lorry covering 30,000 miles per annum carrying a 10-ton load paid a tax then six times less than that paid by the owner of a 1-ton private car covering 8,000 miles a year. This was stark evidence of how road-damaging heavier vehicles were effectively subsidised by car owners. He also pointed out that all road transport users derived benefit from the ratepayers' partial underwriting of the cost of roads, lighting and traffic control. He appealed for what would now be called 'a level playing field' where the various types of road user were concerned.

On 7 May 1963 Marples informed Macmillan that Beeching had met the negotiating committee of the NUR and apparently persuaded them that it would be impossible to implement his plan without redundancies. *The Times* of 10 May 1963 reported that the NUR had settled the date for a strike but had called it off on being offered better terms for their members who would lose their jobs. Beeching was apparently worried about seeming to retreat under union duress, but the Prime Minister was sufficiently alarmed about Beeching's handling of the NUR to urge Marples to raise it at the next Cabinet meeting. Privately, Marples himself worried his boss still more. Prompted by the Chief Whip's fears of how Marples might handle the political implications of Beeching, Macmillan wryly noted that it might be as well to 'remind Mr Marples of the existence of the Cabinet Committee on the Reorganisation of the Railways'. In fact Marples – who was not expecting the first TUCC cases for two or three months, planned an early report to this committee (due on 30 May) and he was already anticipating the arrival of the Buchanan and Crowther Reports. These tensions were not resolved. The next month Macmillan learned that ministers were having difficulty getting the necessary statistics on rail closures. 'This is wrong,' he told Marples on 10 July 1963. A rift began to open between the old allies with Marples protesting that ministers did not need information about closures that were merely possible as opposed to definite. Macmillan, however, thought that these were equally as important as information about definite closure proposals.

On 19 June Marples lunched with officers of the RHA and the Tory Transport Committee. The RHA had generously welcomed the Beeching Report although deeming it insufficiently comprehensive. It was opposed to any railway subsidy whatsoever, being disinclined to endorse the view that railways might have a future and was therefore suspicious of new investment in the railways. It viewed with alarm the diversion of funds from the roads budget to new projects arising from Beeching's railway plans. On 3 July, the Committee on Reorganisation of the Railways, on Butler's recommendation, spawned a sub-committee with a specific remit to 'advise the Minister of Transport on particular proposals for railway passenger closures'. Later, Marples minuted that he and Macleod were agreed that this new body would operate where there were clear political, social or economic issues arising from the distances involved or where another minister had pressed a course of action on him and he could not agree. During the summer of 1963 the Ministry was convulsed with anguished discussions about how to handle growing public unease over prospective service withdrawals. Ministry civil servants pressed the traffic commissioners (who had no constituents to worry about) to prepare maps showing regular weekday bus services but they encountered great reluctance to proceed with this proposal.

Late in July 1963 a doughtier opponent weighed in. This was the Scottish Secretary, Michael Noble, once again. He submitted a brief but powerful memorandum on closures north of the border: he had found discrepancies in the Board's figures and he urged delay. The nub of the problem was a conflict between ministers and the Board over what level of financial information it could practically provide. When they did not receive information or as much as they wanted, they thought it was being withheld. Tempers cannot have improved when the Committee at its 1 August 1963 meeting concluded that board forecasts of the impact of savings were 'on the optimistic side'. An interdepartmental committee on the Beeching Report went further, concluding bleakly that the railways would still be in substantial deficit by 1970. It warned that much political capital might be consumed in pursuit of this uncertain financial outcome.

Wider events now intervened. On 4 June, the War Minister, John Profumo resigned, having belatedly admitted his affair with Christine Keeler. This was the fuse that ignited a fire that would burn slowly beneath the Conservatives and help Labour into office the following year. That summer, scandal filled the air. British newspapers, obsequious just five years earlier when Eden resigned, threw caution to the winds in the era of *Private Eye* and *That Was The Week That Was.* High society parties, some no more than orgies, dalliances with prostitutes by male scions of the supposed social elite and defence leaks offered a bottomless reservoir of salacious and scandalous news. Macmillan, who had perhaps panicked the year before when sacking one-third of his Cabinet, had to demonstrate that he was still firmly in control and he commissioned the famous Denning Report which enquired into the security aspects of Profumo's actions. By the end of July Denning's work was done. Macmillan confided to his diary his expectation that Denning would 'condemn one important and one unimportant minister (or rather, fail to clear him of scandalous conduct)'. The 'important' minister is thought to have been Duncan Sandys (conjectured to be the 'headless man' in a widely publicised photograph) and the 'unimportant' one to have been Ernest Marples. He had fallen far in the Prime Minister's eyes in a bare four months. Marples was under increasing pressure to mitigate the impact of closures even though he had foreseen the societal consequences many of his Conservative colleagues had not seen or had chosen to ignore. Moreover, though unknown at the time, Macmillan's premiership had but a few weeks to run. When it ended, Marples' difficulties could only increase.

Dropping the pilot

The familiar tale of the autumn 1963 Conservative leadership crisis does not belong here. Briefly, Macmillan, feeling his powers waning, had contemplated resignation several times during the summer, even discussing with confidantes a possible October departure. By 7 October he was quite ill, presiding with difficulty over the Cabinet meeting of the following day. His prostate was enlarged by a tumour and his surgeons were taking no chances, removing it three days later. By then the Queen knew he was going but this was the least of the government's problems. Because the crisis had erupted during the annual Conservative Conference the succession battle became an unseemly public spectacle. When the Foreign Secretary Earl Home emerged as winner, a rejuvenated Labour Opposition led by the highly able Harold Wilson was gifted a perfect opportunity. However it was a Tory, Iain Macleod, whose interpretation endured. Macleod's waspish denunciation of the 'magic circle' of Old Etonians who had manipulated Home into office set the scene for the next twelve months in politics.

For Marples, Home's accession was ambivalent. He was an established minister, appointed in the afterglow of Macmillan's 1959 election triumph. He had seen through a massive and largely successful reorganisation of transport. He had not figured in the 1962 'massacre' of Cabinet members carried out so ruthlessly by Macmillan. The stricken Prime Minister may have once had a possibly exaggerated opinion of Marples' ability' but this esteem seemed on the wane. Marples' new chief (who renounced his peerage and eventually entered the Commons as Sir Alec Douglas-Home) had noisily and immediately lost two ministers (Macleod and Enoch Powell) and wished to lose no more. While Marples had been one of ten Cabinet members naming Home as first choice to lead, the capable Macleod had led the Cabinet Committee on the Reorganisation of the Railways, interpreting his role expansively.

The new Prime Minister, a poor match for the supple Wilson in the television age, lacked Macmillan's self-assurance. He fretted over the election prospects from which he had until recently been so far removed. In any case there had to be an election no later than October 1964. Worse, the Beeching closure proposals were now arriving thick and fast: each one would be scrutinised, by ministers and MPs alike, in the light of this impending date.

The changed atmosphere is disclosed in a memorandum from Tim Bligh, now principal private secretary to the new Prime Minister. Bligh implicitly recognised that Home would need time to establish himself with the public which meant a delayed general election; there was also the sensitive matter of Macleod's successor as chairman of the reorganisation committee. By the end of October Bligh anticipated a 'rethinking' of transport policy, eliciting this response from Home: 'Yes, I very much doubt whether we can or should move faster unless it is possible to provide alternative transport which will be seen to work.' The next day Bligh informed the Chief Whip that the 'whole question of transport policy' was now up for consideration. Marples had experienced wobbles by Macmillan but having suffered a nasty shock in October the party was now in a cautious mood. Home's response was to set up a new railway reorganisation committee which met for the first time on 2 December. This was chaired by Lord Blakenham, Chancellor of the Duchy of Lancaster and Deputy Leader in the Lords.

The fate of this committee is interesting. It met just once before being dissolved the next day with its functions taken over by the Road and Rail Transport Committee. This single encounter reveals how far the terrain had shifted away from Marples. It considered just three items: closure proposals for the Woodside to Sanderstead (Surrey) and Pyle to Porthcawl (South Wales) lines; a report, commissioned by Marples, on financial information provided to TUCCs; and the timetable for passenger service closure proposals. The TUCC reaction to the Surrey closure proposal evoked a cynical response in Marples. It deemed as hardship what was to him mere inconvenience. His reaction was to propose a two-year deferral on the grounds that he had recently rejected another London TUCC recommendation and that the just published Buchanan Report had emphasised public transport development, leaving the government open to attack for inconsistency. Even this was not enough for the Road and Rail Transport Committee which extended the deferral to three years and directed the Ministry of Transport to consider raising fares to the economic level in order to see what the market would bear. The Porthcawl service was, as Marples warned, the first of up to fifty lines serving holiday resorts that would come up for consideration. Lord Blakenham directed the committee to consider them as a 'species'. Marples was dismissive of the impact of railway closures on business at seaside resorts, arguing that the vast majority of visitors already arrived by road and that increasing numbers could be expected to do so in the future.

Now on the defensive, Marples turned to an eminent and very senior auditor for a view of what should be disclosed to TUCCs. Sir William Carrington's report concluded that it would not be appropriate to provide them with profit and loss statements, that the information currently supplied was adequate and that the basis on which financial information was provided was sound. More information, he said, would only confuse TUCCs and the public. Every effort should therefore be made to 'remove public misunderstanding' of the methods by which information was supplied. This very much sounded like the prelude to a policy of official obfuscation. Marples must have been pleased because he had commissioned Carrington as a defensive measure but he still had to endure being told that station receipts were not necessarily a true guide to the earnings of a given service. Marples may have been gratified but *The Times* was not. It thundered that no trust should be put in any facts and figures produced by the Ministry of Transport or the BRB which related to a closure proposal going before a TUCC. Ministers themselves wanted full projected profit and loss information yet this was being denied them. Meanwhile regional boards were occasionally divulging the very information TUCCs were blocked from obtaining. Faced with a surviving recommendation from Macleod to bring forward closures, the matter was deferred. Now TUCCs faced objections to no fewer than 129 proposed closures.

After a three-week delay, surprising in a minister who was wont to respond to his old chief the same day, Marples sent Home a seventeen-point memorandum at the end of November attempting to put into context the behaviour of TUCCs. 'They are not there to look at the board's case for closure, just hardship for users. They cannot recommend that I should consent to or refuse closure.' Home was undeterred, conjecturing that if an economically justified main line closure was deferred on the eve of a general election 'accusations of electioneering would swamp the merits of the case'. This fastidiousness had not troubled either his predecessor or the Opposition leader and required Marples to soothe his new chief: 'unless you are thinking of a very late date [i.e. for an election], I would not see much difficulty in arranging the timing as you suggest'. The Prime Minister was worried about main lines but even local closures were contentious and could be electorally damaging in marginal constituencies. One MP, Sir Richard Glyn (North Dorset), wanted the BRB to give the line through Gillingham over to 'us' for running as a private enterprise and fretted about local protest meetings three to four hundred-strong. Glyn wanted no main lines shut until the impact of branch closures had been assessed.

On 16 December, Home convened a meeting of Marples, the Chief Secretary to the Treasury and Selwyn Lloyd, who had returned to the Cabinet as Lord Privy Seal and Leader of the House. Home suggested delaying the programme 'for a short time'. This time Marples resisted, reiterating that it was for the BRB to determine the economic merits of a closure and that the TUCC role was confined to demonstrating hardship. It was Lloyd who grasped the issue, identifying three contentious issues on the railways: lines to seaside towns; lines whose operations did not meet costs; and closures within large conurbations. The seaside lines should be given a reprieve until 1964 to see if they could pay their way. Lloyd went further, arguing that it was futile to ask TUCCs to demonstrate hardship since this was plainly occurring and replacement bus routes through densely-populated areas were not 'a politically acceptable alternative'. The TUCC process did not engage with the problems really at issue and risked being perceived as a 'swindle'. For the first time, a ranking Cabinet member was questioning a key provision of the 1962 Act. Home prevaricated, suggesting a further meeting and asking Marples what he could do to avoid panic about closures while remaining within the statutory framework. He confided to Reginald Maudling, the Chancellor of the Exchequer, in a memorandum that the whole question of the railways might have to return to the Cabinet for further consideration. (Maudling had continued as Chancellor when Home succeeded Macmillan). Therefore, 1963, which had opened as the vindication of Marples' tenure of the Ministry of Transport, ended in some disarray and with questions being asked.

Chapter 14

The Beeching Report

*T**he Reshaping of British Railways*, better-known as the 'Beeching Report', was succinct and clinical, rather like its compiler. It was direct, even blunt, although refreshingly free from 'spin'. It came in two parts, not published simultaneously. Part I consisted of sections tersely called 'Report' and 'Maps'. This appeared on 27 March 1963.

The Report contained a 'hit list' of passenger services and stations proposed for closure. Many people, not necessarily those sympathetic to railways, were stunned by its menacing comprehensiveness. Maps supplemented the lists, showing where the 'axe' was poised to fall. If closure was enacted, sizeable swathes of mainland Britain would be without railways. The lists and maps initially gave the impression of an industry condemned to drastic contraction. A careful reading of the whole text, however, indicated that there was a positive intention to invest in those parts of the passenger system which offered worthwhile financial returns. A number of developments were envisaged for parts of the non-passenger business. The emphasis was on the absolute necessity to adopt a modern commercial approach. Discarding what were hopelessly uneconomic activities, the railways should concentrate on what they could do best. A leaner, more efficient and modern system would take the railways into the future.

The response in some quarters verged on the hysterical as Beeching was lambasted for coolly setting out to destroy Britain's railway network. Among railway enthusiasts, regular railway users and even those members of the public who rarely or never used them there was a feeling that the railways somehow should always be there. This was sentimental and unrealistic but large numbers of people were affronted by the Report and Beeching was vilified as the man determined to destroy the railways. This was understandable although a somewhat mistaken reaction. The purpose of the Report, evident in any close reading, was not to destroy but to reshape Britain's railways with the intention of ensuring their long-term survival. Additionally, Beeching was merely formalising a process which had been going on for years. Between

1950 and 1962 inclusive, over 300 branch lines had closed and 174,000 railway jobs had gone. Beeching analysed a serious problem and proposed a radical solution. It was up to Parliament to endorse or to reject his findings. The process was initiated by a Conservative government which then accepted the Report and approved in principle the drastic measures it proposed. In Opposition, Labour produced some pertinent criticism and implied that the 'Beeching Axe' would be stilled if it came to office. Nevertheless, when Labour returned to government in October 1964, it accepted most of Beeching's rationale and continued implementing closures some of which were highly controversial.

It was evident from the data supporting the Report that substantial parts of the railway system were hopelessly uneconomic. The income generated by traffic on many lines, passenger and/or freight and minerals, did not cover the expense of maintaining the track and signalling let alone the cost of running the trains. Railways have high fixed costs because of their specialised and exclusive permanent way combined with low unit costs where traffic operates in regular and dense flows. Beeching argued that the railways were not playing to their strengths and were carrying much traffic for which they were not the most suitable option. That traffic and those lines and stations that did not cover their costs could not have a long-term future if the railways were to become financially viable. It was essential to ensure that existing lucrative types of traffic should be operated as efficiently as possible and that efforts should be made to attract suitable new and potentially profitable traffic. Judicious electrification of lines with the best earning potential was desirable and operating methods needed to be thoroughly modernised on those parts of the system with prospects of a long-term future. Management and administrative structures required radical overhaul and needed to be operated around much more commercial criteria. This positive element of the Report aroused far less attention than issues concerning closure.

Much of the information in the Report made unpalatable reading and roused argument and criticism from the start. Although other data was also used in compiling the Report, a nationwide traffic survey had been carried out over one week ending 23 April 1961. Beeching denied that this was the only basis on which closure proposals were made. However, the survey took place at a time of the year that gave a misleading impression of passenger usage, especially to leisure destinations such as popular seaside resorts. The line to Skegness, for example, might be used to saturation point at times in the holiday season but be little-used in April. This was just one of many sources of contention in the major furore that ensued. The existing methods used to identify the costs and losses generated by particular parts of the business were known to be primitive and the conclusions frequently incomplete and inaccurate. Opponents of Beeching saw behind him a pro-road government determined to make huge cuts to the railway network and to use any means at its disposal to do so.

The Report informed its readers that a figure of 6,000 paying passengers per week using a branch line would not generate sufficient income to cover even the cost of the train movements. Many branch lines never saw a figure anywhere near 6,000 weekly passengers. It was revealed that if there was no freight generating some additional income a branch line would probably need about 17,000 paying passengers per week in order to break even. What future could such business have?

Beeching identified longer-distance stopping passenger services and the majority of branch line passenger trains as hopelessly uneconomic and argued that they, with the stations operating them, needed to be systematically culled. The revelation that half the route miles of the network carried just 4 per cent of the traffic came as a great shock. Of Britain's railway stations, 50 per cent produced only 2 per cent of passenger receipts. Even the use of diesel trains provided no panacea for unprofitable services. Gleneagles to Comrie and Thetford to Swaffham were just two examples where new diesel trains led to considerably increased usage but not enough, apparently, to put the lines into the black. Nationally, thirty-four stations produced around 25 per cent of total receipts. An astonishing 50 per cent of the system did not generate sufficient revenue to maintain the track and other infrastructure. Seasonal holiday traffic was a major loss-maker despite such trains frequently still being packed. This part of the business would be run down. Of 18,500 main line passenger carriages, only 5,500 were in use throughout the year. Most of the rest were only used at peak holiday weekends and otherwise were stored, earning no revenue while still requiring maintenance for those few occasions when they were actually used. Expensive non-revenue-earning movements were required to shift empty stock to the places it was needed to handle peak demand. Beeching estimated that this fleet of under-used carriages cost nearly £3.5 million annually to maintain but generated only about £500,000 in income. It was proposed to eliminate most of this rolling stock and the summer seasonal trains in 1965. It was asserted that fewer than 25 per cent of holidaymakers now used rail to reach their destination.

A total of 5,000 route miles and 2,263 stations out of a total of about 7,000 were recommended for closure. Long-distance passenger traffic, however, especially on inter-city routes, was mostly profitable and could be modernised and improved to encourage more usage. Closing poorly-used intermediate stations on main lines would help to speed up non-stop trains from which more money could be generated. Outside the south-east, commuter services were, at best, marginal but a case could be made for integrating them with other forms of public transport and doing so with local authority involvement. The Report disconcertingly made it clear that London's intensive and heavily-used suburban network provided insufficient profit margin to justify the new investment it desperately needed as off-peak travel was in decline at that time. Across the country, services on lines that basically duplicated each other needed to be eliminated.

Wagon load and sundries freight traffic made huge losses. The average goods wagon performed only forty-five miles of revenue-earning work per week. Freight trains consisting of non-continuously braked wagons should be eliminated urgently as being hopelessly uneconomic. Over half of the goods depots produced less than 3 per cent of BR's income from freight handling. There could be no justification for retaining so much loss-making business. Closing these depots and drastically reducing the huge fleet of under-utilised wagons would achieve considerable savings.

Block trains consisting of wagons with considerably greater capacity should deliver coal to concentration depots and power stations. The coal handling facilities at small stations should be eliminated. There was a need to persuade unwilling major customers such as the NCB and the Central Electricity Generating Board to cooperate in changing their practices in order to handle larger wagons. The evident reluctance of different nationalised industries to work together was gleefully seized upon by those with an antipathy to State ownership. Coal merchants, many of whom operated on a purely local and small-scale basis, were also extremely reluctant to cooperate in the operation of larger wagons. They wanted to continue with 10-tonners. These were ideal for them, being small enough for their contents to be emptied within the forty-eight hour period BR allowed before 'demurrage' clicked in. This was the charge that BR imposed as a fine for lateness where a customer held on to a wagon, effectively making it unavailable for use elsewhere.

BR handled large quantities of milk, giving this perishable commodity priority to be moved in special trains at express passenger speeds. It did the job well but it was symptomatic of the changing times that grubby-looking, unrefrigerated milk tankers could not compete on image with smart modern-looking chilled road vehicles hurtling with their milk up and down Britain's expanding motorway network. Traffic in perishables had no place under the Beeching regime and BR was determined to get rid of what was becoming unprofitable business. It did so with little finesse. For example, the fish traders at places like Fleetwood and Grimsby were told that the transit of fish by rail was being run down. It was posed it in a very brusque 'take it or leave it' fashion and when it was unsubtly suggested that they make their own arrangements, not surprisingly, the traffic was soon going by road.

Beeching believed that there was great potential in developing what were then known as 'liner trains': bi-modal rail and road traffic providing door-to-door transport for containerised merchandise. These were to evolve into the highly successful Freightliners, transporting containers. The long-distance haulage of these containers was by rail and lorries took over for the short-haul to and from the customer. Beeching was enthusiastic about 'block trains', freight services designed to suit individual companies who could guarantee sizeable and regular flows. Block trains moving commodities like aggregates for road-making, coal on a 'merry-go-round' basis and oil in bulk should be encouraged as should trains carrying new road vehicles. The road lobby was unhappy about Beeching's enthusiastic advocacy of bi-modal container business. It believed that road haulage should have a monopoly of the inland transportation of container traffic.

Beeching also made it clear that the remaining steam locomotives needed to be eliminated as soon as possible. This cut many railway enthusiasts (and others) to the quick and further contributed to the way in which the man was demonised. All too often they ignored Beeching's argument that by eliminating the outdated, inefficient and unprofitable parts of the system and by concentrating on that business for which the railways were best suited, a viable network with a future could be created. In the storm caused by the publication of the Report, the optimism regarding the future of parts of the system was largely lost and there was a widespread perception that the whole exercise was one of negativity and disinvestment. In the Report Beeching explained that while very high fixed costs were associated with the provision and maintenance of railways, this mode of transport permitted the safe movement of dense flows of high-capacity trains with very low movement costs per unit conveyed. Beeching saw a great future for such operations but this optimism was largely lost in the anguished debate about passenger service closures.

Beeching was assailed with a tsunami of criticism for daring to prescribe such drastic medicine for the railways but also for perceived inconsistencies and anomalies within the Report. *The Reshaping of British Railways* quickly became referred to as the 'Beeching Axe', synonymous with butchery. *The Times* commented tartly that Beeching had been appointed by the government to sort out its greatest loss-maker and report to a minister whose interests lay with redirecting resources into road transport. The writer of a letter to the editor of the *Stockport Advertiser* of 29 June 1961 commented, 'Let us hope that Dr Beeching will move in the right direction ... he must remember that any moron can stop a concern losing money by closing it down: the clever man makes it run at a profit.' At the same time, some commentators pointed to the irony that the Report was published at a time when the uncontrolled growth of road transport was clearly generating a host of almost insoluble problems, not least the environmental impact of motor vehicles in a crowded island. If Beeching's recommendations were implemented in full, would they go some way to addressing these issues?

A host of organisations and individuals attempted to question, criticise and counter aspects of the Report, or even the whole thing. Some concentrated on arguing against individual closure threats, but no matter how much resistance there was it was no match for the lobbying power of organisations such as the RHA.

Amazingly, Marples was apparently pleased with the overall tone of the media coverage. The only newspaper that unequivocally criticised the Report was the Communist Party-supported *Daily Worker*. Both Marples and Beeching later admitted to being disappointed with and surprised at the extent of the hostile reception to many specifics and the Report in general. In their different ways both men thought that the essence of the Report was irrefutable. Ironically, there was much vocal opposition from Conservative MPs who had agreed with the principles of the Report and supported it in Parliament and then opposed specific closure proposals which affected their own constituencies. Such MPs, especially in marginal constituencies were anxious to retain their seats and unblushingly put their career interests before party policy. As a general election became imminent, Marples rejected a number of closure proposals and this was political expediency rather than the development of a coherent strategy for the future of the railway industry. Such tactics annoyed those civil servants and railway managers who wanted the closure programme to go through quickly. They also annoyed Dr Beeching.

It is interesting to note that whereas the public criticised Beeching for what they thought he did to the railways, workers in the industry itself blamed Marples. In the 1960s, rundown and filthy steam locomotives could be seen adorned with slogans such as 'Marples wants stuffing' and other sentiments, often more indelicate.

G. Freeman Allen in the editorial for the May 1963 edition of *Modern Railways* commented on Beeching in his usual level-headed way: 'Despite the staring headlines of "bombshell" which greeted it, there are few shattering surprises in the Beeching Plan. Anyone with ears to hear and eyes to read all that has circulated this past year on the state and the future of B.R. can have expected no better than the document's remorseless statistics prove and no less than the surgery proposed to rectify the situation. Unpalatable some of the harsh economic facts may be, but arguable they are not, after one has followed the clear, close reasoning that makes this probably the frankest, most convincing treatise ever produced on railway problems – would that the 1955 Modernisation Plan had been founded on similar realism and economic research in depth! ... The country now knows in fine detail where its money to sustain the present B.R. system has been flooding down the drain and that in future, if it wants trains, it will have to pay at least the full cost of their service in rates and fares. It has no such information about its roads and their users, without which there can be no rational transport policy.'

Freeman Allen argued that the appraisal to which the railways had been subjected should be extended to roads and internal air services. Very presciently, he said that not to do so 'may result in the precipitate elimination of some railway facilities which a broader appreciation of national transport facilities might later show should have been retained'.

Certainly there were anomalies in the Report. Beeching admitted that suburban services around London and the south-east were expensive to operate and, although they carried growing numbers of passengers at peak times, they were only marginally profitable at best. Why then did services in that area emerge almost unscathed where other heavily-used suburban services in the provinces such as Liverpool to Southport and Manchester to Bury were proposed for closure? The reasoning behind the financial problems of these commuter services around the big cities was that they suffered from heavy peak-hour demand which was expensive to provide since much passenger stock was only used during the rush hours. At other times the trains were frequently underused. If this applied to suburban services generally, why then so few proposed closures put for London's network?

Elsewhere, how could a town the size of Mansfield in Nottinghamshire be threatened with the total loss of its passenger services? Some tiny rural communities with ill-used stations were granted a reprieve from closure on the grounds that hardship would be caused. How was it that Prestatyn, a town with a population of at least 10,000, was proposed for closure when many tiny, little-used halts on the Cambrian Coast line to Pwllheli emerged unscathed? Was it seriously proposed that the lightly-used lines to remote places such as Kyle of Lochalsh, Wick and Thurso would actually close, depriving vast swathes of Scotland of their trains? A cottage industry appeared overnight preoccupied with picking holes in the Report and denouncing and deriding Beeching and all his works.

Beeching seemed uninterested in the reduction in costs that could be made by downgrading a line to fall within the 'basic railway' category. He saw the costs of running a line as largely fixed irrespective of the amount and nature of its traffic. Of course simplification of infrastructure and operations might bring about useful economies but they were unlikely to turn a service making a great loss into a profitable one. He seemed dismissive of the 'basic railway' concept and this emphasised the negative reasoning that many people thought permeated the Report. Another criticism concerned Beeching's apparent failure to consider the economic and social changes which were starting to exert an enormous influence on the United Kingdom. An obvious one was the changing situation facing the coal industry. Beeching saw this as an area of business to be developed by the modernised railway whereas demand for domestic coal was already diminishing as was the demand from heavy industry, much of which was in long-term decline. Beeching could not have foreseen that road congestion would, decades later, become chronic enough to lead to a remarkable growth as passenger traffic was effectively forced back to many of the railways which had survived the earlier onslaught. These comments can be made with hindsight. The brief Beeching had to observe precluded concern with wider social and economic developments that might or might not occur in the future. He stuck to that brief but the narrowness of his remit provides valid criticism of the rationale underpinning the Report.

The method of crediting income only to stations where traffic originated was widely criticised. This meant, for example, that Birmingham Snow Hill gained all the income from the considerable number of passengers booking there to travel for holiday purposes to, say, coastal resorts such as Aberystwyth, Barmouth or Pwllheli. Beeching was seen as dismissive of the smaller seaside resorts and some inland holiday centres such as Keswick. In 1962 BR stopped collaborating with holiday resorts for advertising purposes. Ill-feeling was generated by official statements claiming that the railways serving many resorts were loss-making and that the future of seasonal traffic was under review. The Association of Health and Pleasure Resorts was greatly alarmed but attempts to avert the withdrawal of most summer-dated traffic fell on deaf ears. Some resorts, of course, lost their railway services completely, Ilfracombe and Bude being examples.

Also controversial was the issue of the traffic and revenue contributed to main lines by the minor lines with which they were associated. Contributory revenue might be hard to quantify with exactitude but the Report seemed not to take account of this when considering the closure of a line. Take the St Ives to St Erth branch. It is likely that the majority of its passengers would have changed at St Erth into or out of trains on the main line for Plymouth and points east. St Erth itself was too small to generate much traffic. Passengers travelling to or from St Ives and Penzance by public transport would be likely to have gone by bus. How much more business would trains on the Cornish main line have lost had the St Ives branch, which was relatively well-used although allegedly loss-making, actually closed? Similar questions could be asked about the Alston to Haltwhistle, Amlwch to Gaerwen and Langholm to Riddings branches, for example. It is likely that few passengers who had previously changed at the junction to and from main line services would drive to that junction station once their local service was withdrawn. They would be far more likely to do the whole journey by road and the fares they had previously generated would be lost to the railway.

Bernard Hollowood, writing in *Punch* (23 August 1967) made clear his opinion of Beeching: 'Lord Beeching is praised by many for his ruthlessness. He was given a job of making the railways pay, and to this task he applied precisely the same tools that he would use to make a cosmetics company pay. His recipe was to cut out all uneconomic lines. Simple, but utterly naïve and in callous disregard of the convenience of millions. He could make the hospitals or schools pay by similar methods.'

There can be little question that some people suffered when a line, even one which was little-used and hopelessly loss-making, was closed. Journeys previously taken for work, to school or college, for leisure purposes, or visits to hospital, for example, would have to be taken by car, taxi, bus or not taken at all. Some people, particularly non-drivers, in effect became marooned in their own localities. This had a very harmful impact on the life of many rural communities. Railways were part of the social capital. While the well-to-do with their own cars were hardly affected, there were poorer people faced with little option but to migrate to towns and cities. Their homes might be bought up by commuters with cars or for use as second homes and this impacted harmfully on the stock of affordable living places in the district. Local shops, pubs and schools could all go into decline. A settlement where increasing numbers of houses were occupied by those who were essentially outsiders could lose its sense of community life and be priced out of the range of ordinary people. Some people were convinced that it was unspoken government policy to force people to use cars.

The Gloucester to Chalford shuttle service was withdrawn in 1964. The Railway Reinvigoration Society conducted a survey of former users of the service. A large number of them described the replacement bus service as highly unsatisfactory, being slower, more expensive, less convenient for the carrying of shopping and luggage, often overcrowded and frequently late. More than 70 per cent of the respondents said that after the withdrawal of the services, they used other trains much less.

A perception developed and embedded itself that BR did not necessarily tell the truth when putting forward a case for closure. One example will suffice. This concerned the ex-Great Central Railway passenger service from Manchester to Hayfield on the edge of the Peak District. One reason officially advanced for closure was the state of a tunnel near New Mills Central at the beginning of the Hayfield branch itself. Insufficient income was being generated by this service, it was alleged, to justify funding expensive but necessary repairs to this tunnel. When the line closed in 1970, the track remained in the tunnel. Trains which had previously gone on to Hayfield now only went as far as New Mills Central and then ran empty into this tunnel to await time to run back into the station and then return to Manchester. Also when the case was being put forward for closure of the service, it was airily stated that commuters and the significant number of hikers who used trains to Hayfield at weekends would simply detrain at New Mills and use buses to Hayfield. They did not.

Writing in *Last Trains*, Loft (2014) saw the Beeching Plan as not simply a set of proposed railway closures but a commentary on the wider situation in which the United Kingdom found itself in the mid-twentieth century, facing the hard realities of relative decline and the need to reinvigorate the economy. Seven years after Suez, the British public was aware of but resentful about the UK's reduced world power and status. Intense self-absorption led to various nostrums being proposed for arresting and reversing the negative trajectory of Britain's place in the world. Paradoxically, these years saw rising living standards for many and the expansiveness that private motoring brought about. While there were ardent modernisers who would have liked to see the railways, once themselves the epitome of modernity, virtually swept away as relics of the past, others plumped for an essentially reactive response from which emerged what we can now see as the beginnings of the 'heritage industry'. This reaction to the painful descent from greatness involved turning much of Britain into a commemoration, even reconstruction, of an imagined happy but largely illusory past with the nasty bits taken out. An idyll was created referring to the days, perhaps centred on the mid-nineteenth century, when it was thought that Britain had been truly great. For many, nostalgia was preferable to facing the uncomfortable changes and challenges that seemed to be piling up. Britain was a nation losing its way and beating itself up, part of it wanting, albeit fearfully, to recognise relative decline and embrace modernity while hankering to preserve what were seen as the best artefacts and practices associated with the country when it had been at the supposed height of its powers. Railways, and especially steam railways and quaint country branch lines, were among these things.

In this clash of the old and the new, the Beeching Plan encapsulated the paradoxes of the period and was the focal point for a meeting of conflicting forces. The modernisers argued that science and technology could and should be applied to make the world a better place. What was dirty, old-fashioned and inefficient had to be swept away. This included back-to-back and other jerry-built life-expired terraced housing, trams and trolleybuses, 'dark, satanic mills', architecturally eclectic and vulgarly pretentious Victorian buildings and, of course, the steam age railway. Then in with the new – fast arterial roads, motorways, town centres adapted to the needs of motor vehicles, high-rise housing, overspill estates on peripheral greenfield sites, and so it went on.

Loft again: 'The battle over railway closures was first and foremost a political struggle between those who saw the threatened lines as worthwhile social services and those who felt the nation could not afford them. In order to win that battle the government adopted tactics which were effective in the short term but which fuelled suspicion and resentment over time – limiting debate, withholding information, erring on the side of closure. This conflict took place at a time when the romantic nostalgia for the disappearing rural railway co-existed with enthusiasm for modernisation…'

Other evidence of attempts to restore some vitality and sense of direction included the debate about the UK joining the Common Market and the creation of the National Economic Development Council which met for the first time in 1962. This was very much a creature of its times, an economic planning body to bring together business management, trade unions and government to identify and plan measures that would tackle Britain's relative economic decline. 'Planning' was the buzzword. It was easy to draw up plans but less easy to implement them given that Britain was part of a world economy dominated by the unpredictable vagaries of the so-called free market. Other received wisdoms were the need to control public expenditure and to move the nationalised industries towards more commercially orientated methods of operation. Clearly the Beeching Plan fitted into this wider scheme of things by scrutinising the business conducted by the railways, identifying strengths and weaknesses and drawing up a plan for the role they could play in a changing and challenging scenario.

In political terms the Conservative government was clearly on borrowed time by 1963. It wanted to be seen as having fully embraced the modernisation which was such a buzzword at this time but instead it looked like what it was, a tired and beleaguered government. Not all its leading lights were exhausted, however. Marples knew that there were votes to be had for a party seen to be supporting road users and from those who wanted tax cuts to give them more spending power. Such people, and there were many of them, resented what they saw as their taxes being poured into the bottomless pit of an outdated railway system. Marples was well aware, however, of the rub. There were substantial numbers of voters, many of them Conservatives, who had an attachment to railways and did not want to see the network being substantially reduced either in their own constituencies or more widely. In the run-up to a general election, an adroit touch was sorely needed in order to steer a successful path through these and other conflicting pressures.

By contrast, the Labour Party, headed by the astute and energetic Harold Wilson promoted the scientific agenda, 'the white heat of technology' and looked like the party of the future. The negative impressions of the Tory government were only strengthened in October 1963 when Macmillan had resigned as Prime Minister for health reasons and been replaced by Home As Sir Alec Douglas-Home the negative image of Toryism was intensified by this man so easily caricatured as a cadaverous-looking, hidebound aristocratic throwback. He could not help his looks but he did not possess the skills required for his new role. He seemed to lack the sense of the urgent need to create a modernised Britain that was essential for a leader taking his party into what was likely to be a difficult general election. By contrast, the Labour Party had a 'young' leader. Wilson was 'only' forty-six. He was an example of the new meritocracy free from the cronyism and old boys' network image of the elite of the Tory Party. Wilson seemed much more in accord with the prevailing optimistic dreams of the benefits that 'out with the old and in with the new' and technology, innovation and increasing generalised affluence would supposedly bring with them.

No calculation was made of the extra costs which would have to be carried by road transport as a consequence of the withdrawal of railway services. While the Report argued that many parts of the railway system were not covering the direct costs of their maintenance, the same could be said of many roads. This was because the operators of the largest and heaviest lorries were not paying in licence duties and fuel tax anything like the full cost of the damage their vehicles inflicted on roads, buildings and other infrastructure. It added insult to injury that by not paying a more realistic contribution to the costs of their operation, hauliers were able to charge their customers prices that undercut those of the railways. Roads were expensive to build and maintain, especially when used intensively by heavy goods vehicles. The BRB produced a report in 1964 with the title *A Study of the Relative Track Cost of Rail and Road Freight Transport over Trunk Routes*. This claimed that much of the cost of new roads could be saved if they were not designed for heavy vehicles, the cargo of which would go instead by rail. The report argued that axle-loading rather than unladen weight should be used to estimate the damage done to roads by heavy goods vehicles and that axle-loading should be a major yardstick when it came to deciding rates of taxation for such vehicles.

The view expressed in this report was not welcome at the Ministry. Marples was somewhat stung by arguments of this sort put forward by those demanding a level playing field for the railways and earlier, in October 1963, he had appointed a small committee under Lord Geddes, who was a ship owner, to enquire into the commercial road vehicle licensing system. Its report, published in June 1965, involved, among other things, checking a sample of 15,000 lorries and revealed an appalling situation in which many lorries were not only grossly overloaded but the loads themselves were often unstable and potentially hazardous. If this was not bad enough, it was clear that in the haulage industry there was large-scale evasion of limitations on drivers' hours and of safety regulations concerning the vehicles themselves. It was evident that there were many cowboy operators and that the industry needed to be far more scrupulously regulated. Problems have continued to this day around these issues.

The Reshaping of British Railways, Part 2

Part II of the *Reshaping* was individually titled *The Development of the Major Trunk Routes* and did not generate the attention accorded to Part I. It was published on 16 February 1965 by which time a Labour government had replaced the Tories. It stated, rather baldly, that the realistic choice being faced was between 'an excessive and increasingly uneconomic system, with a corresponding tendency for the railways as a whole to fall into disrepute and decay, or the selective development and intensive utilisation of a more limited trunk route system'. A map was produced indicating 'Routes selected for development' and this elicited negative responses. There were many lines still extant which were missing from this map. Railways designated as worthy of development were absent from north-west Scotland; from Wales west of Swansea and elsewhere; and from north Devon and north Cornwall, for example. While there were many other lines on the map, critics jumped to the conclusion that if they were not for 'development' (marked boldly in black) then they had no long-term future. On this basis trains would cease to run in Wales except as far as Swansea; there would be no trains west of Plymouth; East Anglia's only line would be from London to Norwich and the East Coast Main Line would terminate at Newcastle. No wonder this map gave some people palpitations!

The ostensible purpose of this exercise was to identify duplicate trunk routes left over from the largely unregulated competition of the second half of the nineteenth century. Cutting out some routes designated as 'duplicate' would make for more economic utilisation of those that remained and allow resources to be allocated to those lines which were best placed to produce the highest returns, given that money for investment was likely to continue to be limited. The ex-GWR route from London Paddington to Exeter via Westbury and Taunton and the ex-SR line from London Waterloo to Exeter via Basingstoke and Salisbury were cited as examples of lines competing for much of the same traffic. Despite reassurances that a route not selected for development was not necessarily one marked for imminent closure, the map was widely viewed as evidence that official intentions were to move to a greatly slimmed down system, perhaps of something like a mere 3,000 route miles. In *The Organisation of British Railways*, Michael Bonavia (1981) explained that a similar exercise of identifying the parts of the system most worth developing was mooted back in 1949 when road and rail integration were still on the agenda but no progress was made at that time for various reasons. He argued that had such a survey been made and acted upon, the post-war history of Britain's transport system might have been very different. By implication the crisis that developed on the roads and railways in the 1950s and 1960s could have been avoided or at least mitigated.

The identification of a network of lines to be developed was based on estimates of sustained economic growth, population increase and the winning of new traffic especially in the oil and aggregates sectors and with the liner or freightliner concept. These estimates proved to be over-optimistic and could not have been expected to take account of the mass closure of primary industries in the 1980s and 1990s such as coal and iron and steel which had traditionally provided so much business for the railways.

There was much criticism to the effect that the Beeching 'remedy' was fundamentally flawed because he analysed the railway system in isolation from other forms of transport. This, it was alleged, made a mockery of the principles of transport planning on a national scale. The man was reviled but he did the job required of him. This was to produce recommendations for radically improving the economic state of the railways. As Loft (2013) says, '… all Beeching did was to put forward for closure those lines which were, in his view, irretrievably unremunerative'. He could possibly be criticised for some of the theoretical underpinning of his recommendations but the actual implementation of those recommendations was not within his remit. Beeching never had the power to close railway lines. Wider issues were not his concern. If blame has to be apportioned it should be remembered that it was a Conservative government which commissioned the Report and produced the parameters within which Beeching was required to operate. Typically of him, he did not stray beyond those parameters whatever his private thoughts might have been.

A pertinent question in relation to the Report, however, was how to reach an objective means of ascertaining the costs of running any particular stretch of railway since every line was a component of a national network and the closure of any component of the system was bound to have an impact on others. From the day of its publication, doubts were expressed about the validity of the statistics supporting the Report. As the *Observer* acerbically commented on 31 May 1963: '… these intricate costings of branch lines and slow trains have been a precautionary exercise, with a high propaganda content … an important object has been to influence politicians and public'.

Beeching brought an accountant's approach to railway finances and it showed, for example, in the way he did not accept that some unprofitable lines should be kept open to meet unquantifiable but identifiable social need. He probably thought of this idea as messy. With extraordinary artlessness, in 1964 he told a bemused reporter, 'People who can afford to choose won't motor between the main centres of population. They don't now and they won't in the future.' The Report contained a map of stage carriage bus routes and regular express services. This may have been included to give the impression that there was a vast and intensive network of existing bus routes which could easily be utilised by those passengers displaced by the closure of railway passenger services. It was extremely unhelpful because it provided absolutely no information about the frequency of the routes shown. Some of these may have been routes perhaps running only once a week on market days. There were services that were even more infrequent. Beeching's expressed opinion that buses could be a cheap and effective substitute for withdrawn trains probably struck him as a neat solution but was highly naïve and in practice 'bustitution' was messy. Most replacement buses could not easily handle prams nor much in the way of passengers' luggage. Rail replacement bus services were frequently withdrawn after a short time, greatly reducing the quality of life for former passengers who did not have cars but had a need to get about. This was messy for them. There was no statutory requirement for the continuance of rail replacement bus services if few people used them. Inevitably, those whose passenger trains were taken away largely rejected buses, bought cars and turned their backs on railways. There is some evidence that the mere threat to withdraw a service was sufficient to persuade some of its users to make alternative travel arrangements. It would not be unfair however to say that the public took the railways for granted. It was comforting to know that they were there even if they were not used. The newspapers were full of indignant letters addressed to their editors. Even people who admitted that they had not travelled by train in years gave the impression that the threat to close their local line was some kind of personal slight and that they would be severely put out if the closure actually took place.

The passenger-carrying mileage of the railways contracted by 5,700 route miles from 1962 to 1970 and the inhabitants of many often sparsely-populated parts of the country were largely deprived of access to rail transport. Some saw this as a victory for the pro-road lobby happy to force people onto the roads if they needed to travel any distance. No attempt was made to subject the cost of the congestion, injuries and death on the roads, the physical damage done by heavy goods vehicles or the impact of environmental pollution created by road vehicles to similar quantitative scrutiny. Jeremy Thorpe of the Liberals warned the House of Commons against the danger of examining railway policy in isolation from other modes of transport. This, he said, would be 'like a judge making up his mind on the evidence of one expert witness'.

Political pragmatism

Ernest Marples approved most of the closure proposals submitted for his consideration by the TUCCs. Among these were some where there was irrefutable evidence that hardship would be caused. These included the lines to the remote coastal town of Whitby. In February of the election year 1964, Marples conceded that that no lines serving seaside resorts would be closed until the holiday season was over. Roads might have been on the rise and railways on a downward trajectory but politicians remained politicians anxious as ever for the spoils of office. Marples applied a politician's pragmatism to the need to rein back on closures, at least until his party had won the election. The Tory government had run its course and many Conservative MPs were worried that its association with railway closures would prove damaging electorally. Macmillan had earlier attempted to propitiate the unions by ensuring generous payouts to workers made redundant when closures were implemented. This could be seen as little more than a short-term electoral ploy.

Closures Marples refused to sanction in 1963 included Haltwhistle to Alston and Woodside to Selsdon. Others followed including the Central Wales Line and Manchester to Buxton in 1964. Marples was under considerable pressure from MPs of his own party concerned about the damage that might be done to their electoral chances by many of the closures. This sudden conversion of some fellow Tory MPs to questioning the wisdom of closures when they had enthusiastically supported the Beeching Plan in Parliament was simple political legerdemain. Beeching, for his part, deplored such action as unprincipled and based on nothing more than electoral expediency. Evidence that closure proposals could be contentious and politically damaging came in December 1963. A byelection took place at Dumfries and a Conservative majority was cut from over 7,000 to less than a 1,000, the proposed closure of the Dumfries to Stranraer line being a major issue. Loft suggests that Beeching was pressurised to moderate announcing further closure proposals in the run up to the 1964 general election. With his clinical mind and singleness of purpose, it must have irked him deeply to find himself being used as a pawn in political manoeuvrings.

In a speech in March 1964 Harold Wilson stated that the Labour Party's policy was to halt the main programme of closures pending a national transport survey which would relate to planned regional and national expansion and the needs of a national integrated transport policy. Critical to this policy was ensuring that road haulage would not be allowed to cream off the most profitable traffic. This too was legerdemain. To the disgust of the railway unions and others, the incoming Labour government of 16 October 1964 with its majority of only four and despite its pre-election promises, seemed no great friend of the railways. However, again for political purposes it slowed down the closure process, hoping that when the time was right it might call another election and obtain a much larger majority, riding at least to some extent on an apparently more supportive view of the railways. The new Prime Minister, Harold Wilson, was an extremely wily politician, untroubled by principles and, having obtained that larger majority in the election of May 1966, he was happy to act pragmatically.

To return to Whitby, it emerged from the furore around closures to be served by just one line, that to Middlesborough, with a service so infrequent as to deter potential users. Two major routes, the Somerset & Dorset and the Great Central were clearly being run down, seen as 'duplicate' routes. Wilson had to perform a balancing act. The Treasury and many taxpayers who were also electors wanted closures enacted to reduce the losses being made by the railways. Other taxpayers and voters were hostile to specific closure proposals or closures in general. Wilson himself wanted to be seen as a 'moderniser' and part of the modernising agenda was to adapt the role of the railways to fit the challenges of the changing times.

Railway Magazine accused the Labour government of pandering to the trade unions and the TGWU in particular. This union had a huge membership in the road transport and automotive industries and was a very major influence on Labour's income and policymaking whereas the unions representing railway workers had a much smaller membership and significantly less weight in the Labour Party. Ideologically, it might have been expected that Labour, in theory a party in favour of socialist and collectivist solutions, would be sympathetically inclined towards forms of public transport such as railways. In practice there was little evidence at this time of such sympathy.

MPs were lobbied, councils and trade union delegations went to see the Minister of Transport, objections, many eminently reasonable but some plainly ridiculous, were submitted to TUCCs. Research was undertaken and scathing articles written, some merely hysterical but others cogently argued, criticising individual closure proposals or the whole tenor of the Beeching Report. Unflattering effigies of Beeching were paraded and even burned when closures took place and direct action was undertaken when, for example, protestors padlocked level crossing gates against the passage of the last train on the 'Waverley Route' in the Scottish Borders. Of course there were some lines that were reprieved but many people felt they were powerless in the face of forces that were determined to decimate the railways. The particularly contentious closure of the Oxford to Cambridge line generated no less than 1,300 written objections but still went through. This service had not even been recommended for closure in the original Report. Statistics claiming that the saving made by closing 5,000 miles of passenger services was the equivalent of just four days' worth of defence expenditure cut no ice in official circles. Lord Stonham, a Labour peer, produced figures arguing that the total costs associated with road usage amounted to a net subsidy of over £600 million a year, this being four times the annual deficit of the railways. Such revelations did not lead to a reappraisal of the closure process. At a time when 'planning' was the buzzword, the proposal to close services often made a mockery of local and regional planning initiatives. The Oxford to Cambridge line passed through the area designated for the new city that was to become Milton Keynes. Other 'new towns' whose stations were threatened with closure included Corby, Cumbernauld and East Kilbride.

Some serious gaffes were made in closure proposals. In December 1964 the secretary of the Welsh TUCC was provided with official figures supporting a proposal to modify the stopping passenger services between Chester and Holyhead. He was told that the annual movement costs of this provision were £687,400 but he was able to show that these figures were based on the cost of using steam locomotives. The replacement of steam on this service was imminent and shame-facedly the figure was reduced to £505,400. While this may not have been enough to save these trains, it did, of course, cast doubt on other figures produced by the authorities in support of proposals for modification and closure of services.

The method of dealing with closure proposals through the TUCCs became increasingly cumbersome and long-winded as objectors became more sophisticated but it was all too easy to see the laid-down procedure as designed deliberately to discourage informed objections at least partly by withholding or manipulating relevant information. Of course if BR provided detailed information in support of a case for closure, it made them vulnerable to those increasingly skilled objectors who enjoyed unpicking and publicising shortcomings in official information, even if such efforts were not considered relevant to the proceedings of the TUCCs. If they did not provide such information they opened themselves up to accusations about being secretive and conspiratorial. It was easy to be cynical about the whole process when Beeching in a press conference in March 1963 had loftily dismissed the efforts of objectors. While admitting that closure proposals produced strong emotions he assured those present that those emotions died down quickly once closures had been implemented.

Beeching and freight

It was the proposals to close passenger services identified as loss-making that aroused so much opposition to the Beeching Report. What Beeching said about the freight business generated much less controversy. The closure of large numbers of goods depots, over 2,000 in 1963–1964 alone, went ahead so smoothly that it almost seemed as if the public was unaware of this aspect of the changes or that such facilities even existed. These closures were a vital part of the necessary rationalisation that was taking place and contributed greatly to the economies and improvements in efficiency. The general tenor of Beeching's recommendations on BR's freight business was positive and forward-looking, giving the lie to those who consider him as little better than the destroyer of Britain's railways.

The problems facing the freight business in the early 1960s were dire and needed drastic action. Much freight handling had hardly moved on from Victorian times and was chronically outdated and inappropriate for the middle of the twentieth century when road vehicles and the haulage industry had reached such a level of sophistication. It seemed almost as though railway management could not or would not recognise the hopelessly uneconomic nature of so much of its freight handling activity. Many small goods stations received less than one wagon per week. Most wagons ran less than twenty-five loaded revenue-earning journeys per year. The average length of a wagon's journey was only about sixty-seven miles (the advantages of freight transport by rail generally accrue the greater the distance involved).

Coal traffic was marginally profitable but minerals, general merchandise and small consignments made thumping losses.

Less than 40 per cent of coal was carried in through train movements to large customers such as the Central Electricity Generating Board. Regular bulk trainload traffic was the sort of business the railway could handle well and economically. Typically, however, a loaded wagon of coal would be 'tripped' from colliery to sorting sidings and then marshalled into a longer-distance train. This would eventually arrive at a large yard, often on the fringe of a conurbation, whereupon it would be sorted into another trip working which would then deliver the wagon to the customer, probably a domestic coal merchant in a small coal yard serving its immediate vicinity. Some of these yards handled very small quantities of coal. There were about 5,000 coal yards and between them they received just over 28 million tons annually. The busiest coal yards, numbering about sixty, each received over 50,000 tons annually. The small yards had to go and Beeching recommended the establishment of around 250 coal concentration depots. Most small coal merchants did not like the disruption to their hallowed ways of doing things. Beeching was scornful of the typical small capacity and non-continuously brake fitted coal wagon and urged the use of larger, braked wagons that could run at considerably higher speeds and which soon saw the light of day in the successful so-called 'merry-go-round' operations conveying bulk coal to power stations.

In 1961 traffic categorised as 'mineral and merchandise' earned £109.3 million but together it failed to cover its direct costs by over £24 million and its total costs by more than £57 million. Enormous losses were being made on the approximately 59 million tons of wagonload freight. There were over 5,000 facilities at which such traffic could be handled but just 855 depots dealt with 78 per cent of the traffic. Beeching felt that much merchandise traffic could be retained profitably if concentrated in around 100 large depots in conjunction with the development of a Freightliner network and the concentration of consignments of less than a wagonload at new facilities designed specifically for the purpose.

There is little doubt that Beeching's prescription for freight was largely correct. Since his time great economies have been made by virtually eliminating trip working and sorting and marshalling in sidings. Also the use of wagons of much larger capacity and the slightly ironic expansion of the private owner wagon fleet have enabled useful economies to be made. He was wrong in his expectations about the possibilities of the sundries or less than wagonload business which BR clearly regarded as beyond redemption and sought to eradicate. This type of traffic was much better handled by road.

Other areas where economies could be made but which did not necessarily catch the public eye were the protracted negotiations leading to agreements for the single-manning of many diesel and electric locomotives and the introduction of high-speed track maintenance and replacement machinery. Modernisation led to the closure of large numbers of traditional mechanical signal boxes and a considerable reduction in the number of what have come to be known as 'signallers'. Those working in the ultra-modern power-operated boxes now earned wages commensurate with their responsibilities and the sophistication of the equipment they used. A reduced labour force was being deployed with much greater efficiency.

Beeching introduced business and management structures of the sort he was familiar with at ICI such as specialised marketing teams. A corporate identity was introduced as part of the development of a modern market-orientated industry. The name 'British Rail' (rather than British Railways, both 'BR') was adopted in 1964 and subjected to some ridicule as people thought that the second word looked incomplete. Likewise the double-arrow, double-track symbol was interpreted by some as indicating that British Rail did not know whether it was coming or going. Some dubbed it 'the arrow of indecision'.

Beeching in perspective

Beeching was indelibly identified with the Conservatives' railway transport policies and the election in October 1964 of a Labour Government under Harold Wilson was bound to take him out of his comfort zone. He resigned as from 1 June 1965 and returned to ICI, having been ennobled in the New Year's Honours List of 1965. He was able to say that although his reforms had not yet made the railways totally viable, the deficit had decreased despite the award of higher wages to the reduced number of workers in the industry. His claim that the changes that he had proposed, if fully implemented, would enable Britain's railways to be profitable, was and remained an illusion. How could railways be profitable in an economy and society dominated by road usage? The harsh reality is that even if every single closure proposal put forward by Beeching had been implemented the railways would still have made a loss. It took a long time for the truth of this unpalatable fact to sink in.

Beeching may have been appointed while a Conservative government was in office and he may have attracted most of the opprobrium associated with the Report but the bulk of its recommended closures were actually carried out when Labour was in office. Some of the most controversial closures of lines that could now be playing a useful role in the national network took place years after Marples had left office and Beeching was back in private industry. Such closures were the afterbirth, as it were, of their policies and can now be seen to have been fundamentally flawed. Responsibility has to be held by Labour when in office.

In the 1960s many major power-brokers were firmly pro-road and hostile to the railways. They did not accept that an efficient modern railway was capable of making a major contribution to a buoyant economy. We can see now that a significant number of passenger service closures were mistaken but they were products of the dominant ideology of the time and the economic, social and cultural values that it produced which constituted the received wisdom. While the pro-road lobby remains immensely powerful, from the end of the twentieth century there has been an extraordinary renaissance in the usage of the railway system which can partly be accounted for by the fact that the road system has reached saturation point. With hindsight we can see that both phenomena have their roots in the shortcomings of national transport policy since the Second World War. It was a great shame that it was not until the 1960s that politicians of either main party faced up to the crisis of railway overcapacity and road congestion.

Perhaps curiously – or maybe not given the somewhat inscrutable nature of the man – Beeching believed that the same forensic, cost-based analysis that had been applied under his direction to the railways should be extended to road haulage and even inter-city air services. While Beeching was not touting to be the person heading up such a process, he inevitably ruffled feathers with the road lobby for having the temerity to suggest that road haulage should receive the same treatment as the railways. He favoured discouraging the use of private cars for commuting purposes by radically increasing street parking charges and reducing street parking spaces. Additionally, it was his opinion that city dwellers should be required to garage their vehicles and not leave them in the road where they frequently impeded the traffic flow. In some circles Beeching was even described as being anti-road. It is interesting that, among senior Labour Party figures, the avidly pro-road ex-trade union leader Frank Cousins was at the forefront of those who wanted him sent back to ICI. Cousins told Parliament that he had pressurised Tom Fraser, who was Marples' successor, to sack Beeching, an assertion always denied by Beeching himself. There has always been a sense that, since Beeching left the job before the expiry of his five-year term of office, he may have been 'encouraged' to go. Certainly there were strong vested interests that did not want the economics of road traffic and transport subjected to scrutiny of the kind that Beeching had applied to the railways.

It is interesting to note that Macmillan stuck to his guns regarding the appointment of Beeching. In his memoirs written many years later, he described Beeching as 'one of the most able and fertile brains in the industrial and commercial world'. Given the fact that he seems not to have liked the man, this seems a generous tribute. Perhaps he was being disingenuous. In her diaries, Barbara Castle, the future Labour Transport Minister, described Beeching as having '... an arrogance that comes... from a clear mind that sees a logical answer to a situation and cannot tolerate any modification of it to meet human frailty'.

Writing in 1965, G. Freeman Allen in his assessment of the man and his achievements, *British Rail After Beeching* (1966) stated: 'The Beeching regime did far more than lop off the British railway network a good deal of miserably under-utilised, rural network. Dr Beeching's outstanding achievements are: first, to have driven the British public to face the fact that the retention of a national railway system on its historic scale deep into the motor age will cost them an increasingly frightening and unnecessary fortune; and second, to have comprehensively re-educated the management of an industry that before his arrival was shackled from top to bottom by time-hallowed methods and techniques of running and selling its product. In brief, he transformed a browbeaten, rather aimless social service into the makings of an aggressive modern industry'.

In *Beeching. Champion of the Railway?* Richard Hardy (1989) made a robust defence of Beeching saying: '... his famous Reshaping Report was constructive and for us within the system his work changed our thinking, our methods of doing things, our ideas on assessment of managers and our systems – such as they were – of financial control'. He 'saved the railways from financial and organisational disintegration' and, Hardy says, he was a sensitive, courageous man whose failure was not to understand or appreciate the sentimental attachment of many British people to the railways even if they did not actually use them. Hardy highlights the weaknesses in accounting practices which meant that there was a serious shortage of the kind of data which was needed in order to make informed decisions and develop meaningful strategies. He almost eulogises Beeching, describing him as 'considerate, friendly, imperturbable determined and courageous'. He claims that Marples and Beeching enjoyed a good working and personal relationship, recognising that they were both the kind of people who got things done. However he recognised that Beeching lacked personal warmth, perhaps because he was basically shy and undemonstrative and this made him appear aloof, or even disdainful, especially when people he was with did not grasp what he saw as the self-evident and essential logic in his ideas.

Hardy was also generous in his assessment of Marples. 'He was cocky and he knew it but he was very, very shrewd and was humble enough, having chosen well, to put his faith in others and then to support them all the way and all the time … He never ducked from under, least of all when Dr Beeching was at his most unpopular with the public.'

During Beeching's time as a railwayman, considerable savings were made in BR's working expenses despite continuing wage, salary and price increases. Manpower was reduced by 103,000 from the beginning of 1962 to the end of 1964. This was achieved at a time when the level of traffic remained more or less constant and it meant that Beeching presided over increased productivity on the railways to the tune of just over 26 per cent. Losses fell from £104 million in 1962 to £82 million in 1963 and £68 million in 1964, but then increased costs sent them spiralling again. Even Beeching could not make the railways pay. Although he was always more likely to be characterised an axeman, there were definite plusses to his legacy. These included the merry-go-round and Freightliner concepts. The idea of fast, frequent long-distance passenger trains which Beeching advocated was to lead to the 'Inter-City' brand and logically following that, the immensely successful fleet of high speed trains (the HSTs) which transformed long-distance rail travel. BR took on an effective new corporate identity and, behind the scenes, systems for staff appraisal and training and comprehensible accounting and financial arrangements were implemented. Overall, BR put its activities on a much more businesslike standing.

The thrust of *The Reshaping of British Railways* was largely seen as negative, as being about closures whereas Beeching wanted it to be seen in a positive light as a programme for modernisation and the future. It was not in the Report's brief to suggest cost-cutting measures that might have reprieved some loss-making lines. Useful economies could have been achieved by converting some routes to 'basic railways' as advocated by Gerry Fiennes and applied to the long and predominantly rural East Suffolk Line between Ipswich and Lowestoft. However, such measures were not necessarily a panacea. The King's Lynn to Hunstanton line was given similar treatment but it closed in 1969. Railways were traditionally labour-intensive and although the workforce had been declining continuously for decades, over-manning remained on many lines and reflected the continued existence of much outdated infrastructure and working practice. Basic railways at least still provided a service, surely better than no service at all.

BR looked as if it was determined to close some lines come what may and was prepared to employ dubious tactics in order to do so. An example already discussed is the selective culling of trains to render a service inconvenient or almost useless. As usage fell away, it would be triumphantly declared that the line did not pay. Sometimes routes marked for closure but not yet considered by the relevant TUCC were omitted from public timetables. On being challenged, officialdom described such omissions as 'administrative oversights' but no one was fooled. Some lines passed through two or more regions. In such cases, a region in its timetables might advertise just that section of the route lying within its own jurisdiction. For those not in the know, the precise longer-distance nature of the service might not be apparent.

Loft, in *Last Trains*, commenting generally on perceptions of the Beeching Report wrote: 'Beeching and Marples are obvious targets because they were the public face of an apparently proactive period of transport policy-making – a time when government actually seemed to be shaping the transport network rather than breathlessly attempting to keep pace with its development. Add in the secrecy and dodgy figures and it is all too easy to lay blame at the feet of a cabal of anti-railway officials or a conspiracy of pro-road interests.'

It has been said that politics is distilled economics. Insofar as economics is about how wealth is created, exchanged and distributed, it is inevitable that political issues intrude into so many aspects of life. Railways have always operated in a world where political issues and factors have been an important influence and this became more so than ever after nationalisation. In the twentieth century the sphere of operations of the State became ever wider, more complex and expensive. This created the paradox that citizens generally wanted the services provided by the State while resenting having to pay for them through taxation. Because taxes are unpopular, politicians for electoral reasons and the Exchequer for wider financial reasons wanted control over public spending. Taxpayers' money went to run the nationalised industries but as a seriously financially challenged member of those industries, it was inevitable that the railways would be targeted for criticism. The Exchequer was always unhappy with the notion that some services which inevitably made losses had to be kept open because they were deemed socially necessary.

Despite the low general standing of the railways and the cheap abuse often thrown their way, politicians knew that attempts to rationalise them had the ability to arouse strong passions. Proposed closures could mean losses at the ballot box. Particularly contentious were closure proposals for Scotland and Wales for these tended to stoke the growing fires of nationalism. In turn these could generate problems with voters in England. If severely loss-making lines in Scotland and Wales were kept open largely for political considerations, might not English-based voters think that lines in England which apparently made smaller losses might be sacrificed and closed as a political ploy?

In the polity of contemporary Britain, it was easy to see money spent on loss-making railway services as depriving other areas of state provision of necessary funding. Education and health services come immediately to mind. Such an approach was premised on the idea that there is only a finite amount of money available for the government to spend and that the various claimants on funds should see each other as competitors when seeking financial support. This sidesteps the broader political issue of how much overall wealth is generated and the manner in which that wealth is distributed across the entire economy. It became commonplace to hear politicians and the media refer to 'investment' in roads but a 'subsidy' to the railways, indicative of the relative value they accorded to the respective modes of transport and the funding they required.

Given the number of station and even line reopenings in recent years, the rise in passenger usage and the ever-increasing congestion on the roads, it is clear that while drastic action was needed to cut the losses being made by various parts of the railway's operations and to develop the kinds of traffic for which rail was well suited, some at least of what actually happened was a short-sighted, kneejerk reaction underpinned by a deeply-rooted pro-road culture at ministry and government level. While the vicissitudes of so-called market economics can make long-term planning almost impossible, this was short-termism at its worst. Assets were destroyed, some of which were quickly missed but could not be brought back. Sometimes track was lifted and the formation sold off with almost indecent haste and relish. One service, that connecting Peterborough to Spalding, was restored with local authority financial support within a year of initial withdrawal. A policy was pursued of singling double track lines, of reducing quadruple routes to double track, lifting loops into which slower trains could be shunted to allow faster ones to pass and simplifying the layouts at junctions. These made savings but also often increased inflexibility and the likelihood of delays and disruptions. On some such lines, for example Salisbury to Exeter and Oxford to Worcester, track capacity has since been restored at great expense. Diversionary routes were closed, being regarded as superfluous because they duplicated other lines. The former London & South Western Railway (LSWR) route from Exeter to Plymouth was closed as a through route despite the knowledge that the Exeter to Teignmouth section of the old GWR line from Exeter to Plymouth had to be closed on many occasions because of heavy seas attacking the coast. The current HS2 project involves a state-of-the-art partial replacement of capacity destroyed during the 1960s and 1970s.

The seeming obsession with removing what was categorised as surplus track was formalised under the Transport Act of 1968. Money was available to BR for a period of years to rationalise and reduce the overall track capacity. Considerable energy was displayed by BR in demonstrating that this money was being well spent. Uprooting rails and sleepers leaves visible scars. Time and nature softens these scars but for a period the reduction in the amount of track gave the impression of an industry that was visibly shrinking and declining in importance. Very often, of course, coal and goods yards close to stations were turned into car parks, evidence of the changing nature of transport usage at this time as well as the use of alternative domestic fuels.

There were a number of closures as a result of the Beeching Plan which were almost certainly mistaken. It is, of course, a matter of opinion but many people would regard the following closures as being among those that were certainly ill-advised: Harrogate-Ripon-Northallerton; Oxford-Cambridge; the Okehampton to Bere Alston section of the former LSWR route from Exeter to Plymouth; the Matlock to Millers Dale Junction part of the former Derby to Manchester Central line; and the East Lincolnshire line from Peterborough and Spalding to Boston and Grimsby.

It is easy to say with hindsight that this or that particular closure should not have been allowed to take place. It is equally easy to say that Beeching should have taken into account likely population growth and other social changes such as the increase in commuting. The closures meant that some places that grew rapidly from the late 1960s were already bereft of passenger services. It is also easy to say that he should have anticipated the headlong growth of road traffic and the massive increase in road congestion that occurred after his time. All this may be true but even if Beeching had been able to gaze accurately into the future, this was not what he was paid so much money to do. He was not required to prognosticate concerning future social and economic change and his forensic methods of analysis were based on facts, even if some of them may have been of dubious provenance, and not on speculation. It is fair to ascribe to Dr Beeching the initiation of a process of change which helped to ensure that a slimmed-down, more efficient British railway system survived into the twenty-first century. It was not a system, however, which paid its way.

There is little doubt that railway passenger closures disproportionately affected the less privileged members of society. Older people, those without cars who could not or would not use them, low-paid workers and their families and women bore the brunt. Buses often proved to be a poor or inadequate general alternative when rail services were withdrawn and were often reduced or withdrawn because of low ridership. Today's buses are much more user-friendly but back in the 1960s and 1970s they found it hard to handle passengers with any kind of substantial luggage.

Beeching's replacement was Stanley Raymond. Of known pro-Labour sympathies but hardly a radical, Raymond had wide experience in the railway industry. He had masterminded the traffic surveys on which much of the Beeching Report was based and had subsequently become vice-chairman of the BRB. He was of working class origins and had had to fight hard to climb the greasy pole. He was acknowledged to be hard working. He may have been chosen because of his experience in industrial relations. This could have been useful because the future envisaged for the railways was likely to continue to include contentious issues like single-manning of locomotives and considerable reductions in staff levels. Although he largely endorsed the theory underpinning the Beeching Report and did not discount that changed economic and social circumstances might in the future require another examination of the railway system, as far as he was concerned most necessary closures had already been carried out. Raymond was also emotional and impatient, even aggressive, and he fell foul of disagreements with Barbara Castle who was possibly even more bloody-minded than he was. He left his post on 31 December 1967, having been in office less than three years.

Chapter 15

Private Life at the Ministry of Transport

M arples knew how to balance politics and a personal life. Madge told the Belfast Telegraph, 'he regularly walks about 16 miles every Sunday'. Weekdays meant early morning tennis coaching in Maida Vale with Frank Wilde, once coach to Fred Perry. He did not neglect the Wallasey constituency association, assiduously turning up at AGMs and social events. In London, Eccleston Street was an ideal political venue. Guests drawn from the great and the good appeared at glittering dinner parties. The couple featured pictorially in the April 1960 number of *Life*. March 1961 saw *Ideal Home* profile Eccleston Street, featuring the new 'barbecue room'. They flew to Nice for ten days, ideal for the evening train to Les Baux, took an autumn week in Paris and, after spending Christmas 1960 at home, left for Davos on New Year's Eve.

As we have seen, in September 1960 he bravely used the Commercial Motor Show to lament the 'dreadful carnage' on the roads. At October's Conservative conference he was talking about ships, lamenting nationalism and 'flag discrimination'. Just the following week he mused in public on new pedestrians' rights. Michael Foot, soon to return to the Commons as Aneurin Bevan's Ebbw Vale successor, missed the point entirely (*Daily Herald*, 1 November 1960), complaining that he was using the occasion to promote himself. In fact a transport revolution was being prepared, despite fears in the popular, not just the Labour, press ('Marples Fiasco' screamed one *Evening Standard* headline in November). On 26 October Marples tabled a resolution noting the BTC report for the year to 1959 and the Select Committee on Nationalised Industries report on the railways (H.C. 254, 1960). He was careful not to promise publication of the Stedeford Report, whose remit and composition he had announced on 6 April, offering instead a White Paper to ensure the eventual debate would be about his proposals. By late November, press reports of compulsory seat-belts abounded while parking meters were expected to come into use in the City in the New Year. The *Daily Express* (15 March 1961) was the first paper to spot the significance of the Beeching appointment. Dunnett, who observed the two closely, recalled them as 'an admirable team', seeing railway problems from the same point of view. An autumn 1962 interview with Malcolm Muggeridge cemented Marples' status as one of the more interesting, if controversial, members of the Cabinet.

The year 1963 began in familiar mode. In February Selwyn Lloyd lunched at Eccleston Street; on 27 March Marples brought his long-gestating Beeching proposals to the House. These were dramatic enough but now came high political drama of a different sort. The defection of the spies Burgess and Maclean had occurred in 1951; slowly, the press learned how their privileged educational background (Eton, Cambridge) had shielded them; ten years on the Portland spy ring was busted by security services. In 1962 Admiralty employee John Vassall, blackmailed by the Soviets into leaking secrets, was exposed: this embarrassment forced Macmillan to set up the Lord Radcliffe inquiry, presenting its findings on 7 May. In March sex rumours linked the Minister for War, John Profumo, to a well-known good-time girl, Christine Keeler. She had distributed her favours freely, also servicing one Yevgeny Ivanov of the Soviet Embassy. In a personal statement Profumo acknowledged knowing Keeler but denied any 'impropriety'. By June he had admitted this was untrue, resigned as War Minister and later relinquished his seat. The combined impact of these events shaped the public view of politicians; they seemed to enjoy a social life marked by unusual sexual freedom while being indefensibly casual about security. Marples, considered too vulgar perhaps for an invitation to the Astors' Cliveden home where Profumo's Keeler liaison had begun, never moved in the same social circles.

There was another reason for politicians to be wary. The first fortnightly edition of *Private Eye* was published in 1961, targeting the same British establishment from which its own well-informed reporters hailed. November 1962 brought the first Saturday night showing of BBC's *That Was The Week That Was*; less forthright than *Private Eye* but equally willing to lampoon those in authority and enjoying a much larger audience. It might not have mattered but for a shift in popular press coverage of politics. At Eden's resignation newspapers had been generally disposed to support the government in international affairs, especially if British troops were involved, an inclination crossing partisan allegiances. By 1963 there was less deference. There was perhaps even boredom with a Conservative government twelve years in office.

Marples went climbing in Derbyshire that May, visited the Chelsea Flower Show and at the end of the month flew to Lyons for a Beaujolais tour, returning by way of Paris and Brussels. The first hint that the Profumo affair might have an impact on him came on 12 June; Michael Kemp of the *Sketch* rang his office seeking information on Keeler. His private secretary parried the call but this could only provide temporary relief. On 17 June, attending the Commons Profumo debate, he was warned by Chief Whip Martin Redmayne that there were rumours circulating about him. Redmayne feared Deputy Opposition Leader George Brown might refer to them when winding up the debate. In the event Brown did not do so but Marples was sufficiently concerned to warn Ruth, who was due to join him later at a dinner. The rumours (relayed via Cheadle MP William Shepherd) arose from high society parties hosted by Hod and Mariella Dibben, a couple known for varied and voracious sexual appetites. They suggested either that he might be the 'headless man' pictured (in a widely circulated photograph) being pleasured by the Duchess of Argyll or that he was the individual, clad only in a Masonic apron, requesting a beating if his performance failed to provide the anticipated pleasure. Of these shenanigans Marples flatly denied any knowledge.

The next day Shepherd suggested that a law officer meet his source. But, Marples wrote privately, 'he was [so] shaken by my firmness' he agreed to check his informant again. Marples told Redmayne he would chase down the story and by 19 June Shepherd conveyed the 'encouraging news' of a lack of evidence connecting him with the rumours. On 20 June the source of the rumours was revealed as Keeler's companion Mandy Rice-Davies, who had told a *Mirror* reporter: 'I left early and afterwards met someone who told me it was Ernest Marples'; her inability to recognise the government's most photographed minister was remarkable. The Solicitor General quietly advised Marples to keep a record of his movements. That same day Macmillan's all-male Cabinet had discussed the affair, drawing entertaining disclosures from new War Minister Duncan Sandys.

The next day's *Daily Express* carried an article about the 'Man in the Mask'. While Marples blamed Rice-Davies, forty years later Keeler herself owned up, blaming Stephen Ward (*The Truth at Last*, 2002, 213). Marples privately believed the ministers concerned were Christopher Soames and Sandys. Buffeted by rumour and dreading each day's press, a fearful Cabinet put Home Secretary Henry Brooke in charge of coordinating its defence. Marples that day refused the *Express* an up-to-date photo, suspecting they wanted to compare it with a fake one in their possession; even Shepherd now knew 'I was in the clear'. Two days later, his showbusiness friend Hughie

Green, who 'knew a couple … at the party', tried to get a guest list. This came to nothing.

Macmillan's Commons statement that day announced a judicial inquiry under Master of the Rolls Lord Denning: 'to examine, in the light of the circumstances leading to the resignation of the former Secretary of State for War Mr J.D. Profumo, the operation of the Secret Service and the adequacy of their co-operation with the Police in matters of security; to investigate any information or material which may come to his attention in this connection and to consider any evidence there may be for believing that national security has been or may be, endangered; and to report thereon'. Wilson's challenge to this format focused on its failure to require evidence on oath. Denning eventually reported but not before the autumn, by which time Profumo was the least of the Cabinet's problems.

On 27 June the *News of the World*, securely in the Conservative hands of Sir William Carr, reported that the masked man was neither a Cabinet minister nor an MP. This should have dispelled Marples' concerns, but now he had Denning to deal with: his lordship was interviewing all Cabinet members. He first saw him on the afternoon of 28 June, learning the next day that Denning proposed interviewing Hod and Mariella Dibben. *News of the World* reporter Cyril Jones briefed Marples about Mariella's impressive range of sexual tastes. Its 30 June issue carried these, revelling in salacious detail. A relieved Marples learned that Denning agreed it was 'better to tell in private than have it dragged out in public'. That evening he updated Tim Bligh, Macmillan's private secretary; the next day he saw Denning again, promising to send him a 'complete set of daily diaries with supporting documents'.

Denning and his assistant, ex-civil servant Thomas Critchley, worked at top speed. Then on 9 July Ann Bailey turned up at their office as a voluntary witness. Bailey's interview with Denning appeared in Tom Mangold's *Daily Mail* 2013 and 2020 articles and his February 2020 television programme (*Keeler, Profumo, Ward and Me*). Mangold quotes Critchley's description of Bailey '… 40ish, very painted with a bright vivacious manner who spoke quietly and fluently and plunged straight into her tale'. She claimed to have been paid during a long sexual relationship with Ernest Marples who, that same day, was enjoying a leisurely lunch with Geoffrey Crowther. Apparently Bailey held little back, charging that Marples wore women's clothing during sex; that he liked being whipped; that his 'difficult' sexual requirements meant she sometimes needed an assistant; that after their relationship ended he wrote her a series of 'annoying, obscene and filthy letters'; that their liaison was conducted at 33 Eccleston Street. Bailey also mentioned her child to Denning. Marples had been 'very good to her, seeing her at once' at the time of her son's birth: apparently she did not allege he was the father.

Critchley told Mangold that he and Denning had concluded 'every word of her story was true' and the two then began to worry about the security implications. Now Marples was perhaps the most prominent Cabinet member after Macmillan. His exposure might, on top of the other scandals, have caused the government to collapse. On 26 July, in a fatal misstep, financially and for her status in Denning's eyes, Bailey took her story to the *People*. A week later it made her existence known.

Denning and Critchley had misconstrued the significance of Marples' Privy Council membership. Perhaps also these two British establishment products were shocked by anything other than 'normal' sex delivered from the missionary position? Denning's final report would allude to 'vile and revolting' sexual activities. Mangold records Critchley's conviction that a newspaper was behind Bailey's approach, hoping for corroboration once Denning (who enjoyed security services assistance) had confirmed her tale. Marples soon confirmed Critchley's fears. Allegations were already swirling overseas. On 19 July Bligh gave Marples two telegrams making allegations about him, forwarded from Athens by the Foreign Office.

On 24 July, Marples heard about Denning's visitor: 'the name I would remember was Anne Sylvester (now Bailey)' who alleged 'abnormal sexual practices' over many years from wartime to 1961. The Marples papers contain a handwritten letter from Denning, asking him for an undertaking not to proceed legally against her. This, Marples, perhaps under solicitor's advice and in a rare typewritten letter, declined. When first confronted with Bailey's allegations Marples dismissed them as 'irrelevant' but Denning was having none of it. He wanted to see the two of them together and make up his own mind. Marples saw that Denning believed Bailey; meeting her would test his own sincerity. He feared a press leak. Denning overrode his violent protests: the allegations related were a quarter-of-a-century old; Bailey was a 'bloody liar'.

Knowing that the story had been leaked, Marples spoke to deputy editor Rothman of the *People*. His paper had bought the story, intending to suppress it. Marples confirmed the Bailey liaison but insisted it was not recent. He had first met her in wartime (actually 1938), recalling an attractive woman 'in battle dress'. He disputed all her other charges. He believed he had not seen her since 1959 and even then not for sex. Rothman undertook to publish nothing *unless* Denning mentioned Marples in his report.

An appointment was made for the confrontation which would happen at the Home Office. Apart from the learned judge and the two principals, only Critchley would attend. Marples arrived to find a woman two stone heavier (in his estimation) than he remembered. He had also discovered (from the security services?) that she had twice (1946 and 1952) served time in Holloway prison. His friends, including Hugh Massingham, concerted their efforts to influence Denning and discredit Bailey, in particular over her contacts with the *People*. Had she contacted the paper before or after seeing Denning? Did her solicitor know of her threats to go to the press? Marples checked his official and personal diaries, realised the date of his last 'association' with Bailey was crucial, resolved to 'pluck victory from the jaws of disaster' and grimly awaited Sunday's papers.

So all-consuming was the Profumo affair and Marples' attempt to avoid being politically destroyed by it, it is easy to forget he was still Minister of Transport, and a controversial one. Beeching had created headlines in the spring, but by July roads, not rail, dominated the press. The 'Marples must go' campaign had backfired, with the ratio of those thinking he was doing a 'good job' highly favourable at over 55 per cent. He later gloated: 'I remember as Minister of Transport that a lot of people thought I had changed too many things too soon. But they took credit for the results when it was all over. But when that lot opposite [i.e. Labour] got into office the new sticker on cars was "Come back Marples, all is forgiven".'

On 30 July Marples met Denning and his legal counsel who were pursuing several lines of inquiry and corroboration. Marples told him 'my wife and I have carefully and conscientiously reviewed my activities … Looked … at my movements and … associations to see whether I had done anything which might endanger national security'. This provoked Denning's interest: he expressed a wish to meet this loyal wife, visited the marital home on 31 July and presumably asked some highly personal questions. Marples noted he was 'much impressed'.

The next afternoon, Marples had to steel himself for the Home Office confrontation. In the Mangold version, Bailey jumped up, but Marples spoke first. 'Eh, Ann,' he said in a broad Lancashire accent, 'You've changed,' and the two shook hands like old friends. Privately (according to his own notes) his reaction was different: 'she was *enormous* (how I hate fat girls)'; adding

'When Denning asked her to describe the 'practices' she related them in detail. I asked her if she performed these practices on her ex-husband. She replied that she provided these for most of her clients'. Critchley records Marples' belief that 'Bailey would do all in her power to gain Lord Denning's acceptance of her story so that, well embroidered, she would be able to sell it for a sensationally large sum of money.' Denning still insisted his staff had not told the papers, but the worldly Marples knew better: 'I knew in my heart that the press would be told.'

After the confrontation Marples met Denning alone. He admitted an association from the beginning of the war but disputed the charge of 'weird' sexual practices. The notes he made contain contradictions; had their last meeting been in 1949 or 1959? Politically it mattered a lot. He left in despair, convinced neither Denning nor his counsel believed him and he was no further forward after another meeting the next day. But then, remarkably, he was invited to dine at Denning's Cuckfield (Sussex) home. Dinner was followed by twenty minutes with his lordship in a private study, about which his notes reveal nothing. It was now 3 August. Had this news been published it must have dented the Denning reputation for probity on which Macmillan was depending.

Mangold suggests Denning and Critchley held different views of their recent discoveries: Denning thought he must deal faithfully in his report; Critchley was more sensitive to the government's position and the country's reputation abroad. Left alone after his ordeal, Marples gradually drew together a coherent defence which distanced him from matters of security. His notes record '... apart from Jack Profumo I never met any of the leading personalities in the Profumo affair'. Profumo had dined at Eccleston Street (in a lunch party of five) in 1955 and at Christmas 1960. To Marples the key question was: had his private life endangered national security? It was obvious that it had not done so. Denning sent two handwritten sets of notes to him on 12 and 13 August. Then on 16 August came what he considered a blackmail attempt when a woman rang his office reporting hearing his name in an overheard pub conversation.

Five days later came another, more plausible, blackmail attempt. The *News of the World* proprietor William Carr visited him at 33 Eccleston Street 'as a friend', telling him, 'Ernest you are in trouble.' Marples records Carr urging him 'what you have got to do is to act quickly before Denning finishes his report ... alter your evidence if necessary ...' (!) By now however Marples had grown more confident in handling Denning: he could plausibly dispute the end-date of the Bailey relationship which she had put at 1961, embarrassingly recent; he could prove from passports that she had lied about a meeting in 1956 when he had been abroad on honeymoon; he had learned that she had no fewer than sixty-one convictions for fraud and false pretences. However Carr's visit was followed by a new approach from Rothman, less secure from a party point of view. The canny Marples took precautions, arranging for shorthand notes to be taken by PC Williams of Norbury police station on 3 August. (Williams' transcript may be found in the Marples papers, 7/3/2.) Rothman informed him that the *People* had paid Bailey £25 and promised £100 but it had no intention of publishing her story. 'We bought her out … to shut her up' he assured Marples. He believed she had been to Denning 'once or twice before she came to us'. Marples, alert to the importance of the sequence of events, spent time trying to extract it from Rothman, but the journalist's remarks are incoherent. There was however a hint of menace: if the foreign press should get hold of the story his paper would use it. Then, in an extraordinary aside, he said, '… you might be contemplating resignation … if we can be in on the story …'. Like Carr he was surprised Marples was waiting for Denning's work to be complete; he thought he might resign before the story 'blew abroad' to save Macmillan embarrassment. Marples countered, accurately, that he had not yet finished giving evidence. He wondered why Bailey had approached the *People* and not the *News of the World*, from which Keeler had extracted no less than £20,000.

By 12 August 1963 Marples felt confident enough to write to Macmillan in his own hand (MPLS 7/3/1) informing him he intended 'going it alone'. He drew on his old loyalty to his chief: '… it's my job … to help you – not to hinder you', adding 'something must be done to stop trafficking in scandal for reward', which hope he placed in the newly reconstituted Press Council. Mangold reports a crisis meeting two days later between Macmillan, Critchley, Denning and Bligh at Admiralty House. Critchley's notes record Macmillan disowning any wish to influence the final report. Nor did he did want the conduct of individual ministers relegated to confidential annexes. Denning replied he was satisfied that none of the evidence showed national security had been endangered and would so report. 'This,' comments Mangold, 'was an outright lie.' Unfortunately Mangold then misquotes Macmillan's diaries where, on 2 August, he wrote: 'I fear that Lord Denning's report … will condemn one important Minister … this will be another great shock and make my position impossible.' In fact Macmillan wrote 'condemn one important *and one unimportant* minister' (or, rather, fail to clear him of scandalous conduct). This shows the Prime Minister understood, as Critchley and Denning did not, that ministers of transport are distant from matters of national security.

Denning's report (September 1963, Cmnd. 2152), a best-seller when it emerged in September, dispelled Macmillan's fears. It alluded tantalisingly to the Marples story, labelling it as 'other evidence', 'scarcely relevant to my terms of reference', concerned with the 'private lives of public figures'. His options had been either to investigate it thoroughly and reach conclusions or ignore it on the grounds that it might stimulate a witch hunt. He had concluded it was his duty 'to hear all witnesses and thoroughly sift the evidence in case there may be a security connection however remote and to avoid any criticism that I did not do so'.

He continued: 'Among the many witnesses who volunteered evidence on these unrelated matters was a woman who claimed she had a relationship with a public figure. After exhaustive investigation it was proved to me and I am abundantly satisfied:

1. That whatever the relationship was, it had nothing to do with the Profumo episode and that such acquaintanceship as there was ended over 10 years ago. There was not the slightest evidence that "national security has been or may be endangered."
2. That she is an accomplished liar who now has a considerable criminal record and has served terms of imprisonment.
3. That before she had completed telling her story to me, she started negotiating with one or more newspapers to sell her story about the acquaintanceship. She claimed that her motive in volunteering her statement was in the public interest, but in my opinion her real motive was to join in pursuit of the large sums of money certain women are reported to have received from newspapers for their stories.'

Denning's report has since been widely criticised. Unquestionably he accepted the Marples version in its entirety including a focus on security to the exclusion of all other considerations This wise and upright judge appears to have been unduly swayed by political factors.

By 23 August, with Denning's first draft on the Prime Minister's desk, the storm had passed. Marples wrote heartfelt letters of thanks to Mark Schreiber and Rex North who had advised him. Schreiber's had been the analytical mind charting the path out of the labyrinth. On 27 August Marples felt able to travel to Paris on Ministry of Transport business; at the height of the crisis, fighting for his political life, he had been forced to cancel a similar trip to Poland. September brought an overnight stay at St Thomas' Hospital for what must have been a deferred operation. By 9 October 1963, he was in Scarborough, winning from the party faithful the biggest ovation of five ministers speaking that day at the Conservative Party Conference. That same day a Profumo echo surfaced with *The Times* obituary of the untimely death of fifty-one-year old William Asquith, head of William Asquith Ltd. Marples annotated marginally: 'He *was* the real Man in the Mask. Another casualty of the Profumo affair?' By now however politics had shifted back to issues of power and influence. Illness had forced Macmillan out and the murky handling of the succession had plunged the Conservative government into new obloquy. The very lack of social connections that had shielded Marples from the core Profumo affair now excluded him from any weight in the choice of Macmillan's successor. As the partisan *Sunday Citizen* put it on 20 October 1963: 'Note that Health Minister Enoch Powell, Transport Minister Ernest Marples and Postmaster General Reginald Bevins were never involved in the so-called consultations to find a new leader. Why not? Because this was strictly a blue-blood decision. Old Etonian Macmillan picked Old Etonian Home.' The *Citizen* thought Marples would resign in disgust but he would serve a full year under Douglas-Home. By autumn 1963 it was back to normal. A Beaujolais dinner on 12 November: the opening of Knutsford motorway services and the M6 stretch from J16 to J20 on 15 November; a Commons statement on Buchanan (27 November) and an appearance on BBC's *Panorama*.

Chapter 16

After Beeching: Barbara Castle and The Railways

L abour's successor to Ernest Marples as Minister of Transport had been Tom Fraser, who in turn fell victim to a Cabinet reshuffle to be replaced by Barbara Castle, who assumed office on 23 December 1965. Harold Wilson saw that Labour's record around transport was uninspiring given that decisive measures needed to be taken and he wanted someone who would get things done. He knew that Castle was tough and that she was probably the best person available who could turn the situation around. She came unwillingly from Overseas Development with absolutely no experience of the transport industry. However she was a person of great energy and focus and she quickly brought this to bear on her new portfolio. She was feisty and not the sort to be easily browbeaten. She needed this quality because, as she said in her memoirs, there were permanent officials at the Ministry of Transport who were 'closure mad'. They probably also thought that a woman would be a pushover. Castle only held the post for just over two years but made a major impact in that time. She was aware that many people believed the closure process had now gone far enough. Wilson's choice of Castle for this job, even if it was only intended to be a short-term tenure, was a shrewd one and he likened her to the 'tiger in the tank' which was making such an impression as a contemporary advertising slogan for Esso. Where Macmillan had wanted a 'swordsman' in Ernest Marples, Wilson saw Castle as a 'tiger'. He told her that it was her job to produce the integrated transport policy that Labour had promised in its manifesto.

In her diaries Castle had acerbic comments to make about the Ministry of Transport. It seemed to have no sense that transport should be planned holistically. Its work was dealt with under the auspices of three deputy secretaries with little cooperation between the three fiefdoms. The secretaries dealt respectively with highways, urban policy and the rest – an antediluvian portmanteau consisting of railways, ports, shipping and nationalised road transport. It was crystal clear that roads and highways was the one with status.

Castle was unusual as a Transport Minister for two other reasons. Firstly, she argued that transport needed to be planned and treated on a national and integrated basis. Secondly, and this was ground-breaking, she totally accepted the argument that subsidies were required for parts of the system which could never be made to pay but which provided essential social needs and, unlike her predecessors, she was prepared to do something about it. 'Socially necessary' was the phrase often applied to such services. It had become very clear that the closure of services had not achieved anything like the expected level of savings nor would further closures be likely to do so. Despite this positive attitude, many advocates of railways criticised her because she gave her consent to some significant line closures, did not implement controls over road haulage which might have prevented more freight traffic being lost by the railways and did not put any restrictions on road and motorway building programmes.

In her diaries, Castle wrote: 'I outlined the general direction of my policies: the need to come to terms with the motor car without allowing it to ruin our environment. This, I argued, meant an expanded road programme … the preservation of an adequate rail network with subsidies for non-paying but socially necessary lines; the diversion of freight traffic from road to rail; and the encouragement of public transport, particularly in urban areas.'

The Labour government of which Castle was a leading member faced an almost unprecedented set of challenges. No sooner was it in office than a serious balance of payments crisis became clear. International relations were dominated and destabilised by the increasing involvement of the USA in a war it could not win in Vietnam, while Britain faced the constitutional problems posed by the actions of the white minority in what was still Southern Rhodesia. A lengthy and acrimonious strike of seamen inflicted damage on the UK's international trading arrangements. A sharp devaluation of sterling in late 1964 and the consequent economic crisis caused the then Governor of the Bank of England, Lord Cromer, to tell Wilson unequivocally that the government had no option but to abandon the implementation of some of its most precious election promises, especially that of abolishing prescription charges. Any minister trying to promote the interests of his or her priorities in such a situation needed to be bloody-minded. Castle possessed this quality in abundance.

Castle quickly set up a joint steering group. The activities of this group were intended to be far more transparent than the Stedeford Committee which had been notorious for its opacity. The new group was composed of members from the Ministry, other government departments and BR. It set to work identifying loss-making activities, scrutinising management and operational structures and considering options for savings on the railway infrastructure. Six White Papers on various aspects of transport quickly followed. Among other matters they outlined the measures the government intended to apply to modernise the railways, to integrate publicly owned road and rail services and to subsidise 'socially necessary' railway passenger services out of public funds. Other operations would be expected to pay their way. Grants would be provided for services losing money, initially on an individual basis, if there were demonstrable social and economic reasons why they should continue and if it was unreasonable to expect BR to continue providing the service without financial support. The grants were payable for three years only, after which for them to continue it would have to be proved that continuing support was justified. In March 1967 Castle published a map showing the lines she envisaged having a long-term future as part of 'a stable railway network'. This caused some alarm because the system was slimmed down to 11,000 miles which was considerably less that the system envisaged after the cuts associated with Beeching had been implemented. This plan reversed some of Beeching's proposals for closure such as Settle to Carlisle, Par to Newquay and Scarborough to Hull but some lines which then seemed to have an assured future such as Exeter to Okehampton and Cambridge to St Ives subsequently closed.

Castle soon became aware that despite all the organisational changes that had rained down on the railways in the preceding period, there were still many mediocre managers at all levels and a fully reciprocated aversion of senior railway management to the Ministry. None of this was helpful for an industry which needed to be thoroughly overhauled if it was to meet the challenges of the late twentieth century.

The relationship between Castle and Stanley Raymond as head of BR was hopelessly acrimonious. Their clash of personalities was such that nothing fruitful was ever going to emerge, both being jealous of their respective fiefdoms and suspicious of the other's motives. Castle had been born into a middle-class family, had been educated at grammar school and Oxford and united the radicalism of Labour's generation of 1945 with the belief in the virtues of planning that was so prevalent in the 1960s.

Raymond was a died-in-the-wool career railwayman. Time and time again they clashed especially over issues concerning how nationalised transport should be organised and financed.

The subsequent Transport Act of 1968 was immensely detailed and a landmark piece of legislation. It wrote off a large part of the railway's accumulated debt to a total of £153 million. The 'commercial' and the 'socially necessary' passenger services were identified and separated with the latter being grant-aided on the decision of the Minister of Transport. This was the first time that a minister had taken action on this issue as opposed to talking about it. It was clear that service closures were not the magic bullet that would solve the loss-making of significant parts of the railway network. Making public funds available for particular lines which met the required criteria relieved the railways of the requirement of achieving the impossible target of breaking even or actually making a profit. Many services that might have qualified for grant aid had already been withdrawn and there was a sense that Castle's measures, although welcome, were a case of closing the stable door after the horse had bolted. As it was, a grant of aid was no guarantee that a service would survive in the long-term. Among those which received aid only to close later when support was withdrawn included Penrith to Keswick, Bridgend to Treherbert and Maiden Newton to Bridport. The Central Wales Line was reprieved. It was a long route which was expensive to maintain and passed through few centres of population that generated much traffic. The reprieve owed something to political expediency given the rise of Welsh nationalism. Its closure would have deprived large tracts of highly rural country of rail services but the hard reality was that its survival meant that other probably better-used lines elsewhere closed.

The idea of railways being subsidised to operate loss-making but socially necessary services was anathema to politicians and civil servants with pro-road sympathies. Castle had a very difficult relationship with her permanent secretary, Thomas Padmore, who was notoriously hostile to railways. Castle, who was not then a motorist, did not allow herself to be dominated by the pro-road lobby but she made significant enemies and was eventually given a new portfolio. It is a moot point as to whether her promotion to Secretary of State for Employment and Productivity was a consequence of covert moves within the corridors of power to subvert somebody regarded as a nuisance or because Wilson, as Prime Minister, wanted someone of proven toughness to front legislation intended to curb the power of the trade unions.

The seriously loss-making railway sundries (less than wagonload) goods business was handed over completely to the recently created National Freight Corporation which was also given the responsibility for BRS. In due course the National Freight Corporation came under the jurisdiction of a new body known as National Carriers Limited which was very much road-orientated and the sundries traffic continued to ebb away from the railways. The then unprofitable Freightliner business was also placed under the National Freight Corporation. Castle wanted to do something to stem the flow of freight traffic away from rail to the roads and increase coordination between the two modes. Radically, she proposed to overhaul the existing licensing system for private sector lorries and the owners of large vehicles would be granted licenses on the basis that they could prove they were providing a more economical and reliable service for the commodities they handled than was possible on the railways. She brought in tighter regulations concerning lorry drivers' working conditions, including, controversially, the tachograph. It was a brave try but Castle herself was frustrated at only achieving partial success in the face of sustained hostility from the haulage industry, the mandarins at the Ministry, the Conservative opposition and elsewhere. With the election of a Conservative government under Edward Heath in 1970, the road haulage industry breathed a huge sigh of relief.

Passenger Transport Executives were established in the major conurbations and placed under the control of Passenger Transport Authorities (PTAs). Ernest Marples, although no lover of railways, had recognised that action was essential to stem the decline of public transport facilities and its deleterious effect on the quality of life in the major urban areas. He had been involved in preliminary discussions about the creation of some kind of authority on Merseyside, in Birmingham and Glasgow. Castle went much further. She saw planned and coordinated local transport systems as essential for much-needed urban regeneration.

The PTAs, which were composed of representatives appointed by local authorities and by the Minister, would plan and oversee the creation of efficient integrated public transport systems and management tailored to meet local need while the Passenger Transport Executives would manage their operations. The Act represented a positive approach to urban public transport. One of its early outcomes was the highly successful Tyne & Wear Metro. Other projects originated in this period went on to make a major contribution to urban life in a way that could not have been foreseen ten years earlier. However they did not necessarily arrest the declining use of public transport as a whole or the continued seemingly inexorable rise of road traffic.

In the context of the present study, Castle should be credited with identifying a core railway system with a long-term future. This represented a positive change from much of the railway system being treated as a basically outdated mode of transport fit for little else but to be run down. Castle should also be given credit for doing and not just talking when it came to the concept of a public service obligation, of public funding for loss-making services which clearly met an identifiable need. While this did not in itself prevent some further closures, there was a sense among railway workers at all levels that they were no longer part of an undervalued industry in terminal decline. In 1974 the Railways Act introduced the Public Service Obligation Grants which were a requirement of European law. A new culture was beginning to emerge which was to make the closure of railway passenger services almost unthinkable. Coordination of public transport in the major conurbations under local authority control saved many loss-making suburban railways and bus services and went some way towards providing an effective local transport infrastructure to attract greater usage. A new optimism was beginning to emerge.

Although Castle clearly had more sympathy for railways than was usual among Ministers of Transport, critics noted a 'creeping' process whereby some lines not recommended for closure mysteriously appeared on the list of proposed withdrawals. Probably the most notorious of these was that from Oxford to Cambridge. It would seem likely that there would be a demand for a fast and frequent diesel service between the two university cities, perhaps extended to Norwich in the east and Bristol or Cardiff in the west. In the summer of 1964 the timetable showed three through trains in each direction. One of these was an 'express' taking two hours for the seventy-seven miles and the other two, calling at a host of wayside stations, taking about two-and-a half hours. It was usually quicker to travel between the two cities via London. The line ran through a part of the country experiencing population growth, especially the designated new city of Milton Keynes and could have provided connections to trains on the West Coast, Midland and East Coast Main Lines. It was divided between three regions, none of which appeared to be enthusiastic about promoting the section for which they were responsible, never mind the rest. The closure proposal aroused stormy protests including some from heavyweight critics at the two universities but it went ahead. The Bletchley to Bedford section retained its service because of the difficulty of bus replacement and much later the Oxford to Bicester section reopened. Controversy has continued to rage over the issue and moves are afoot to recreate the route and restore services.

In retrospect, there was much that was inconsistent about Castle's decisions regarding the retention or closure of passenger services. The service to Redditch was reprieved, Redditch being designated for large-scale population growth, a consideration rejected in the case of Bletchley as part of the new 'city' of Milton Keynes but served by the Oxford to Cambridge line. Castle expressed concern about maintaining services to small seaside resorts and she refused consent for the closure of lines to Skegness, Whitby and North Berwick, for example. Among places losing their services were Clevedon, Padstow and Aldeburgh. She reprieved lines such as Penrith to Keswick and Maiden Newton to Bridport but always made it clear that such reprieves were conditional on future economic trends. Both lost their services after she had left office, Keswick in 1972 and Bridport in 1975. Many lines in the north-west of England were reprieved and have continued to this day, most of them having seen encouraging increases in usage.

Castle has been criticised for giving her approval to ninety-one partial or total withdrawals of passenger services. Some say that she should have simply stopped both the railway closure process and the motorway building programme but neither was going to happen in the context of the times. However, she identified the basis of what can now be seen as a stable network. The idea of providing public funding for necessary but unprofitable rail services took root and enabled the survival of many of what are now seen as vital parts of the system. Much needed investment and public transport coordination in the conurbations resulted from policies she initiated and implemented, often in the face of open hostility. Under Ernest Marples, 1,436 miles of the network lost passenger services. With Barbara Castle at the helm 606 miles lost theirs. It is a mixed record but it is not unfair to speculate about the fate that might have befallen the railways had Castle not become Minister of Transport and acted as she did in the period immediately after the Beeching era. Castle went off to another very demanding and controversial post when Wilson gave her the job of drawing up legislation to clip the wings of the trade unions through the Industrial Relations Act. In April 1968 she was replaced by Richard Marsh. During his short term of office in a job he had not sought, he consented among other things to the closure of the 'Waverley Route' from Edinburgh to Carlisle, the Taunton to Minehead and Barnstaple to Ilfracombe lines, all of which were controversial closures. By this time long delays were manifesting themselves in some closure proposals. An example was the line from Alton to Winchester. Over five years elapsed between initial proposal and closure, a delay of such length not only damaging BR's finances but provoking all manner of negative responses especially in the immediate neighbourhood of the line.

As far as roads were concerned, Castle was pragmatic. She recognised the personal benefits that had been brought about by the growth of private motoring and knew that it would be political suicide to take serious measures to curtail the freedom of movement that cars could offer. She famously said that she was not going to be a King Canute trying to force car-users back to rail when so many lines and stations had closed. Like all Ministers of Transport from the 1950s and since, she steered clear of formulating and attempting to implement policies to bring road traffic fully under control but introduced a tranche of safety measures despite almost hysterical protests that she was infringing individual liberty and persecuting the poor downtrodden motorist. The permanent installation of the 70mph speed limit, the breathalyser and the compulsory fitting of seat belts in new cars resulted in deaths from road accidents beginning to fall (8,000 people died on Britain's roads in 1966 when people could drink as much as they wished and then get behind the wheel and drive as fast as they wanted). The National Bus Company was created under the Transport Act bringing together the major non municipally-run bus companies and providing them with assistance with fuel costs and fleet replacement. That any of these measures were carried out at all was all the more creditable given that the Labour governments elected in 1964 and 1966 had to deal with economic problems of crisis proportions, considerable labour unrest and an intensely volatile period in international relations.

Labour, theoretically a socialist party, might be expected to prefer the collective nature of public transport to that of privately-owned lorries and cars and to initiate measures of transport coordination. As we have seen, this was by no means consistently carried out in practice. Working from within the ranks of the party in favour of road vehicles, against measures giving preference to railways and the concept of comprehensive transport integration and coordination had been the TGWU. This union organised large numbers of lorry drivers, bus crews and workers in the automotive industry all of whom were opposed to developments which might have a restrictive impact on the industries in which they worked. Frank Cousins, general secretary of the TGWU, was a particularly forceful advocate of the road-based interests of his members. Barbara Castle once said of Cousins that his socialism stopped at the door of a lorry. The TGWU could muster a huge card vote at the Labour Party's Annual Conference. It also had a sizeable number of sponsored Labour MPs and its views had to be taken into account in policymaking. Such views might conflict with those of the railway unions which were also affiliated to the party, but being smaller than the TGWU they had less clout. Cousins is purported to have once told Castle, probably not totally in jest, that if he had his way, he would close all the railways down. Certainly the TGWU was bitterly hostile to the creation of the National Freight Corporation.

The deficits continued to mount up and 1967 was a disastrous year financially. The economy was depressed and this impacted on the revenue of the railways. Despite praiseworthy economies a loss of £153 million was made in 1967 compared with £134.7 million in 1966. Green shoots were evident, however. Main line electrification was spreading and the 'sparks effect' was attracting more passengers. More diesels were entering service. The last standard gauge steam locomotives were withdrawn from service in 1968. Container-carrying trains were starting to make an impact, merry-go-round coal trains from pits to power stations meant much more efficient handling of this important traffic, 100-ton oil tank wagons were in use and, for passengers, new Mark II coaching stock came into service on long-distance routes. The rate of closures was slackening. In 1969, the BRB had a working surplus of £48.5 million. The railway workforce fell from 520,000 at the beginning of 1960 to 296,000 at the close of 1968. In the same period passenger stations and freight depots declined from 7,450 to 3,235, freight wagons from 945,000 to 437,000 and passenger coaches from 40,500 to 19,500.

In 1970, 275 route miles of passenger services were closed, 23 in 1971, 50 in 1972, 35 in 1973 and none in 1974. In March 1973 BR presented a report to the government titled *The Future of British Railways*. This argued forcefully against the implementation of any major cuts in the future and this was, of course, the exact opposite of the thrust of the Beeching Report of just ten years earlier. Almost empty trains continued to trundle along a number of rural backwater branch lines but any serious attempt to tackle this situation was now distinctly a non-starter for political reasons. There was a realisation that one small closure here and another there would only effect a very minor reduction in railway losses but might have significant social repercussions. This was a remarkable turnaround. Was it an endorsement of the necessity of the doctor's medicine which had now completed the cure required of it or evidence that common sense was now prevailing? The age of railway closures was almost over but few would have predicted the subsequent reopenings of stations and services, both heavy and light rail.

David Henshaw, in *The Great Railway Conspiracy* (1991) argues that railways never stood a chance in the world of 1960s realpolitik. 'The road transport pressure groups – the car manufacturers, the road builders, the oil companies and ancillary companies … were ranged against a nationalised yet virtually powerless railway industry. Aided by the Ministry of Transport, they succeeded, by the late 1960s, in bringing the railway system to its knees.' It is perhaps debateable whether the railways were brought quite as low as Henshaw suggests. Certainly there were extremists who would not have turned a hair if the railways had all been ripped up and turned into roads. It is true that they were perceived as old-fashioned in the 1950s and 1960s which was the age characterised by a perhaps excessive obsession with change and modernity. It took the unwelcome intervention of the Middle East oil crisis of 1973 to force the powers that be to take a more supportive attitude to the remaining network and see it as an asset rather than as an outdated mode of transport which was simply a drain on government finances.

Richard Beeching, ennobled as Lord Beeching, died in 1985 and, many years after he had left the railways, was asked if he regretted producing the plan that had led to the closure of so many lines. We shall never know how serious he was when he responded by saying that he wished that more lines had been closed.

Chapter 17

Seeking a Role, 1964–1978

The general election of 15 October 1964 returned Labour to office with a narrow majority. While the Liberal revival continued, bringing them nine MPs, Labour polled strongly, gaining sixty-five seats, mostly from the Conservatives. This marginal defeat thrust the Tories into Opposition for the first time since 1951. In Wallasey Marples retained his seat with a respectable 6,121 majority, though the Liberals, absent since 1951, surged to almost 20 per cent of votes cast. His 1950s majorities, gained without Liberal opponents, had clearly flattered him. Safely returned, Marples was rewarded with the position of Shadow Technology Minister by Sir Alec Douglas-Home, now adjusting implausibly to the role of Leader of the Opposition. Labour's narrow majority fuelled instant speculation about a swift return to the polls. This situation unsettled Home who was widely expected to retire or face an early leadership challenge. He probably had little appetite for a return bout with the wily Wilson.

Home directed Edward Heath to reformulate party policy and soon handed him the Shadow Chancellor portfolio, responsibilities that clearly boosted his succession chances. Then, in February 1965, knowing that it had been damaged by Home's 'emergence' as leader and Prime Minister, the party adopted a new procedure, giving the future choice of selecting the leader to Conservative MPs. That same month Home directed Marples to make a 'special study' of computers (in practice a twenty-three-day course devised for him by the three major British computer companies). Marples made sure the press knew about this while also happily ranging across other policy areas (see 'What I would do with the Telephones', *Sunday Telegraph*, 20 June 1965). In July Home resigned, triggering a contest between Maudling, Heath and Enoch Powell with Maudling assumed to be the favourite. It was, however, Heath who won. Marples might have been expected to back Heath, whose relatively humble background he shared; instead, like most of the Shadow Cabinet, he opted for Maudling, his former Cabinet colleague. Marples never explained this preference, but the ex-Chancellor was collegiate while

Heath was autocratic. The affable, gregarious Marples would have sought in vain for any vestige of personal warmth in Heath. Heath did not record his view of Marples but was frustrated by Wilson's successful identification of Labour with the cause of modernity in the public mind. Marples, as Shadow Technology Minister, may have seemed a potential rival.

This invites speculation as to why the ex-Minister of Transport did not throw his own hat into the ring at this time. Doing so is a common ploy of those seeking to raise their profile and in 1965 Marples certainly retained political ambitions. He was, arguably, the best-known figure in the Conservative Party. Was he still bruised by the snobbery which ten years earlier had almost ended his government career? Was his image still that of a publicity-seeking dilettante? There is no record of him even considering a leadership bid. The clubbable Maudling was lazy and complacent, traits observable in the contest preceding his narrow defeat by Heath that same month. Marples' dual failure, neither standing nor picking the winner, would in time blight his political career. For now he retained his place in a Shadow Cabinet largely unchanged from Home's time. Its meetings filled him with gloom; he wrote later of how 'destructive' they were.

The Labour bloodhounds might still be on the scent of his business interests: one of them, the Newham MP Arthur Lewis, even forced publication of all Marples Ridgway public sector contracts gained after public tender (a list unaccountably unpublished in Hansard). Privately, Warburgs, who had demanded a 'put' option in 1960 when he had sold his shares in the company, were minded to compel reacquisition now that he was out of office. It was forced instead to carry overdrafts locked up in Sudanese, Ethiopian and Libyan debts which it had been told were to finance UK contracts. It later lamented that 'as Mr Marples came back into the picture he increasingly assumed some moral responsibility for this'. The heat was taken out of the situation when Marples Ridgway and the bank reached a new agreement in May 1966. This foresaw liquidation of the company by the end of the 1968 financial year, a date postponed by mutual agreement.

Now however Marples had a new political passion, even an obsession. Asked by an amused Harold Macmillan if he had found the philosopher's stone, he replied affirmatively. As a shadow minister he chaired the Conservative technology policy group which had been set up on Macmillan's advice with a brief to develop party policy in that area. The Conservatives were out of office for now so he identified a new goal: establishing the scope, relevance and meaning of technology for British government. During the first quarter of 1965 he travelled round the UK, visiting the country's computer industry, several universities and looking at technological collaborations in industry. This seems to have been a period of great optimism for him. He had a new interest and there was every reason to think the party would back him in pursuing it; he was in demand on the lecture circuit (where his agent George Greenfield conjured many bookings) and in the press; January 1965 even brought a live interview on television with Malcolm Muggeridge. Meanwhile, publishers competed for a book from him on 'the political reconstruction of Great Britain', provisionally dubbed *Britain Must Go*. Despite its urgent title it never appeared, though it remained under active discussion as late as autumn 1969. All political speculation was subordinate to the thought that an election, with its enticing prospect of renewed office, must come soon.

Marples relished baiting Labour's new technology minister Frank Cousins, an ex-union leader rarely comfortable in the atmosphere of the Commons. Cousins' only lasting mark was the Science and Technology Act 1965 that set up research councils: this was the emptiness Marples yearned to expose. July 1965 brought a Supply Day used by the Opposition for a technology debate. Marples seized his chance to puncture Wilson's identification of science with socialism, lampooning government efforts in science-based industries. He alleged 'they had not the slightest idea what to do with the Department of the Minister of Technology'. The following week he was speaking on Post Office services. Such hopping about revealed the growing restlessness of a man of action who for the first time in seven years had no department to run.

He was not the first former minister to find Opposition frustrating. Eventually he resolved this by switching his focus away from politics but before that he made one more try in a new role. His reflections have in the half-century since become the commonplaces of historians: 'One of the reasons for the success of certain European countries after the Second World War was that everything they stood for was destroyed and they started anew … it behoves us to have some sort of violent change, and then we can start anew and do well. This applies to the Post Office.' His speeches in the mid-1960s oscillate between defensive rhetoric about his ministerial record and presenting himself as a moderniser. They attempt retrospectively to give some coherence to his time in government, positioning himself as a disrupter who always sought a new approach. 'We should start *de novo*,' he insisted. As technology spokesman he was unpersuasive, too prone to wander down memory lane. Was he the defender of the Conservative record or an iconoclast? In less than a year it would become apparent that his leader viewed him as indelibly part of his party's *ancien régime*. However, one more political opportunity awaited him.

In September 1965 Heath granted him a one-year sabbatical to produce definitive proposals for the Shadow Cabinet which might form the basis of government when the Conservatives returned to office. Was this his leader's ploy to remove him from the scene? If so, he was adequately supported, departing with Central Office backing and his colours nailed to the mast: 'I hope to be able to present Mr Heath and the Shadow Cabinet with some hard, definite proposals which will contribute towards giving Britain a new impetus under the next Conservative government.' He and Mark Schreiber – a Conservative Central Office secondment – left, with secretarial support, for a ten-week visit to the USA and Japan. In the States they ranged widely from the East via the mid-West and finally to the West Coast. Everywhere the pattern was the same. They met government departments, big technology companies, university staff and large industrial concerns. Then in late October they flew on to Japan, where their tour described a similar arc. They took in Hong Kong and even a helicopter ride above US troops defending Vietnamese rice fields from the Vietcong. At home, a mainly Conservative press still adjusting to a Labour government closely followed their progress. In their absence the Conservatives released a new technology policy document. Was it a warning shot from Heath? This maladroit step before Marples' return was not received well. William Rees-Mogg in the *Sunday Times* sniffed 'one can only hope that he will be able to develop a set of proposals which will make up for some of the deficiencies of Mr Cousins' ministry. This document does not contain them'. Wilson was bound to notice the avid press interest and in October packed Cousins off to the States for his own eight-day tour. Marples and Schreiber returned just before Christmas 1965, their return celebrated even in the *Daily Mirror*.

Stimulated by his findings, Marples made known his wish to 'lie low for some time and write a book'. The Central Office hierarchy, keen to exploit his newsworthy trip, found this unwelcome: party officials wanted a quick and partisan win from 'his long absence'. When they learned that he wished to reorganise government and the economy on the more technological basis he had discerned in the States, scepticism deepened. They also thought that they detected a familiar Marples trait: insufficient appreciation of the need to carry colleagues with him. They were, however, impressed by his eagerness to help as an early election approached. He even contributed, perhaps for the first time since 1951, to the party manifesto -- a passage promising war on 'waste in government'. He loyally played his part, addressing the 1922 Committee in February and appearing as 'the irrepressible Marples ... with a message of perpetual change from Japan' (the *Observer*) in a party-political broadcast a week before polling day, which Wilson had called for 31 March 1966.

As this date approached Marples pondered his prospects. A Conservative victory might yield him the Board of Trade; otherwise it would be a book, a byelection and the House of Lords. If however he held his seat but the Tories were out he might stump the country and become chairman of Central Office. His handwritten undated notes (MPLS 8/3) give the impression that he was oblivious to Heath's antipathy, yet 31 March dramatically revealed there would be no return to Cabinet rank. The long-anticipated election proved a Conservative rout, transforming Labour's fragile Commons majority of four into an impregnable ninety-six. Wilson's canny campaigning portrayed the Conservatives as disruptive and divisive and capitalised on the feeling that Labour needed longer to prove itself in office. The result, and what came next, would intensify Marples' alienation from the political world.

In Wallasey he had done well to hold onto his seat. His 22,901 votes barely outpolled those of Labour's R.C. Truman on 22,312. This time the Liberals, with 7,202 votes, may well have saved Marples' bacon. After twenty-one years in Parliament, his majority was reduced to a pitiful 589. In nearby Bebington Geoffrey Howe went down to defeat, while across the Mersey Tory Liverpool had become a Labour stronghold. Marples might now, like Maudling, have retreated into business, retired or taken more walking holidays. He still enjoyed influence, as the erection of an M62 pedestrian footbridge (popularly attributed to his membership of the Manchester Ramblers' Association) suggested. He also had a new walking companion, the rather less trim Richard Beeching. Their conversations dwelt on the unfitness of Parliament for facilitating economic progress (Nora Beloff, writing in the *Observer* on 'The Importance of Ernest', 24 April 1966). But he chose instead to double down on Parliament and seek Heath's backing for a new roving role, advocating a 'total systems analysis' of the party machine. This infelicitous and tactless initiative, extended just two days after the disastrous election result, could not have been more poorly timed. He would soon discover the chasm between his leader's plans and his own daydreams.

Humiliated at the polls, Heath now turned on his own party and purged the entire Shadow Cabinet. The clear-out was so thorough it left no place for Marples, Sandys or John Boyd-Carpenter. This was, transparently, a clean break with the Macmillan era and all those symbolising continuity with it. Marples may not have enjoyed Shadow Cabinet meetings but he regarded them, with the concomitant front bench responsibilities, as his due. Heath's reshuffle was almost laughably inept. It excluded talented figures he would eventually need when he became Prime Minister, yet it left in post the one person he loathed and might now have legitimately disposed of: the Party Chairman, Edward Du Cann. Marples, not yet sixty and armed with a renewed political passion, might have become the hub around which a new Conservatism would revolve; now he was excluded and, for the first time in almost a decade, was not part of the leadership. Either he misjudged Heath's feelings about him, or he overestimated his own centrality to Conservative politics. The leader's icy press release reads 'Marples leaves us and I have asked him to continue with the work he began in the last Parliament in the development of technology'. This might easily have been done from within the Shadow Cabinet – indeed, that would have facilitated it. The reshuffle was a crude display of power that failed to accommodate personal expectations.

Marples avoided any overt display of bitterness. 'You'll hear more of me', he cheerfully informed the *Evening News* (20 April) hinting, implausibly, since he had already had one, at a leader-sponsored sabbatical. He would not, he pointedly added, return to business, 'except for my vineyards of course'. He had a backbench role and was expecting a 'big job' in the next Conservative government. Newly free of collective responsibility, he was now available for major interviews and got them (Francis Boyd, 'Mr Marples will not play by "Etonian" rules', the *Manchester Guardian* 21 April; Nora Beloff, as above). He made the most of it, but Heath's inner team was dominated by career politicians. To the *Observer* he disclosed that he was in politics for the 'kicks' and conceded he could easily withdraw to pursue other interests. Coincidentally, 1966 was his year to be President of the *Compagnons de Beaujolais*.

Heath would later become famous for a U-turn. He made a small one on 19 April, announcing that Marples would after all have 'a role' reorganising Conservative Central Office where things were (Marples darkly warned the *Daily Sketch*) 'archaic and medieval'. If Marples had 'a role', what lay ahead for the Party Chairman, Edward Du Cann? This new arrangement took less than a year to unravel; if Marples had cool relations with Heath, those with Du Cann were positively icy. Anticipating authoritative criticisms of

Du Cann's later, chequered business career, Marples viewed him as slapdash. The two made no progress with developing a new advisory position for him. If Du Cann feared Marples was after his job, Marples did nothing to reassure him to the contrary. He is the likely author of an anonymous summary in the chairman of the Conservative Party's papers, 'Some Important Points in Events leading to the Resignation of Ernest Marples' (CCO 20/1/15). By May he was pressing Du Cann for a 'reconnaissance' to define Central Office objectives followed by a feasibility study to be carried through by someone with technical knowledge – not Du Cann then. They lunched several times, but, to Marples' intense frustration, there was little follow-up.

He stayed in the public eye with a rousing speech on technology at the Conservatives' Blackpool conference that October. It brought the jaded faithful to their feet but may have endeared him neither to Heath nor the chairman; even a three-way meeting of the principals later that month failed to produce results. Marples's pamphlet *No Choice but Change* soon appeared, its title borrowed (he claimed) from a remark made to him personally by Sir Alf Ramsay following England's catastrophic 1953 football defeat by Hungary. This edited version of his Blackpool conference speech was an extended plea for a low-tax economy and the widespread adoption of new technology. He followed it up with 'The Marples Report', three substantial interviews for the *Daily Mirror* on the country's weak economic performance. They read like job applications. When Cousins resigned in June 1966, even his favourite fox had shot itself.

By 6 February the following year, Marples had had enough. He denounced the amorphous position that he found himself in and made sure the world knew about it. This bombshell sharpened the image of an Opposition floundering after demoralising defeat and fuelled speculation he might soon replace Du Cann. He popped up on the Home Programme's *The World at One*, where presenter William Hardcastle mischievously stirred up old snobberies, remembering 'a senior Cabinet minister' who had murmured 'Mr Marples was the sort of man who looked as if he was wearing a brown suit even when he wasn't'. Bury St Edmunds MP Eldon Griffith, put up to defend the leadership, opposed Marples for chairman, citing his poor communication skills and lack of tact. However, he acknowledged that the row might alienate the younger and technologically minded. An unchained Marples was interviewed by the BBC's Alan Watson and *The Frost Programme*. Business offers started to flow, suggesting the talents unwanted in Parliament might yet be accommodated elsewhere. Heath made a lame defence of

Marples's decision while complaining that 'he found it not possible to give specific advice on points put to him', a statement that prompted a private reproach. Still, he kept his communication channels open via mutual friend Willie Whitelaw and within a month secured a meeting. The press, led by Charles Greville in the *Daily Mail* (8 February), followed the story with glee.

Back at Central Office, Du Cann was left to field considerable grassroots discontent. Many constituency officeholders (and not a few MPs) were disturbed at the impression that was being created. Marples decided to strike, calling a press conference, for which his notes ('Potential Statement', nd., MPLS 1/4/4) survive. The present party leadership, he charged, did not understand the real needs of Britain and had no use for his accumulated knowledge; the party was failing to use its time in opposition to work out a philosophy for Britain. When press questions piled in he stayed just on the right side of loyalty. Would he take the chairmanship of the party? No comment. Would he stay with technology? Yes. Would he stay on for his full parliamentary term? Yes. How did he see his future with the Conservative Party? No comment. He was not finished. On 26 February came the announcement 'Marples breaks his silence' on *The Week in Westminster*. He told its listeners that he would 'always resign if he couldn't do anything. By nature I like doing things'. In contrast to Enoch Powell, then campaigning for smaller government, he had no objection to big enterprises as such, but 'if it is big then for heaven's sake let it be efficient'. More damaging still to the party was an article in the *Sunday Mirror*, pitching him as a grassroots champion with 'messages of support' pouring in from 'all over the country'. Not until Ronald Butt of the *Financial Times* weighed in, rejecting the Marples version and disputing that organisational reform was a priority for the party, was there any press comfort for the leadership. Alone among political editors, Butt found the affair 'not very significant'. Heath, the most technocratic Conservative leader ever, might have nursed a grievance; instead he moved rapidly: proposing Marples to head a new unit to develop ideas for speedy and effective government decisions; better value for money and systems changes in the public sector; management of best practice and various recommendations for training and measures to promote staff motivation. Within a month Whitelaw had brokered an exchange of lengthy draft letters between them. Marples concluded, 'I accept these with pleasure, enthusiasm and loyalty. I am glad to be back, continuing my work.' With hindsight it seems he sold himself too cheaply: the problem of a think-tank *within* Central Office nominally subject to a jealous chairman remained unresolved. But now, for a time, things went well: he briefed the south-east Area Conservative annual meeting on the aims of his new unit; he was given platforms on innovation; he gathered around him talented people (above all, David Howell) who in time would make their mark.

Heath's failure to use Marples effectively may just boil down to poor personal chemistry. The Conservative leader was famously unclubbable; the publicity-hungry Marples was his opposite. These two grammar-school boys ought to have hit it off, but Heath had fluffed his opportunity in April 1966 when he might have installed Marples as chairman, leaving Du Cann to take the blame for a heavy drubbing at the polls. As chairman, Marples would always have sought publicity but he was utterly loyal, as Macmillan, had he been asked, would surely have confirmed. The same could not be said of Du Cann, as Heath would eventually discover. Ironically, Heath replaced him with Anthony Barber before the year was out.

Marples' October 1967 speech was his last to the Conservative Party Conference; as *Innovation and Renewal,* it also became his last party publication. This is the book he never wrote, his *apologia pro vita sua. Innovation and Renewal* combined all his post-1964 themes. Drawing heavily on Post Office and Transport experience, he jeered at the Labour government for abandoning socialism without embracing capitalism, specifically its 'best elements': the price mechanism, the profit motive and individual ambition. In a world where everything was subject to constant renewal, innovators themselves were the hardest people to find and innovation the most difficult habit to acquire. Research, however important, represented only about 10 per cent of innovation: also needed were venture capital in the hands of those equipped to judge projects technologically; risk-taking managers who lived on high returns; close cooperation between universities, financial sources and industrial enterprise. Labour, he concluded, might have appropriated the vocabulary of change but could never make it real.

More profound issues now drew attention. Easter 1968 sundered the Conservatives over race with Enoch Powell's infamous speech foreseeing bloody consequences from immigration. Heath, like much liberal opinion at the time, was appalled and Powell was eventually expelled. Marples himself was pro-immigrant (as it would have been put at the time), willing even to publicise Mohinder Loomba, an opponent of Powell's in Wolverhampton South-west, and the Jewish Bernard Delfont, to illustrate success in business ('Marples on Money', the *Mirror Magazine,* October–December 1969). As chairman he would have been a natural ally for Heath. Ruth privately told her correspondents that she thought that most Wallasey activists were behind Powell even if he had been 'rather naughty': she thought his support was a coded expression of discontent with Heath. The political process, once all-consuming for Marples, was losing its charm: he turned up in the Commons less and less, leading some observers to wonder if he saw it as an obstacle to economic progress, a pardonable view with Labour apparently secure in office. Among Conservatives, interventionist views at odds with his transport record were being canvassed: 'there is, then, a great deal to be said for a long-term policy of seducing motorists out of their cars and into public transport', wrote the author of an April 1967 Conservative pamphlet. Nominally he was still preparing his party for the technological challenges it would face in government; in practice, Central Office papers speak less of a 'Marples Unit' and more of the 'Public Sector Research Unit' (PSRU, its official title). He did not join fact-finding missions undertaken by Schreiber and Laurence Reed to the Netherlands, Italy and the USA in 1967 and in 1968 and seems to have mulled over the possibility of an extended stay at the US Brookings Institution, which would certainly have required him to step down from Parliament. He was still theoretically in charge of the PRSU and in the months before the 1970 election, approached Wilson on its behalf for permission to observe the work of government departments. Wilson, grumbling about press stories that the Opposition was being prevented from preparing detailed plans, blocked it.

The Unit was now effectively run by David Howell who ensured its six-monthly reports to the leader continued: a new Conservative government would need to hit the ground running. Central Office frustration with it took the form of efforts to bring its seconded staff back in house. When in early 1969 Maudling was deputed to meet Schreiber and Howell, his complaints echoed Heath's of two years before: 'we are at a loss to get anything very specific out of them' (Conservative Political Archives, CRD 3/14/9). Four months later Schreiber came up with a proposal for personal tax self-assessment which would be the Unit's last product. Certainly, Marples absences had escaped neither the Labour Prime Minister nor Maudling, who acidly observed, 'Marples has now more or less retired to labour in his vineyard.' It was Marples' own fault for giving contradictory signals. To the *Sunday Telegraph* magazine he speculated about devoting himself full-time to Fleurie, yet he had transferred management of the wine shipping business to Fortes. He was still campaigning, addressing the UK chapter of the American Chamber of Commerce (the speech recorded in *Anglo American Trade News*), and successfully moving a 'No Confidence in Her Majesty's Government' motion at the Oxford Union where his opponent was Anthony Wedgwood (later Tony) Benn, Labour's new technological lodestar.

Heath might be unwilling to make use of Marples but he was deadly serious about returning to office. In September 1969 he caused Robert Carr to convene a fortnight-long conference at Sundridge Park on the theme 'preparation for government'. There Shadow Chancellor Iain Macleod joined eleven MPs (among them Douglas Hurd, James Prior, David Howell and Paul Channon), eighteen industrialists (including Christopher Bland and Lord Beeching) and Mark Schreiber of the *nomenklatura*. Even Thomas Padmore, Marples' old Ministry of Transport private secretary attended. Marples was invited to join Heath to discuss Sundridge Park over dinner and also invited to a post-Sundridge Park seminar. When Heath followed Sundridge up with a more purely political Shadow Cabinet conference at Selsdon Park, Wilson amused himself by mocking 'Selsdon Man'. However, he had missed a shift in Heath's thinking: the earlier technological drive to transform government had given way to a belief in releasing market forces.

By now Marples had acquired respected elder statesman status. He became a Fellow of the Institute of Chartered Accountants and then was elected a Fellow of the Royal Society of Arts. He was lunched by David Astor, Donald Trelford and Patrick Seale, the hierarchy of the *Observer;* Seale followed up with an invitation for him to be an occasional contributor. In autumn 1969 *Any Questions?* teamed him with Richard Marsh, Adam Faith and Marghanita Laski. Asked about drivers convicted of drink-driving, he fortunately opposed a lifetime ban. February 1970 brought a BBC *Nationwide* film unit to the Marples' Belgravia home.

In January 1970 Marples wrote to Macmillan recalling their time at Housing: 'happy days because they were constructive and active'. Macmillan, now widowed, fondly remembered 'that great adventure which we shared together'. Steadily bringing out his memoirs, he enjoyed visits from the Marples couple to lighten his loneliness. Macmillan was then seventy-six and had last dined at Eccleston Street on 5 December 1963. Photographs of the sixty-three-year-old Marples, never in short supply, show an ageing man, even though his good physical condition (apart from raised cholesterol) impressed doctors at the Institute of Directors medical centre. One non-medical observer (Arthur Hopcraft) thought he had 'the constitution of a camel in the body of a whippet'. As if to confirm medical opinion his

November 1970 weight was an unchanged nine stone five pounds: a year later he would feature as a Hyde Park jogger in BBC2's *Man Alive* after receiving permission to log with a 'J' the trees on his jogging route; by then car fumes and Hyde Park Corner traffic had put an end to his London cycling.

He used his continuing political fame to promote products he believed in. October 1970 found him in Glasgow praising Minalka, a diet supplement and he arranged to be pictured training with Rangers players while he was there. Like National Hunt jockey Lester Pigott he used regional TV to promote the anti-rheumatism merits of Minalka, produced by the company E.R. Squibb from Moreton in the Wirral. His business interests diversified. Now he became International Director of Purcolator Services Inc. (USA) and Director of Purcolator Services (UK); Director of international affairs in Europe for the American Courier Corporation (ACC); chairman of Minalka (UK) and of Boase Massimi Pollit, the advertising agency.

June 1970 brought the longed-for general election, the first to enfranchise eighteen-year olds. Marples's only national role was an *Any Questions* appearance, though as a prominent north-western figure he featured in the *Today* Programme's Liverpool-based regional coverage. The Conservatives' modest majority of thirty-one was enough to make Edward Heath Prime Minister. His famous manifesto preface had affirmed 'Nothing has done Britain more harm in the world than the endless backing and filling which we have seen in recent years. Once a policy has been established, the prime minister and his colleagues should have the courage to stick with it.' He lived up to this declaration for less than two years. Once established in No.10, Heath thanked Marples 'for all the hard and imaginative work which you did in helping us to prepare for government', warm words that could not disguise the absence of a 'big job' offer. It was not even clear that Heath thought there was a big job to be done. The new Prime Minister's idea of bringing business techniques into government was to sharpen procurement practices (the 'Marks and Sparks' touch as the *Observer's* Nora Beloff termed it, following engagement of Marks & Spencer boss Derek Rayner). Better purchasing procedures were a far cry from revolutionising technology in British manufacturing, the cause Marples had espoused on losing office. Worse, the job of fertilising Whitehall even with these residual business techniques fell to the 'minister in charge' of the Civil Service Department, Lord Jellicoe, a minor non-Cabinet figure, who had not even attended Sundridge Park. Marples lunched with him soon after, generously offering to help but he must have felt crushed by his exclusion. Press reports hinted that Heath viewed Marples as 'too disrupting' for the job. If true this was bizarre: disruption was the whole point.

There was some consolation. David Howell became parliamentary secretary under Jellicoe. In PRSU days Howell had hoped to be the chief of staff in a putative Prime Minister's department. Howell affectionately told Marples, 'if the new style of government had a founder and inspirer it is you', adding that the day they met was 'the most fortunate in my life'. These sentiments might not have endeared him to the new Prime Minister. In October Heath wrote to Marples again, now enclosing his new White Paper *The Reorganisation of Central Government* where Marples' pre-election contributions were acknowledged. The most tangible and enduring of Heath's administrative reforms came in 1971 in the form of the Central Policy Review Staff (CPRS), based in the Cabinet Office. While this had not been a specific Marples recommendation (his later, rather tactless, recollection that Heath was given 'a list of what should be done but he chose not to do it'), it did employ Mark Schreiber, so Marples had two acolytes at the centre. For now, he confined himself to the observation that the new administration had too many whips, while lamenting the absence of entrepreneurs in the Civil Service Department: the cerebral Howell was hardly that and nor was the aristocratic Schreiber.

The 1970 Wallasey campaign had been a conventional joust of meetings in schools and halls. Marples' majority of 3,111 reflected the national swing. Labour had lost over a thousand votes while the Liberals' poll of 5,577 was respectable. This was a four-way contest with 'Anti-Common Market' candidate J.D. Hill on 2,946 votes, almost matching the Marples majority. It seems Heath's pro-European inclinations, not to mention those of Marples himself, were starting to reverberate locally. This result paled before his 1950s triumphs but he put a brave face on it by celebrating twenty-five years as Wallasey MP with the Conservative Association's ladies' branch in July.

Nearly 3,000 Wallasey votes against the 'Common Market' were well-aimed, for Marples was well-known for being pro-entry. 'I always believe that we should have joined the Common Market at its beginning,' he told the House in one of his last speeches. The Wallasey constituency embraced the site of Gandy Belts, a company which sent brake linings to the Continent but feared to expand in case high EEC tariffs blocked the way. As Transport Minister Marples had enthusiastically participated in channel tunnel planning, backed Macmillan's ill-fated 1963 application and acquiesced in Wilson's later unsuccessful attempt. For a vineyard owner (one of only two Englishmen in that happy position) self-interest and conviction coincided. Marples knew Heath meant to succeed where his predecessors had failed and thought this the last chance: 'if we do not get in now, we shall never do so'. During the tense Commons debates preceding entry he jocularly offered a bottle of his own 1970 vintage to anyone prepared to vote for the Common Market. He approved of the Common Agricultural Policy (once even breaking a 'pair' to do so), freely pointed to faster rising living standards in member states and approved the terms when agreed, albeit with some reservations about the impact on pensioners and the low-paid. 'If we go it alone, we shall be a small unit. If we join the Six, we shall be part of a large unit.'

Common Market entry and race were new issues defining a new decade where Marples ceased to be a household word. He could still be heard on Radio 4 (as it now was), or on *Any Questions?* At the beginning of 1971 there was a postal workers' strike (led by Tom Jackson whom Marples knew): Marples ensured he was pictured hand-delivering supplies to Manchester pharmacists. The 1972 resignation of Home Secretary Reginald Maudling forced a reshuffle on Heath and, once again, Marples' name figured in press speculation. But that March, disaster struck. Driving in a rush for a three-line whip, Marples failed to stop and report that he had hit another car, causing £30 of damage to its wing, bumper and lights. Marples, driving for forty-seven years, was ordered to appear in court the following month to give reasons why he should not be disqualified. He claimed to have returned to the location of the crash only to find the damaged car had gone. An adjournment did not help: he suffered a £50 fine, endorsement of his licence for failing to report an accident and a £10 fine for failing to stop. The magistrate observed that he could have reported the crash to one of the PCs on duty at the House. Suspicions persisted that he failed to report the incident because he had been drinking, though his solicitor Charles Brandreth pleaded in mitigation Marples' anxiety about business problems. These were increasingly acute: the day after his court appearance he left on a European business trip. Faced with having to explain why he should not be disqualified, he entered a guilty plea on both charges. His licence was eventually restored but the fines stood. *Punch* later reported an ad offering his 1970 estate for sale. Despite this bad publicity, in 1973 he was elected President of the Electric Vehicle Association of Great Britain. He could still show some real chutzpah.

In March 1973 he was elected one of three Freemen of Wallasey. The 1972 Local Government Act had amalgamated the metropolitan borough of

Wirral (which contained the county boroughs of Wallasey and Birkenhead) within the metropolitan county of Merseyside. Marples was unimpressed, telling the local paper he would promote Wallasey instead. In February 1973 his absence from office was noted in a sharp attack on the government by Reginald Bevins ('Where have all the good men gone?', *Spectator*, 3 February 1973). Even in October 1973 he was still being prodded to write his memoirs. In Wallasey he knew his race was run, soon writing to Heath informing him he would not stand at the next election. This news appears to have reached the press first, going by the usual career reviews. Heath's courteous reply of 26 June 1973 acknowledged 'the work which you did in Opposition on the machinery of government', adding that this had to be kept 'fairly private' at the time, a remark which may have elicited a rueful smile.

Marples had been tidying up his business commitments. The previous year he had settled all debts of Ernest Marples et Cie to the Guaranty and Credit Corporation S.A. February 1973 brought an emergency general meeting of Marples Ridgway to wind up the company and appoint Ridgway liquidator. By an agreement dated 6 February, Warburgs paid Marples £232,923, which was split between three beneficiary accounts. Soon afterwards exchange controls forced them to get Bank of England permission to repay £120,000 to a Liechtenstein bank. The company had thrived, especially overseas; its most recent UK venture was the Liverpool approach road to the second Mersey road tunnel, opened by the Queen in June 1971. October 1972 brought bad publicity when the scaffolding of a concrete bridge linking to the M4, a Marples Ridgway project, had collapsed, resulting in fifty injuries. Ridgway himself settled with Libyan litigants over a historic dispute and a similar resolution was achieved for the company's Ethiopian transactions. This cleared the way for full absorption of Marples Ridgway into the Bath & Portland group in 1974. More personally poignant was Marples' June 1973 decision to sell the Fleurie chateau while retaining a part-management role. He kept Les Laverts.

He was still an MP with business interests. Since early summer 1972 he had been grumbling that three-line whips scheduled for Mondays curtailed his activities as ACC director. He pleaded the need to sort out 'urgent business' in France to successive Chief Whips. Though distracted, his political antennae remained acute: when news of his resignation broke he did not disguise his view that 'Parliament isn't doing very well at the moment'. By late September he was writing to Chief Whip Francis Pym to report a 'sullen mood' in the Wirral, not outright hostility but 'a very deep feeling that we are a hopeless, helpless and obstinate government'. He thought the outlook in the north-west must be 'pretty bleak unless someone pulls an ace or two out of the pack'. When it came to the famous policy U-turn of the Heath government in 1972, Marples had enthusiastically backed the new orientation, having been unsympathetic to the old. He had, for example, been advocating incomes policy for at least a year (letter, *Financial Times*, 21 April 1971). His very last intervention in the House came on 26 November 1973, a question to Education Secretary Margaret Thatcher requesting information on schools' heating fuels. Meanwhile he continued conscientiously to do an MP's quieter work. One constituent, Tommy Wisbey, had ended up in prison. Marples corresponded with him and offered him employment as part of his rehabilitation, but Wisbey was not released until 1984, long after Marples' death.

Wallasey Conservatives had chosen Lynda Chalker, ex-head girl of Roedean, thirty years his junior, as his successor. The 1972 Local Government Act's formation of a new Metropolitan Borough of the Wirral was bound to accelerate its urbanisation. Wallasey itself remained marginal until the years of the Thatcher landslides, eventually succumbing to Labour in 1992. Urbanisation and other trends secured the entire Wirral peninsular for Labour thereafter. Now an already bumpy road to retirement was disrupted further. Marples habitually stored his wine in Arch 42 under a Brixton railway viaduct. On 22 January 1974 the structure was shaken by a blast which damaged six adjacent terraced houses, trapping a middle-aged woman in her bed. Arriving three hours later the couple salvaged 130 cases which they transferred to a flat in Harwood Court. Despite his instant attribution of the explosion to gas, the police believed the cause was an electric fire located too close to a cardboard case, triggering this unfortunate chain of events. Marples was right, as SEGAS later confirmed. Ruth's comment, 'yesterday was just not our day' captured the situation perfectly.

Remarkably Marples kept to his commitment to fly the next day to meet Tom Paine, now General Electric vice-president, to discuss alternative power sources. That same winter the country experienced the oil price shock, precipitating an energy crisis. Then there followed a miners' strike aimed against wage restraint. On 7 February 1974 Heath called a snap general election to resolve (as he saw it) the issue of who should govern Britain: the shivering country would go to the polls on 28 February. To the *Manchester Evening News*, Marples bluntly lamented the 'personal clash' between Wilson and Heath. 'They have never got on well, even privately … ' The day after the election was called, news broke that thirty Harwood Court tenants (in both furnished and unfurnished apartments) were fighting a notice to quit. Marples' intention had been to move them out while carrying through an extensive modernisation of windows, heating and hot water systems as well as installing new lifts. The job needed to be tackled as a whole: it could not be managed flat by flat. By now there was a Labour government, albeit by a narrow margin. That March Putney MP Hugh Jenkins (now also Minister for the Arts) took up the tenants' cause, vowing 'to pare the claws of capitalism'. In Wallasey Lynda Chalker had held the seat against Labour by 2,492.

It was then standard practice for retiring Cabinet ministers to be given a peerage but as the months passed after Heath had been apprised of Marples's intentions, signals indicated that he might not be thus elevated. The Marples couple consulted Martin Redmayne, a former whip who undertook to discover Heath's intentions. Ruth was pessimistic. 'Ted Heath hates your guts' she told him. After waiting and waiting even Marples himself thought Heath could 'stuff' the honour (Marples Papers, 8/1). He faced the prospect of humiliation. Finally, the 5 April 1974 dissolution honours made him Baron Marples of Wallasey, commemorating nearly thirty years representing his Wirral seat. Telegrams arrived from all three of the Prime Ministers under whom he had served, from Lynda Chalker and many others. He borrowed his coat of arms from that of the now defunct Borough of Wallasey and took his seat on 15 May 1974. The Right Honourable Alfred Ernest Marples, having been created Baron Marples of Wallasey in the County of Merseyside for life was, in his robes, introduced between Lords Chesham and Brecon. He would never address the House of Lords.

Ruth recorded some of what happened next in her undated memoir (MPLS 8/1), later writing that his last years were 'not particularly happy or fruitful'. From about 1975 his health was starting to fail. Ruth described his 'extreme fatigue, tiredness, lack of concentration and loss of memory'. For the first time in their marriage he grew lazy: she had (in her words) 'to carry him'. While some visitors found his judgement 'unbalanced', neither she nor anyone else thought of speaking to a neurologist although, as she later reflected, 'he had been declining mentally for some years'. When in 1977 one was finally consulted, he concluded (in Ruth's words) 'Ernest's brain was "physically shrinking", "becoming that of a child"'. He had Alzheimer's disease, a term for which neither she nor anyone in her circle then had an adequate vocabulary.

As early as 1974 there were signs of trouble. One June day while he was jogging in Richmond Park, it came on to rain. He jogged back to his car and was foolishly tempted to try some wine he kept there. He then drove home, passing a red traffic light and drawing the attention of the police. They breathalysed him and found 187 milligrams of alcohol per millilitre in his blood. His case was heard in October at Marlborough Street magistrates' court where he was fined £45 plus nominal costs. This time, probably inevitably, he lost his licence. His post-hearing statement, 'I still say the only way to be really safe is not to take a drink at all if you are driving' availed him naught. Nor was it the end of his motoring troubles. His beige Range Rover was towed away from a House of Commons no-parking area on 1 November.

Wilson returned to the polls in October 1974, hoping to enhance his narrow majority of February. He achieved a 2 per cent swing and there was little sign that voters wished to restore the Conservatives to office. As the results came in Marples lamented the animosity between Wilson and Heath, telling the *Edinburgh Evening News*, 'I think he [Heath] is going to be a loser again'. In Wallasey Lynda Chalker had done well to defy a modest Labour surge. Marples ended a miserable 1974 by breaking his thumb three weeks before Christmas: there would be no Davos or Zermatt this year.

From 1975 the couple were plagued by financial problems. When he was younger, Marples had comfortably juggled political and business interests. It is tempting now to attribute the increasing chaos engulfing his handling of money to a lack of grip as Alzheimer's tightened its hold. After his Maureen Cleave interview for *Drive* magazine that spring, Marples had to press them for his fee. The distinguished Eccleston Street Visitor Book finally petered out on 28 May. This was the prelude to a dramatic flight from the country. The couple had 'slipped away' (in the words of Willliam Hickey of the *Daily Express*) from Belgravia to set up in a 'sumptuous penthouse' in Monte Carlo. In Marples' own (later) words, they had 'scarpered'. Richard Stott alleged that they 'left by the night ferry with his belongings crammed into tea chests, leaving the floors of Eccleston Street littered with discarded clothes and possessions'. To the *Daily Mail* he offered a political explanation that its readers would find congenial, denouncing the iniquities of the Wilson government, its social contract and 'financial gestapo' and grumbling that he ought to have left years ago. The UK, he fulminated, had 'ceased to exist'. Not everyone bought this line. A decent job offer (such as the chairmanship of BR, mused the *Observer*'s William Davies), might have detained him but Wilson was no more likely to offer it than Heath. There matters might have rested but for investigative journalism. That May the couple were already settled into a new life, allowing Marples to be guest speaker at a Monte Carlo club lunch. He wrote to Margaret Thatcher naming Sidney Towning as custodian of his UK interests, predicting he wouldn't be back for 'a very long time'. The new party leader, like her predecessor, was unenthusiastic about ghosts from the Macmillan era. By June Ruth felt settled enough to write a round robin to friends explaining their sudden departure.

Marples had always enjoyed a surprisingly warm relationship with the Labour-supporting *Daily Mirror*. The ex-Postmaster General and Transport Minister was an inexhaustible source of photo opportunities and stories and he was engagingly non-partisan. Perhaps the paper was attracted by the very qualities which (in the eyes of Conservative MPs) ruled him out for a top Tory job. The *Mirror*, now edited by Richard Stott, still had a nose for a story and on 2 July 1975 led with a screaming front-page splash, 'Why Marples had to go, *EXCLUSIVE*'. Thirty years on Stott hilariously recalled confronting Marples in France in his 2007 memoir *Dogs and Lampposts*. Its reporters (Stott and a photographer) had door-stepped the 'visibly stunned and angry' man in Monaco. Three days before the end of the tax year, he had faced in the *Mirror's* words 'a whacking great tax bill', the culmination of a 'running battle' with the Inland Revenue which was chasing him for thirty years' back tax from Eccleston Street and for capital gains tax on his Putney properties. It was a gleeful Labour scoop, upstaging the gullible *Mail*. Meanwhile, the *Mirror* continued, Marples' Harwood Court tenants had presented him with a long list of ninety-two defects that needed righting pending legal action. The *Mirror* illustrated their complaints with a picture over the caption 'dilapidation'. The heart of the problem was his leasing company Penhale Estates with which he would not finally settle until July 1976, and out of court. Marples' plan, charged the *Mirror*, had been to sell the flats as a single job lot to Vin International for between £500,000 and £1 million. Vin International would in turn have refurbished them, selling them on, perhaps for up to £2.5 million. The key to the transaction was tax avoidance: Marples would incur capital gains tax of 30 per cent on the Vin transfer, while Vin, an offshore company based in Liechtenstein, would be liable only for stamp duty of 2 per cent.

The *Mirror* believed the scheme fell through in February 1974 when the Conservatives lost office because the Inland Revenue had to be seen to tighten up under a Labour government. Meanwhile, in a separate action Marples was being sued for a six-figure sum by Bankers Trust International. This arose from an agreement with his French wine shipping company Ernest Marples et Cie.

Marples had been unimpressed by his personal taxman. 'The man was a socialist – I could tell' he declared, unwisely, to the *Mirror*. Appended to the story was, for the first time in print, the name of chartered surveyor and Ecclestone Enterprises director John Holmes. Holmes, in a bitter dispute with Marples and suing for wrongful dismissal, was claiming £70,000 in damages. Only in November 1975 did Marples manage to foreclose two mortgages of Holmes in St Austell: they had cost him £61,000. After the appearance of this report the Treasury froze Marples' British assets. Not until November 1977 did he pay £7,600 to the British government in settlement of his breach of exchange control regulations.

His finances were thus threatened from three different directions: Harwood Court tenants had doubled down on their battle to secure improvements to their rented accommodation and had now taken legal advice. Wandsworth Council subsequently offered to buy the entire block of 129 flats for an unknown amount but Marples had rejected their offer. Ernest Marples et Cie was the second source of trouble. Finally there were debts: to Clifford Tees & Gale (Architects & Surveyors) which he hoped to extinguish with sales of Harwood Court and 33 Eccleston Street. He needed to raise the Harwood Court rents as well. Marples had felt it 'his duty' to resign all UK appointments when he left the country (the only apparent exception his presidency of the Mobile Radio Users' Association). This would have included the vice-presidency of the Camping Club which had reappointed him only in March 1975 and his Ramblers' Association posts.

Faced with a challenge, Marples could somehow still be enthusiastic. Ruth thought he was 'working like a beaver' earning money both for the UK and himself. June 1975 found him in Nigeria pitching for an engineering project. He recorded his relief in focusing on it rather than having a 'continuous battle with the Revenue on the taxes levied by the Socialist Party on those in England who wish to work', but the strain was starting to tell. That month the couple seem to have reached a crisis in their marriage. Ruth's moving letter regretted 'we are not making each other happy'; they even seem to have contemplated separation after he assailed her with accusations of bossiness and even bullying. Eccleston Street, scene of so many social triumphs, was put up for sale early in 1976, the blurb reading 'scheduled [listed] Georgian, penthouse on top, lift to all floors'. BP wrote to Ruth in October informing her that they were disposing of the 'British Ensign' which she had launched at Cammell Lairds twelve years earlier.

Marples could still make plans, telling Macmillan in March 1976, 'I am at this late stage considering writing my memoirs', and seeking advice from John Anderson that June, tempting him with documents on Keeler and Rice-Davies, and his shabby treatment by Heath. His driving disqualification had expired in October 1975 and in January he persuaded Ruth to request renewal of the international permit. Given her growing concerns about his health she must have had some misgivings but Marples deluded himself in the belief he was 'in great shape, physically'. From early December 1976 until late April 1977 the couple were in Davos where Marples' physical vigour seemed undiminished: he resumed skiing five weeks after a heart attack.

By early 1978 his decline was unmistakeable. He made a will (witnessed by David Patrick Rosling and Frederick Carrick Lindsay Dobson on 8 February 1978) leaving Ruth all real and personal property. In mid-June 1978 he was discharged from the Princess Grace Hospital, Monaco, under a heavy drug regime, a responsibility that must have fallen entirely on the indefatigable Ruth. It was a brief reprieve, for he relapsed and died on 6 July 1978 from a coronary brought on by the debilitating symptoms of Alzheimer's. The gross value of his estate was £575,856 but the debts were substantial. The Bankers' Trust debt had been settled two years before, and a month later he had settled out of court with Penhale Estates, the property company running Harwood Court. After settling other debts, £388,166 remained. *The Times* obituary was written by Peter Utley. It spoke eloquently of 'the superiority of a vigorous and largely untutored natural intelligence', recalling him rather as 'a man of action than as the exponent of a consistent and coherent political creed'. The less forgiving *Daily Mail* bluntly reflected the Establishment view: 'the most incorrigible self-publicist the Tories have ever produced'.

His memorial service was held at noon in St Margaret's Westminster on 7 November 1978. The front row was occupied by three former Prime Ministers – Harold Macmillan, Lord Home and Edward Heath. Hughie Green joined them. The tribute was given by Lord Hailsham who, as Quintin Hogg, had been associated with Marples since at least 1946 when they shared a Birkenhead political platform; they were of an age. Hailsham remembered 'a friend of infinite versatility', lauded his boyishness and hailed him as a genius. He did not shun hyperbole (attributing to him the invention of STD) but the list of Marples' achievements and interests during his times at Transport and Housing was impressive enough. In a happy flourish Hailsham suggested Marples would have 'climbed up to Heaven by the most difficult route, using pitons and carabiners all the way'. He mentioned the Profumo affair, a jarring note for some. Lynda Chalker (second choice once Macmillan, pleading failing eyesight, had declined) read one lesson, Mr Speaker George Thomas the other; David Howell (who had helped Ruth plan and organise the service) and Johnny Tierney were ushers. The text of the order of service included the *No Choice but Change* speech which had, when delivered live, brought the 1968 Conservative conference to its feet. Privately Hailsham wrote to Ruth recalling Marples as 'a genius and one of the most lovable of my colleagues'. A future Prime Minister Margaret Thatcher in a handwritten note recalled him 'vividly as he was during his peak political years as Minister of Transport; full of ideas, enthusiasm and determination'. Ruth continued to guard his memory. She pressed the Dean of Westminster for a memorial tablet in the wall of St Margaret's, Westminster. He refused, pleading that shortage of space meant this honour must be confined to those with 'an active and close connection' to the Church. Ruth, angrily fearing Establishment revenge beyond the grave, guarded his legacy into her old age, rebuking *Daily Mail* editor Paul Dacre for publishing an article claiming Marples had been the 'Man in the Mask'. She died on 1 November 2014 at the age of ninety-five. Her husband Ernest Marples lies buried in a family plot in Wythenshawe Cemetery, Manchester.

Bibliography

Allen, G. Freeman (1966) *British Railways after Beeching*. Shepperton: Ian Allan.

Austin, C. and Faulkner, R. (2015) *Disconnected! Broken Links in British Rail Policy*. Addlestone: OPC.

Bagwell, P. (1974) *The Transport Revolution from 1770*. London: Batsford.

Bagwell, P. and Lyth, P. (2002) *Transport in Britain. From Canal Lock to Gridlock*. London: Hambledon & London.

Blake, R. (1970) *The Conservative Party from Peel to Churchill*. Harmondsworth: TBS.

Bonavia, M. (1971) *The Organisation of British Railways*. Shepperton: Ian Allan.

Bonavia, M. (1981) *British Rail. The First Twenty-Five Years*. Newton Abbot: David & Charles.

Boocock, C. (1998) *Spotlight on BR. British Railways 1948–1998. Success or Disaster?* Penryn: Atlantic.

Booker, C. (1969) *The Neophiliacs. A Study in the Revolution in English Life in the Fifties and Sixties*. London: Collins.

Buchanan, C. (1958) *Mixed Blessing. The Motor Car in Britain*. London: Leonard Hill.

Campbell-Smith, D. (2011) *Masters of the Post: the Authorised History of the Royal Mail*. Harmondsworth: Penguin/Allan Lane.

Catterall, P. (ed.) (2011) *The Macmillan Diaries: The Cabinet Years, 1950–1957*, vol. 2, *Prime Minister & After*. Basingstoke: Macmillan.

Clough, D.N. (2013) *Dr Beeching's Remedy. A Cure for a Century of the Railway's Ills*. Hersham: Ian Allan.

Clough, D.N. (2014) *The Modernisation Plan. British Railways' Blueprint for the Future*. Hersham: Ian Allan.

Conservative Party Archive (n.d., references begin CCO, CRO). Oxford: Bodleian Library, University of Oxford.

Creer, S. (1986) *BR Diary 1948–57*. Shepperton: Ian Allan.

Denning, Lord (n.d.) *Report of the Inquiry into the Security Aspects leading to the Resignation of the former Secretary of State for War, John Profumo*. London: HMSO, Cmnd. 2152 (this inquiry's papers, now lodged at the National Archives, will not be released until 2049).

Marples, Ernest *Personal and Political Papers 1940–1978*.

Dyos, A.J. and Aldcroft, D.H. (1971) *British Transport. An Economic Survey from the Seventeenth to the Twentieth Century*. Leicester: Leicester University Press.

Evans, H. (1998) *Downing Street Diary: The Macmillan Years*. London: Hodder & Stoughton.

Faulkner, R. and Austin, C. (2018) *Holding the Line. How Britain's Railways were Saved*. Manchester: Crecy.

Fiennes, G. ([1967] 2015) *I Tried to Run a Railway*, 2nd edn. London: Head of Zeus.

Freeman Allen, G. (1966) *British Rail After Beeching*. London: Ian Allan.

Glover, G. (1987) *BR Diary 1958–67*. Shepperton: Ian Allan.

Gourvish, T.R. (1986) *British Railways 1948–1973. A Business History*. Cambridge: Cambridge University Press.

Hamer, M. (1987) *Wheels Within Wheels. A Study of the Road Lobby*. London: Routledge & Kegan Paul.

Hardy, R.H.N. (1989) *Beeching: Champion of the Railway?* Shepperton: Ian Allan.

Harris, S. (2016) *The Railway Dilemma. The Perpetual Problems of Ownership, Costs & Control*. Addlestone: Ian Allan.

Heath, E. (1998) *The Course of my Life*. London: Hodder & Stoughton.

Henshaw, D. (1991)*The Great Railway Conspiracy*. Hawes: Leading Edge.

Hennessey, P. (2007) *Having it So Good*. Harmondsworth: Penguin.

Hillman, M. and Whalley, A. (1981)*The Social Consequences of Railway Closures*. London: Policy Studies Institute.

Historic Hansard online, https://api.parliament.uk/historic-hansard/index.html.

Horne, A. (1998) *Macmillan 1891–1956*. London: Macmillan.

Jones, R. (2020) *Beeching. Britain's Railway Closures and their Legacy*. Horncastle: Gresley Books.

Joy, S. (1973) *The Train that Ran Away. A Business History of British Railways 1948–68*. Shepperton: Ian Allan.

Keeler, C. (2002) *The Truth at Last*. London: Pan.

Kynaston, D. (2008) *Austerity Britain 1945–48. A World to Build*. London: Bloomsbury.

Kynaston, D. (2008) *Austerity Britain 1944–51: Smoke in the Valley*. London: Bloomsbury.

Kynaston, D. (2010) *Family Britain 1951–57*. London: Bloomsbury.

Kynaston, D. (2015) *Modernity Britain 1957–62*. London: Bloomsbury.

Lamb, R. (1995) *The Macmillan Years: The Emerging Truth,* London: John Murray.

Loft, C. (2013) *Last Trains. Dr Beeching and the Death of Rural England*. London: Biteback.

Macmillan, H. Lord Stockton (1971) *Diaries. Riding the Storm, 1956–1959*. London: Macmillan.

Mangold, T. (2020) *Keeler, Profumo, War and Me*. BBC broadcast, 2 February.

Manoochehri, J. (2009) *Social Policy and Housing: Reflections of social values*. PhD thesis, University of London.

Mullay, A. (2006) *Railways for the People. The Nationalisation of British Railways in 1948*. Easingwold: Pendragon.

National Archives, Kew (references begin AV; CAB; CUST; MT; PREM), https://.nationalarchives.gov.uk/.

Oxford Dictionary of National Biography (2004) Oxford: Oxford University Press.

Pearson, A.J. (1969) *The Railways and the Nation*. London: George Allen & Unwin.

Perkin, H. (1976) *The Age of the Automobile*. London: Quartet.

Plowden, W. (1971) *The Motor Car and Politics 1896–1970*. London: The Bodley Head.

Pryke, R. and Dodgson, J. (1975) *The Rail Problem*. London: Martin Robertson.

Reakes, G. (1956) *Man of the Mersey*.

Royal Mail Archive (references begin with POST), https://postalmuseum.org/collections/the-archive/.

Setright, L.J.K. (2003) *Drive on! A Social History of the Motor Car*. London: Granta.

Sked, A. and Cook, C. (1992) *Post-war Britain. A Political History*, 4th edn. Harmondsworth: Penguin.

Spectator magazine.

Starke, D. (1982) *The Motorway Age. Road and Traffic Policies in Post-war Britain*. Oxford: Pergamon.

Stott, R. (2007) *Dogs and Lamposts*. London: Metro.

Thomas, D. St. J. (1960) *The Rural Transport Problem*. London: Routledge & Kegan Paul.

Thomas Symonds, N. (2015) *Nye: Political Life of Aneurin Bevan*. London: I.B. Tauris.

Thorold, P. (2003) *The Motoring Age. The Automobile and Britain 1896–1939*. London: Profile.

Williams, C. (2009) *Harold Macmillan*. London: Weidenfeld & Nicholson.

Wragg, D. (2004) *Signal Failure. Politics and Britain's Railways*. Stroud: Sutton Publishing.

Ziegler, P. (2010) *Edward Heath*. London: Harper Press.

Index

Aims of Industry 80
Allen, G. Freeman 203, 220
ASLEF Strike 1955 132
Attlee, Clement 19, 20, 32-3
Austin Seven 71
Automobile Association 94, 97

Beeching, Dr Richard 163-6, 175-6,
    219-25
Benn, Tony 86, 154, 256
Bevan, Aneurin 28-30
Bevins, Reginald 36, 58
'Big Four' Railway Companies
    101-7, 109, 111, 115
'Bluebell Line' 145-6
Bonavia, Michael 210
Boyd-Carpenter, John 84, 86, 189
British Rail 218
British Railways 116-8, 121-5,
    135-148
British Railways Board 172-3, 179-80
British Road Federation, 79-80, 82,
    97, 126
British Road Services 75, 78
British Transport Commission
    114-8, 132-4, 136, 142, 148,
    159-66, 172
Buchanan, Colin 87-9
Butler, Reginald 32, 38, 129, 152-3,
    184

Castle, Barbara 96-7, 126, 220,
    236-44
Churchill, Winston 29, 31-2, 36-7,
    104, 121, 128
Cousins, Frank 219-20, 243, 248-9
Crowther, Sir Geoffrey 88

Dalton, Hugh 109, 115
'Deltic' 132-3
Denning, Lord 51, 192, 229-31
Diesel and electric locomotives
    119-20, 132, 137-42
Douglas Home, Sir Alec 193-6,
    208, 286
Du Cann, Edward 251-2, 253-4
Dunton Green to Westerham
    branch 147

Eden, Sir Anthony 47, 51

Fiennes, Gerald, 124, 129, 178
Floods of 1953 43
Fraser, Tom 220
Freight Transport Association 80, 126

Geddes Sir Eric 100-1
General Elections
    1945 19, 109, 113
    1950 16-18
    1951 33-4

1955 47
1959 144, 149
1964 246
1966 250
1970 257-8
February 1974 261-2
October 1974 263
Great Central Main Line 143
Guillebaud Committee 136,
    157-8, 161

Hailsham, Lord 266-7
Hardy, Richard 220
Heath, Edward 246, 252, 253-4,
    257-8, 260
Henshaw, David 245
Hollowood, Bernard 205

Joseph, Sir Keith 90

Kirk & Kirk (Builders) 21-2, 24, 31

Labour Government 1945-51 20,
    23, 28, 32-3
Lewis, Arthur 247
Lloyd, Selwyn 196
Loft, Charles 206-7, 211, 222
London Transport 106, 110, 112

Macleod, Iain 193, 220
Macmillan, Harold 36-8, 41-9, 56,
    136-7, 149-50, 157-8, 165-8,
    181-2, 191-3
Marples, Ernest
  Business interests in Construction
    Industry 48, 151-3
  Domestic life 20-1 and *passim*
  Early life 13-14

Early working life 14-15
Early involvement in building
    trade 15-6, 24-5
Enters Politics & Parliament 17,
    19, 22
Housing Policy 22-5, 28-32, 36-9
Marples, Ridgeway & Partners
    24-5, 39-40, 50, 151-2, 247, 260
Marriages, 15-7, 50-1
Parliamentary Private Secretary,
    Housing & Local Government
    36-45
Parliamentary Private Secretary,
    Pensions 47
Postmaster General 53-63
Shadow Technology Minister
    246-7
Wallasey 17-19, 26-7
War service 16
Marsh, Richard 242
Midland & Great Northern
    Railway 146-7
Miles, Sir Percy 37, 153, 168,
    175-6, 190
Model 'T' Ford 71
Motorways 92-3, 154-6

National Fright Corporation 240
Noble, Michael 168, 192

Oxford to Cambridge Line 215, 241

Passenger Transport Authorities 240
Post Office 54-63
Powell, Enoch 150, 254
Premium Bonds 56
Profumo Affair 51, 192, 227-9, 235
Pro-Road MPs 67

Railway Executive 114, 122-3, 126
'Railway Interest' 99
Railway Modernisation Plan 1955
    127-33
Railway Nationalisation and the
    Labour Party 109-13
Railways in World War One 100
Railways in World War Two 108
Railway Strike 1919 68
Railways Act 1921 68,100
Raymond, Sir Stanley 121, 225,
    238-9
Rees-Mogg, William 249
Riddles, Robin 141, 168
Road Haulage Association 69, 75,
    83, 111, 127, 156-8, 191
Road Lobby Pre-1914 65-6, 101
Road Lobby post 1945 80-2, 84-5,
    93, 126-7
Robertson, Sir Brian 135, 149,
    159-62, 175

Select Committee on Nationalised
    Industries 1960 156
Sharp, Evelyn, 61
Smeed Committee 90-1

Society of Motor Traders &
    Manufacturers 67, 79, 85, 126
Steam Locomotives 118-21, 139-42
Stedeford Committee 153, 162-6
Stonham, Lord 190, 215
Strauss, George 182, 186, 188
Suez Crisis 190, 215

Thatcher, Margaret 267
Thorpe, Jeremy 213
Transport Act 1947 75, 113-1
Transport Act 1953 78, 122-3
Transport Act 1962 184
Transport Act 1968 95-6
Transport & General Workers'
    Union 80-1, 214, 243-4
Transport Holding Company 95
Transport Users' Consultative
    Committee 115, 146-8, 174,
    183-4, 195, 216

Watkinson, Harold 136, 149-50, 154
Wilson, Harold 56, 117, 176, 186-9,
    209, 214, 236, 250, 255-6, 263
Woolton, Lord 26, 40
Wythenshawe 71